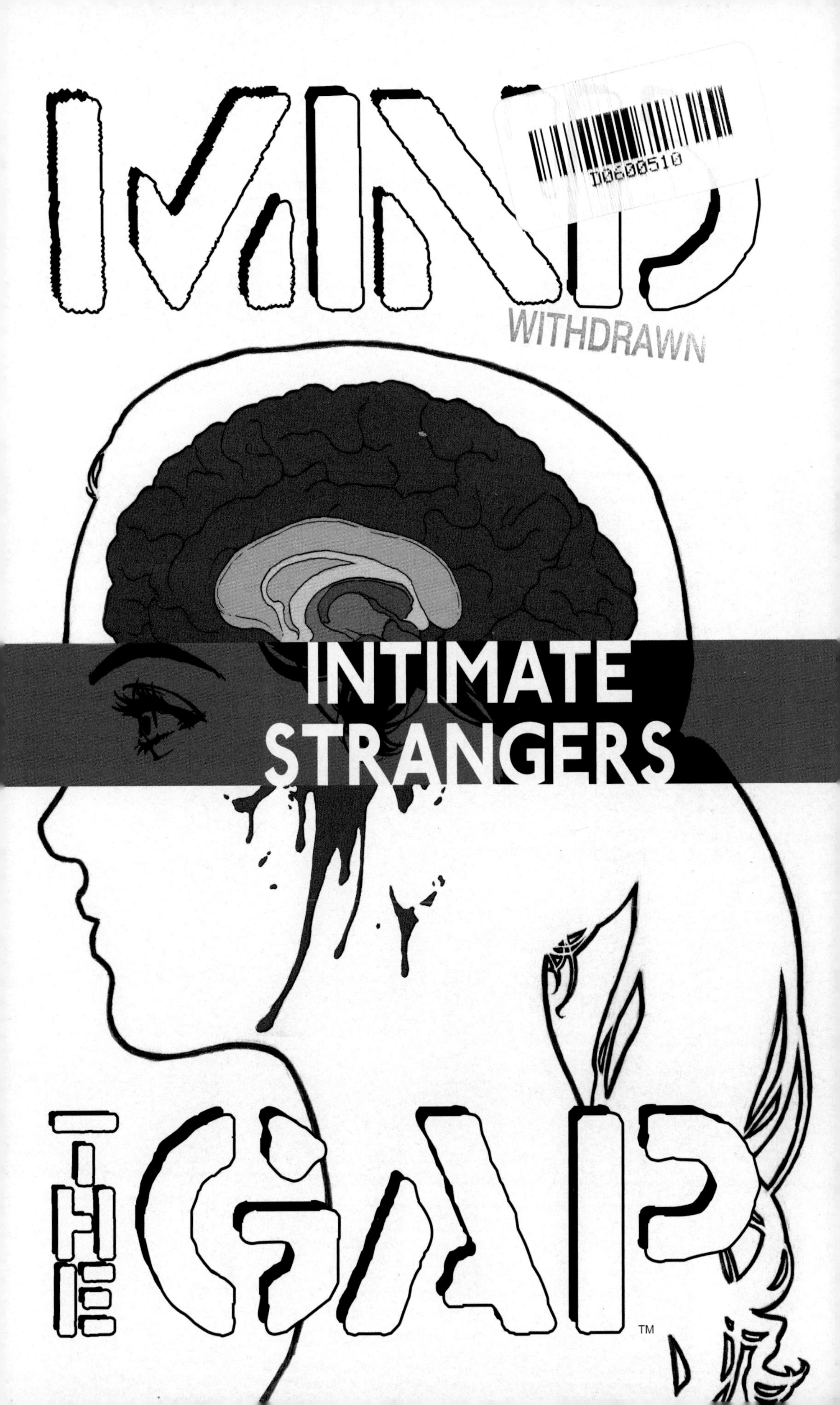
MIND
THE GAP
™
INTIMATE
STRANGERS

"HELLO"
BY LIONEL B. RITCHIE, JR.
© BRENDA RICHIE PUBLISHING [ASCAP] AND
BROCKMAN MUSIC [ASCAP] ALL RIGHTS RESERVED

"FUCK YOU"
BY CHRIS BROWN, BRUNO MARS,
ARI LEVINE, PHILIP LAWRENCE,
THOMAS CALLAWAY
© WB MUSIC CORP. [ASCAP], NORTHSIDE
INDEPENDENT MUSIC PUBLISHING, LLC [ASCAP],
WESTSIDE INDEPENDENT MUSIC PUBLISHING LLC
[ASCAP], LATE 80'S MUSIC [ASCAP], MARS FORCE
MUSIC [ASCAP], MUSIC OF WINDSWEPT [ASCAP],
TOY PLANE MUSIC [ASCAP], MUSIC FAMAMANEM
[ASCAP] AND GOD GIVEN MUSIC [BMI] ALL RIGHTS
ON BEHALF OF ITSELF AND LATE 80'S MUSIC
ADMINISTERED BY WESTSIDE INDEPENDENT
MUSIC PUBLISHING LLC ALL RIGHTS RESERVED

"NO RAIN"
BY GLEN GRAHAM, RICHARD SHANNON HOON,
ERIC BRADLEY SMITH, THOMAS ROGERS STEVENS,
CHRISTOPHER JOHN THORN
© EMI APRIL MUSIC INC [ASCAP], HEAVY MELON
MUSIC [ASCAP] ALL RIGHTS RESERVED

"MONEY"
BY ROGER WATERS
© HAMPSHIRE HOUSE PUBLISHING CORP [ASCAP],
ROGER WATERS MUSIC OVERSEAS LTD. ALL RIGHTS RESERVED

"JAIL HOUSE ROCK"
BY JERRY LIEBER, MIKE STOLLER
© SONY/ATV SONGS LLC [BMI] ALL RIGHTS RESERVED

"DON'T YOU [FORGET ABOUT ME]"
BY KEITH FORSEY, STEVE W SCHIFF
© USI A MUSIC PUBLISHING [ASCAP],
USI B MUSIC PUBLISHING [BMI] ALL RIGHTS RESERVED

"NOW. HERE. THIS." [c] of Jeff Bowen, Hunter Bell and Susan Blackwell

"DIAMONDS ARE A GIRL'S BEST FRIEND"
BY JULE STYNE, LEO ROBIN
© MUSIC SALES CORP [ASCAP] ALL RIGHTS RESERVED

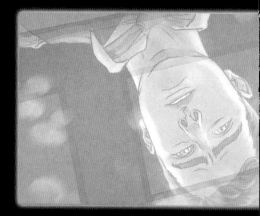

MIND THE GAP, VOL. 1: INTIMATE STRANGERS
ISBN: 978-1-60706-598-2
First Printing

Published by Image Comics, Inc. Office of publication: 2134 Allston Way, 2nd Floor, Berkeley, CA 94704. Copyright © 2012 Jim McCann. Originally published in single magazine form as MIND THE GAP #1-5. All rights reserved. MIND THE GAP™ (including all prominent characters featured herein), its logo and all character likenesses are trademarks of Jim McCann, unless otherwise noted. Image Comics and its logos are ® and © 2012 Image Comics, Inc. All rights reserved. No part of this publication may be reproduced or transmitted, in any form or by any means, (except for short excerpts for review purposes) without the express written permission of Image Comics, Inc. All names, characters, events and locales in this publication are entirely fictional. Any resemblance to actual persons (living or dead), events or places, without satiric intent, is coincidental. For information regarding the CPSIA on this printed material call: 203-595-3636 and provide reference # RICH - 454789. International Rights / Foreign Licensing -- foreignlicensing@imagecomics.com. PRINTED IN USA.

image®

IMAGE COMICS, INC.
Robert Kirkman - chief operating officer
Erik Larsen - chief financial officer
Todd McFarlane - president
Marc Silvestri - chief executive officer
Jim Valentino - vice-president
www.imagecomics.com

Eric Stephenson - publisher
Todd Martinez - sales & licensing coordinator
Jennifer de Guzman - pr & marketing director
Branwyn Bigglestone - accounts manager
Emily Miller - administrative assistant
Jamie Parreno - marketing assistant
Sarah deLaine - events coordinator

Kevin Yuen - digital rights coordinator
Drew Gill - art director
Jonathan Chan - production manager
Monica Garcia - production artist
Vincent Kukua - production artist
Jana Cook - production artist

Written by
Jim McCann

Art by
Rodin Esquejo,
with Adrian Alphona (Issue #5 pp5-21)

Colors by
Sonia Oback,
with Rodin Esquejo (Issue #2 pp4,5,14-20),
Arif Prianto (Issue #4 pp16-24),
and Beny Maulana (Issue #5 pp1-3, 22-26)

Letters by
Dave Lanphear

Production and Graphic Design by
Damien Lucchese

Edited by
Rob Levin

Cover by
Rodin Esquejo and Sonia Oback

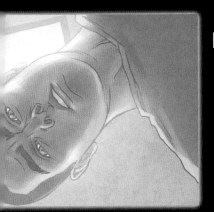

MIND THE GAP created by
Jim McCann

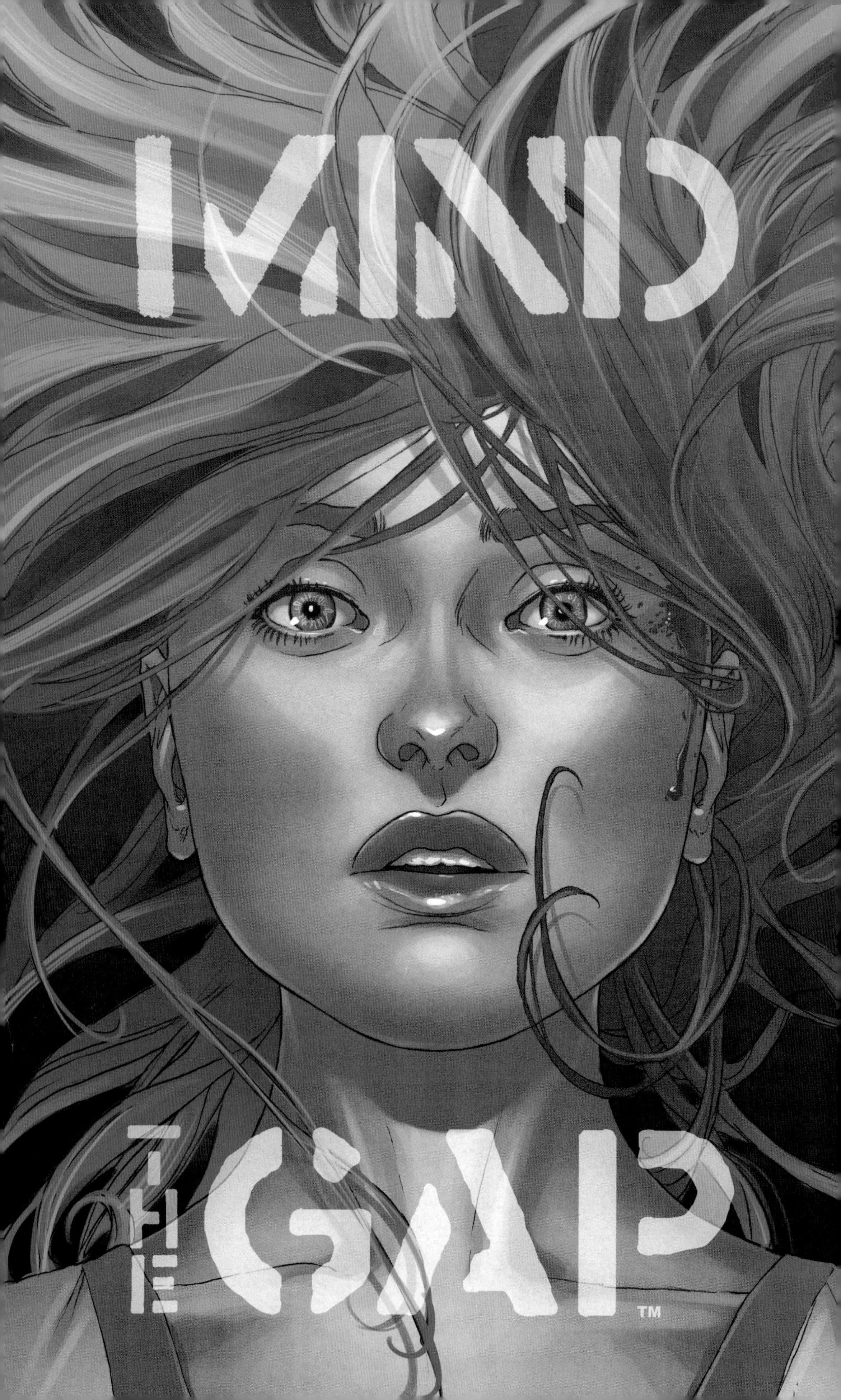
MIND
THE
GAP
™

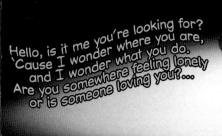

Hello, is it me you're looking for?
'Cause I wonder where you are,
and I wonder what you do.
Are you somewhere feeling lonely
or is someone loving you?...

Hello, is it me you're looking for?
'Cause I wonder where you are--

Damn it.
Did it
again.

E, I'm
gonna kill you.
You earwormed that
song with my ringtone.
And woke me from a
pre-show nap!

Hhhh...
hhhh.

Elle?
Sweetie,
what's
wrong?

Elle?!

Hhhheeeh.
Nnn...

click

C'mon,
c'mon.

Elle

Call Failed

Shit!

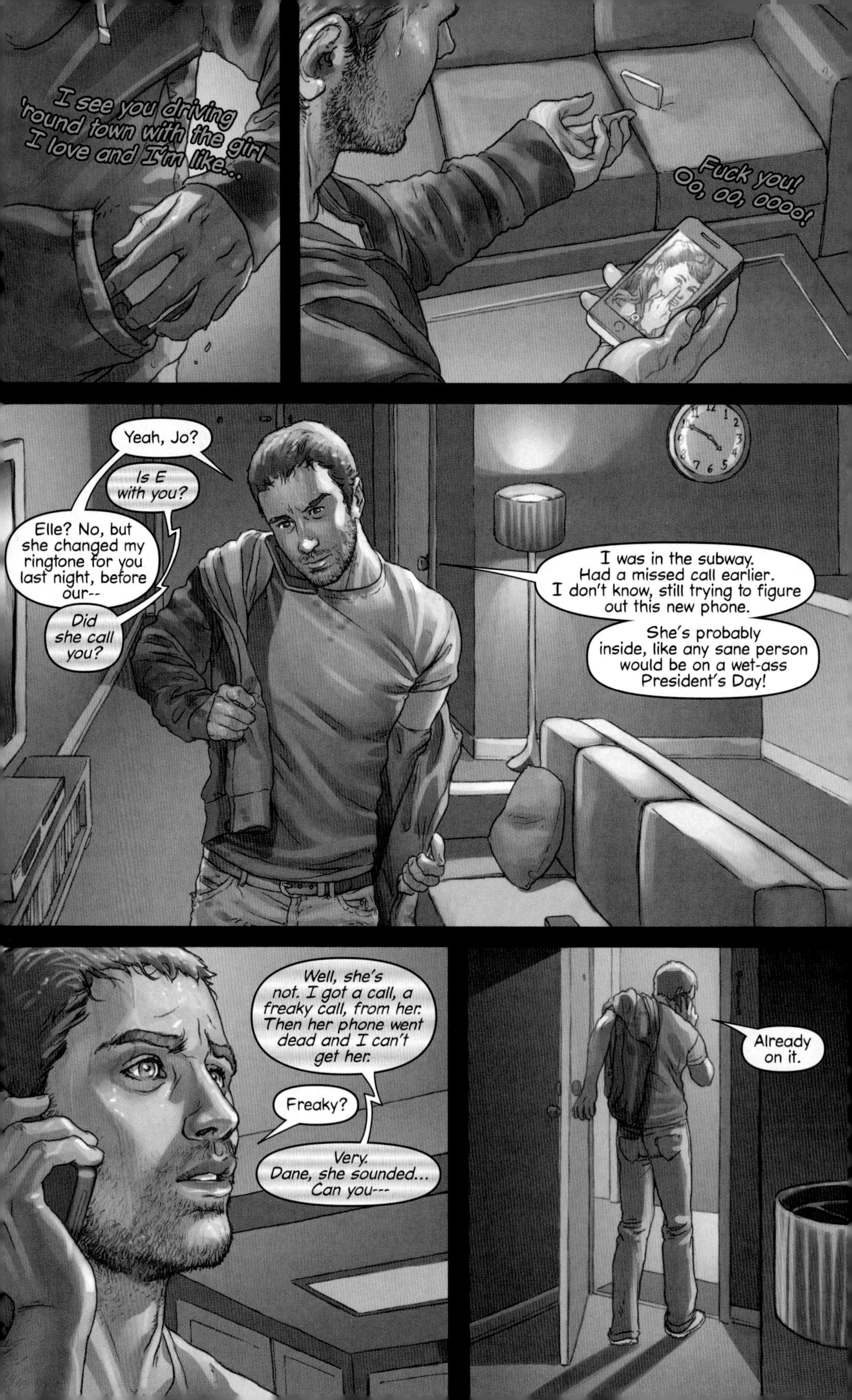
I see you driving 'round town with the girl I love and I'm like...
Fuck you! Oo, oo, oooo!
Yeah, Jo?
Is E with you?
Elle? No, but she changed my ringtone for you last night, before our--
Did she call you?
I was in the subway. Had a missed call earlier. I don't know, still trying to figure out this new phone.
She's probably inside, like any sane person would be on a wet-ass President's Day!
Well, she's not. I got a call, a freaky call, from her. Then her phone went dead and I can't get her.
Freaky?
Very. Dane, she sounded... Can you---
Already on it.

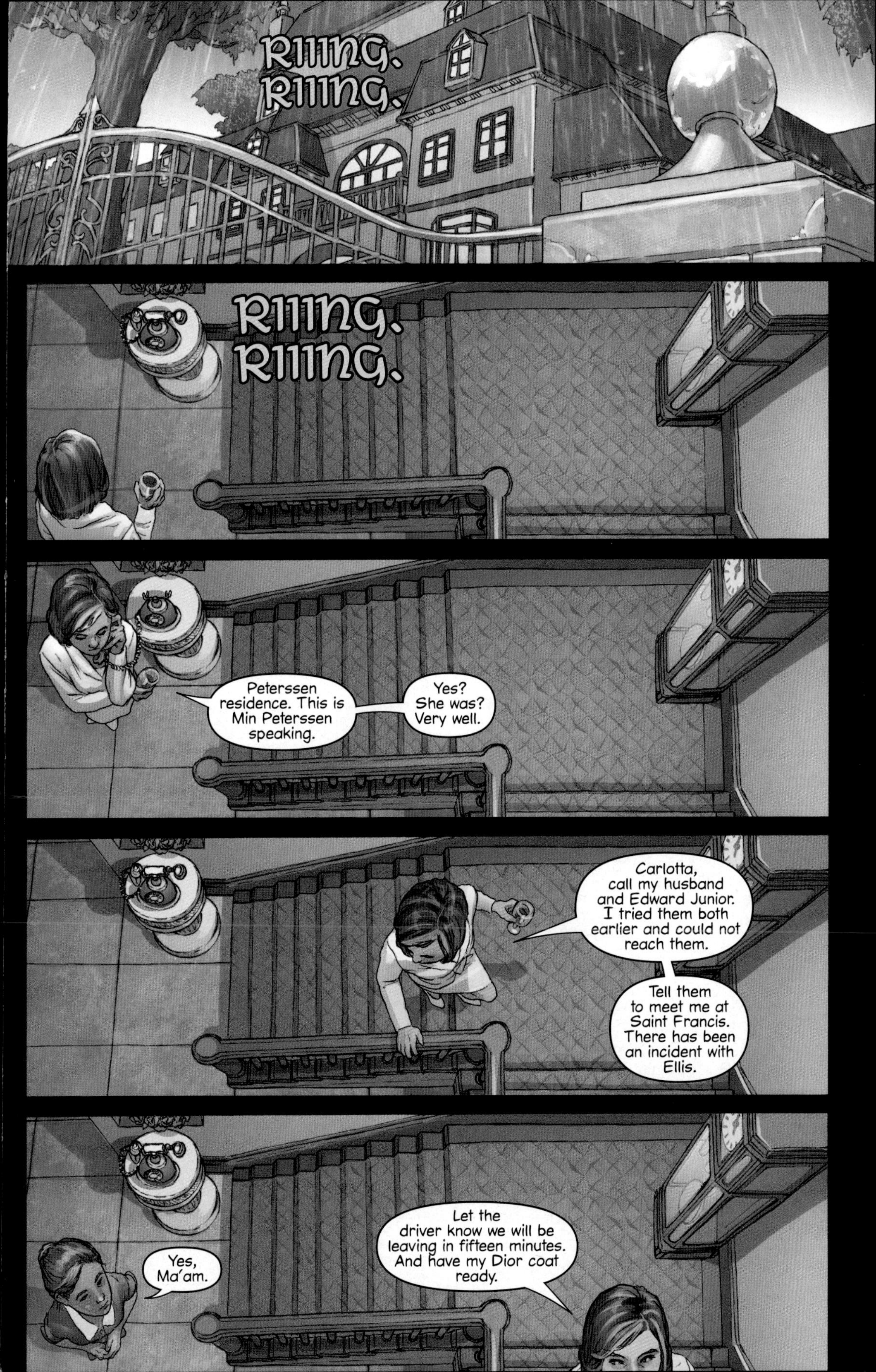
RIIING. RIIING.
RIIING. RIIING.
Peterssen residence. This is Min Peterssen speaking.
Yes? She was? Very well.
Carlotta, call my husband and Edward Junior. I tried them both earlier and could not reach them.
Tell them to meet me at Saint Francis. There has been an incident with Ellis.
Let the driver know we will be leaving in fifteen minutes. And have my Dior coat ready.
Yes, Ma'am.

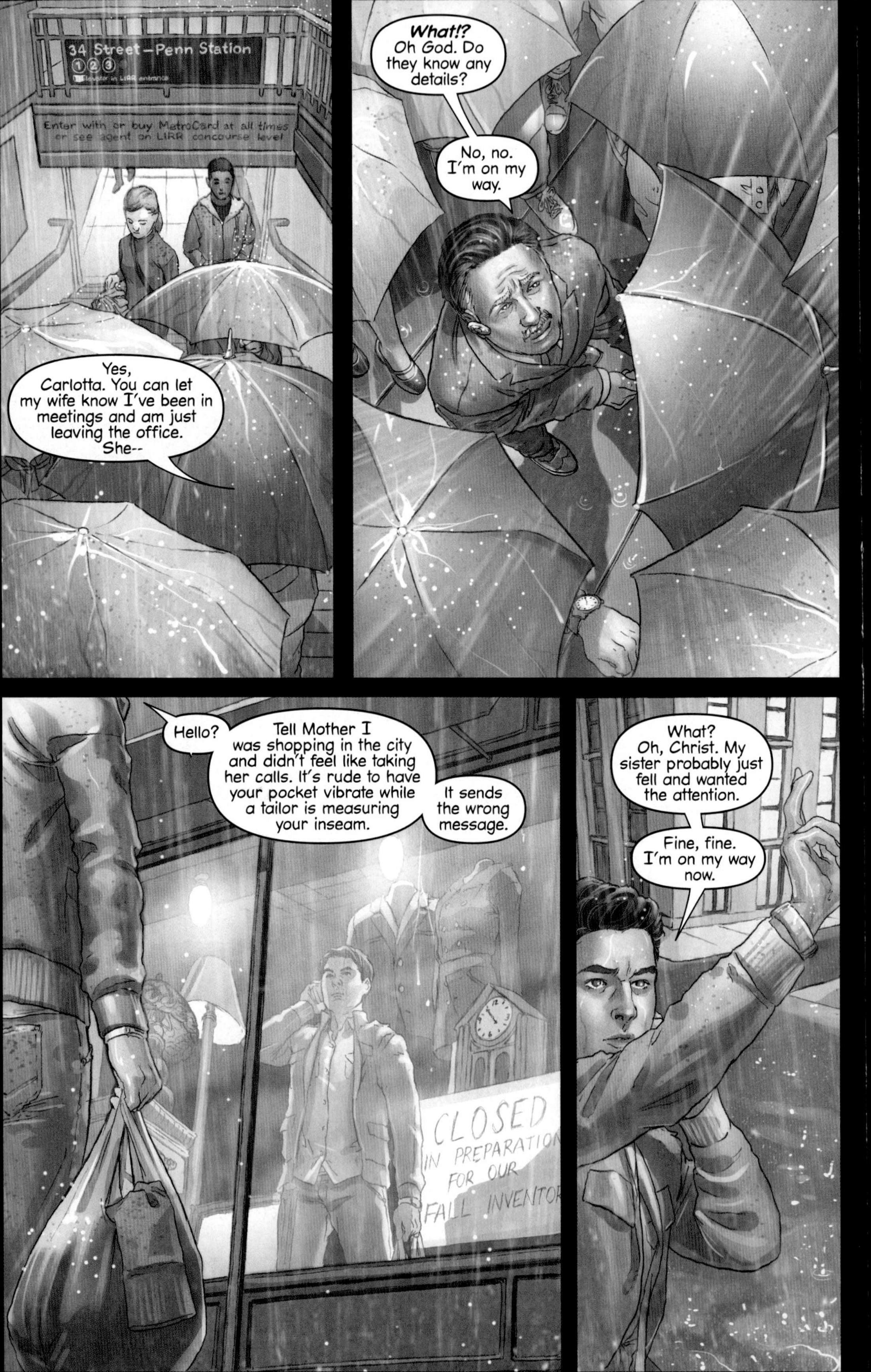
34 Street—Penn Station
Enter with or buy MetroCard at all times or see agent on LIRR concourse level
Yes, Carlotta. You can let my wife know I've been in meetings and am just leaving the office. She--
What!? Oh God. Do they know any details?
No, no. I'm on my way.
Hello?
Tell Mother I was shopping in the city and didn't feel like taking her calls. It's rude to have your pocket vibrate while a tailor is measuring your inseam.
It sends the wrong message.
CLOSED
IN PREPARATION
FOR OUR
FALL INVENTOR
What? Oh, Christ. My sister probably just fell and wanted the attention.
Fine, fine. I'm on my way now.

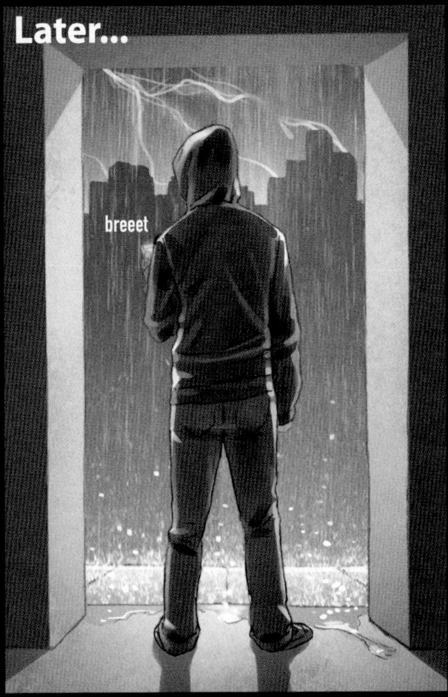
Later...
breeet

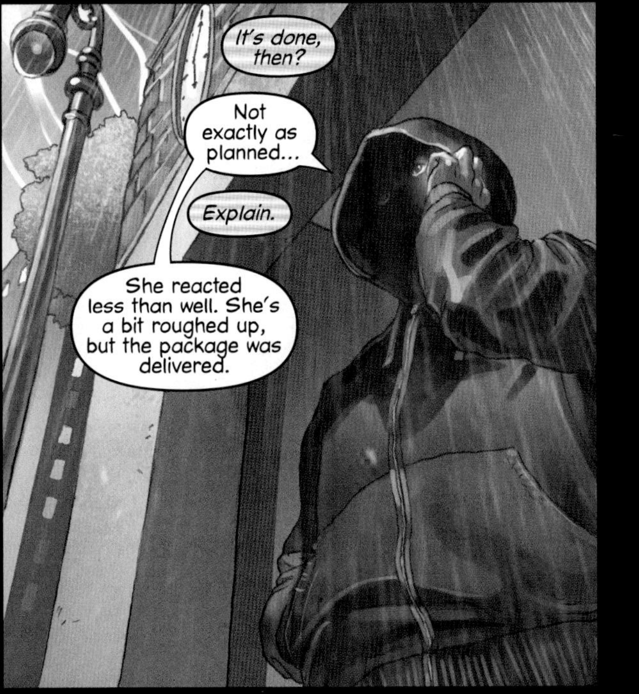
It's done, then?
Not exactly as planned...
Explain.
She reacted less than well. She's a bit roughed up, but the package was delivered.

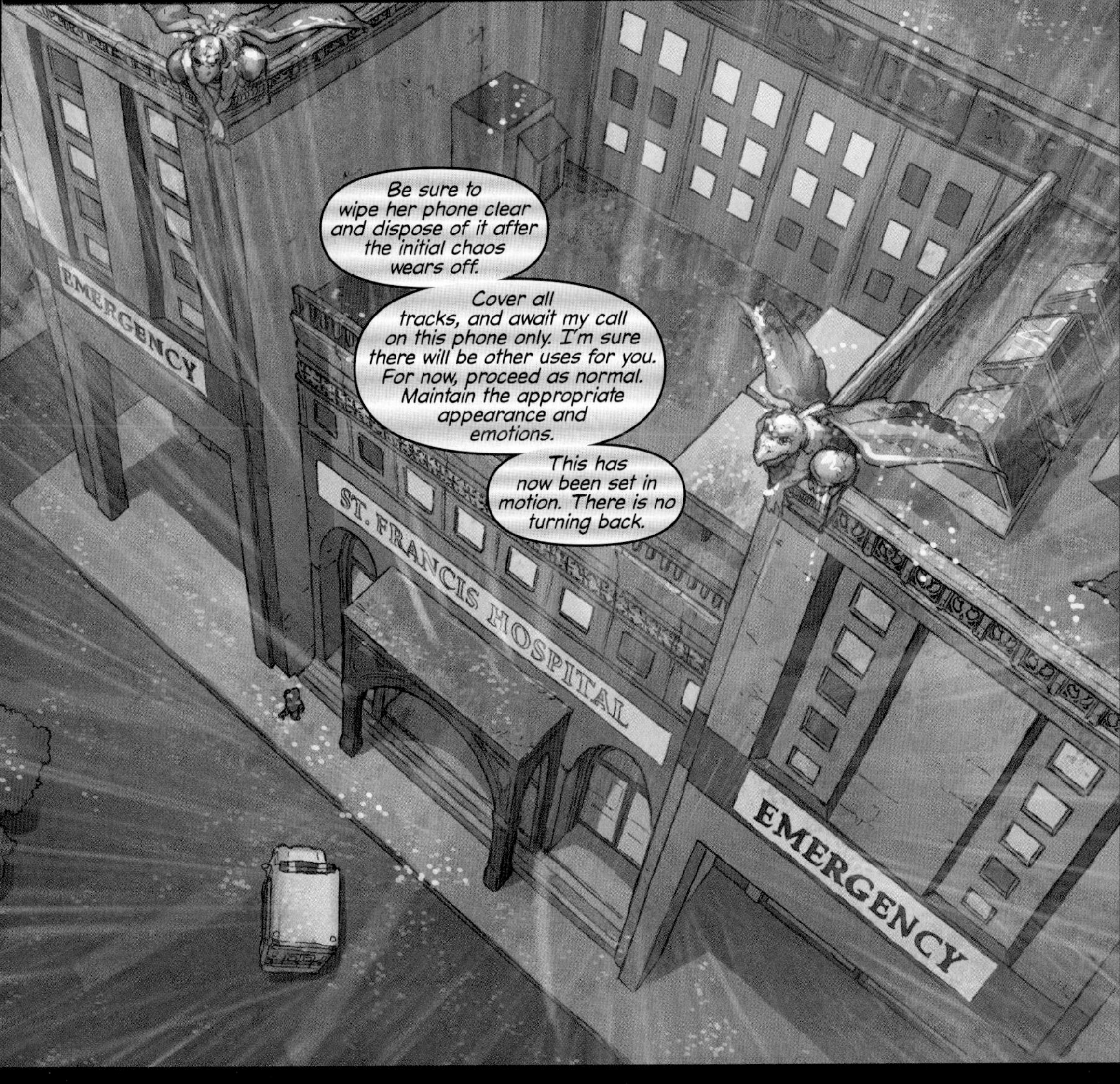
Be sure to wipe her phone clear and dispose of it after the initial chaos wears off.
Cover all tracks, and await my call on this phone only. I'm sure there will be other uses for you. For now, proceed as normal. Maintain the appropriate appearance and emotions.
This has now been set in motion. There is no turning back.
EMERGENCY
ST. FRANCIS HOSPITAL
EMERGENCY

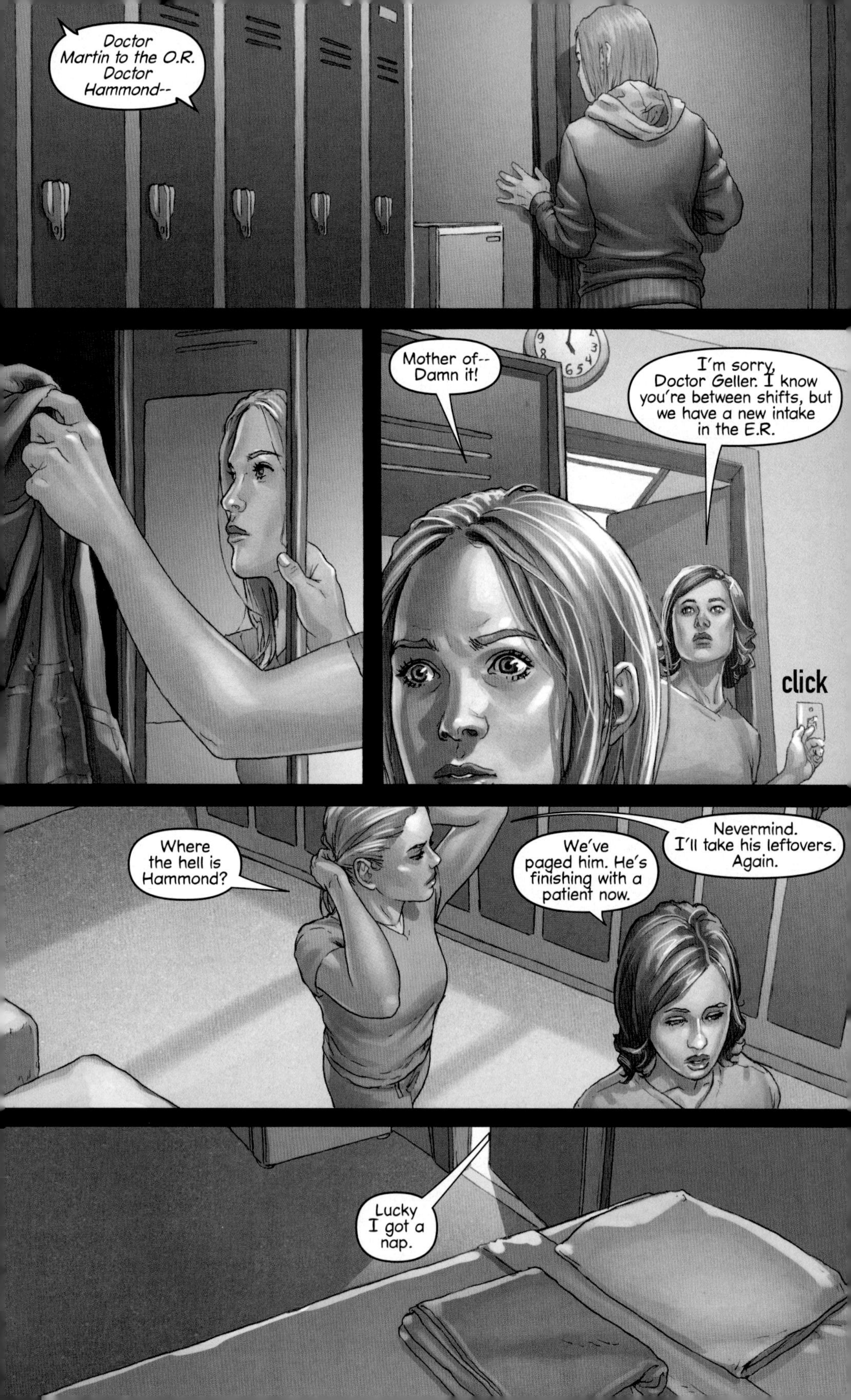
Doctor Martin to the O.R. Doctor Hammond--
Mother of-- Damn it!
I'm sorry, Doctor Geller. I know you're between shifts, but we have a new intake in the E.R.
click
Where the hell is Hammond?
We've paged him. He's finishing with a patient now.
Nevermind. I'll take his leftovers. Again.
Lucky I got a nap.

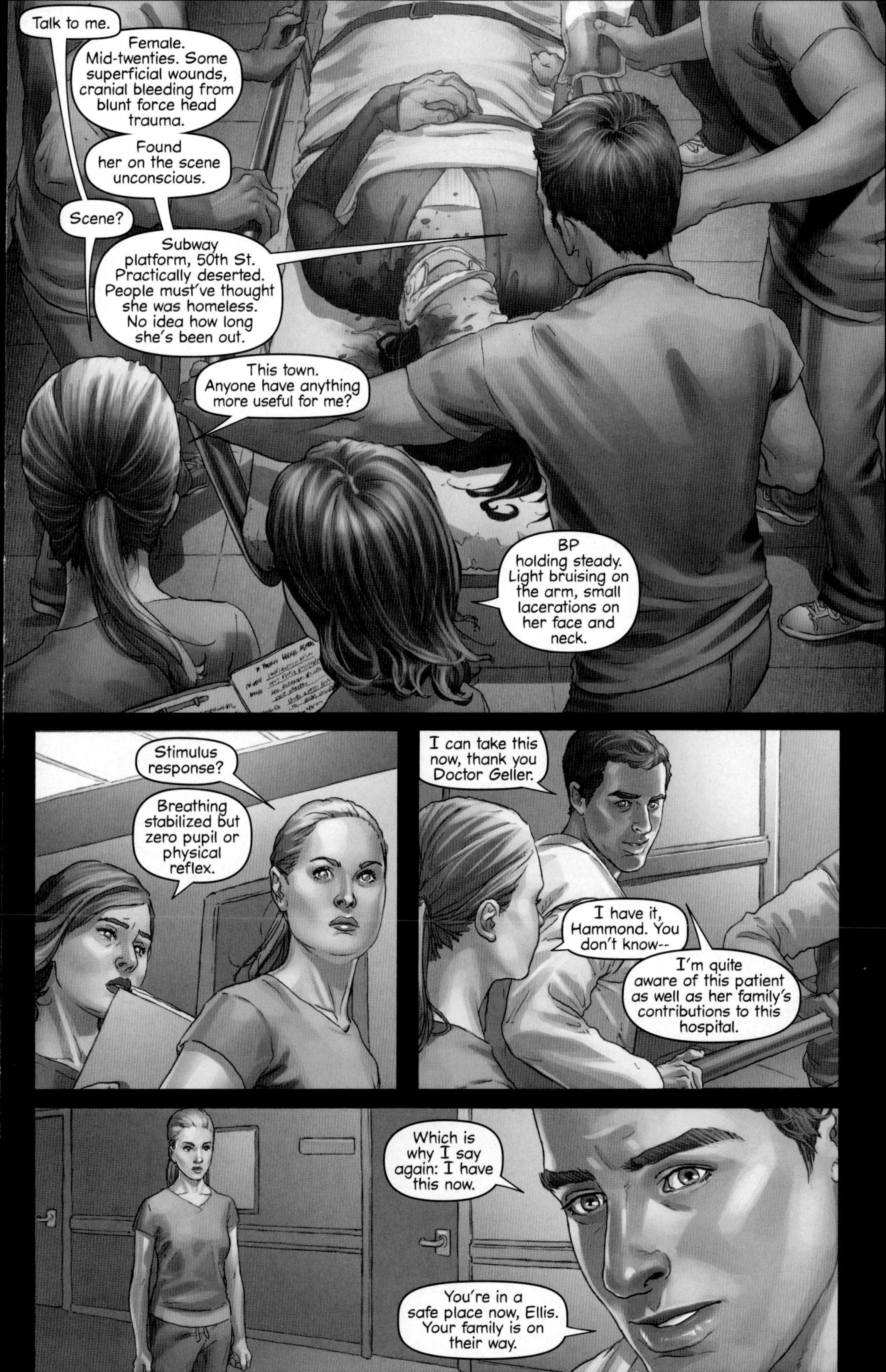
Talk to me.
Female. Mid-twenties. Some superficial wounds, cranial bleeding from blunt force head trauma.
Found her on the scene unconscious.
Scene?
Subway platform, 50th St. Practically deserted. People must've thought she was homeless. No idea how long she's been out.
This town. Anyone have anything more useful for me?
BP holding steady. Light bruising on the arm, small lacerations on her face and neck.
Stimulus response?
Breathing stabilized but zero pupil or physical reflex.
I can take this now, thank you Doctor Geller.
I have it, Hammond. You don't know--
I'm quite aware of this patient as well as her family's contributions to this hospital.
Which is why I say again: I have this now.
You're in a safe place now, Ellis. Your family is on their way.

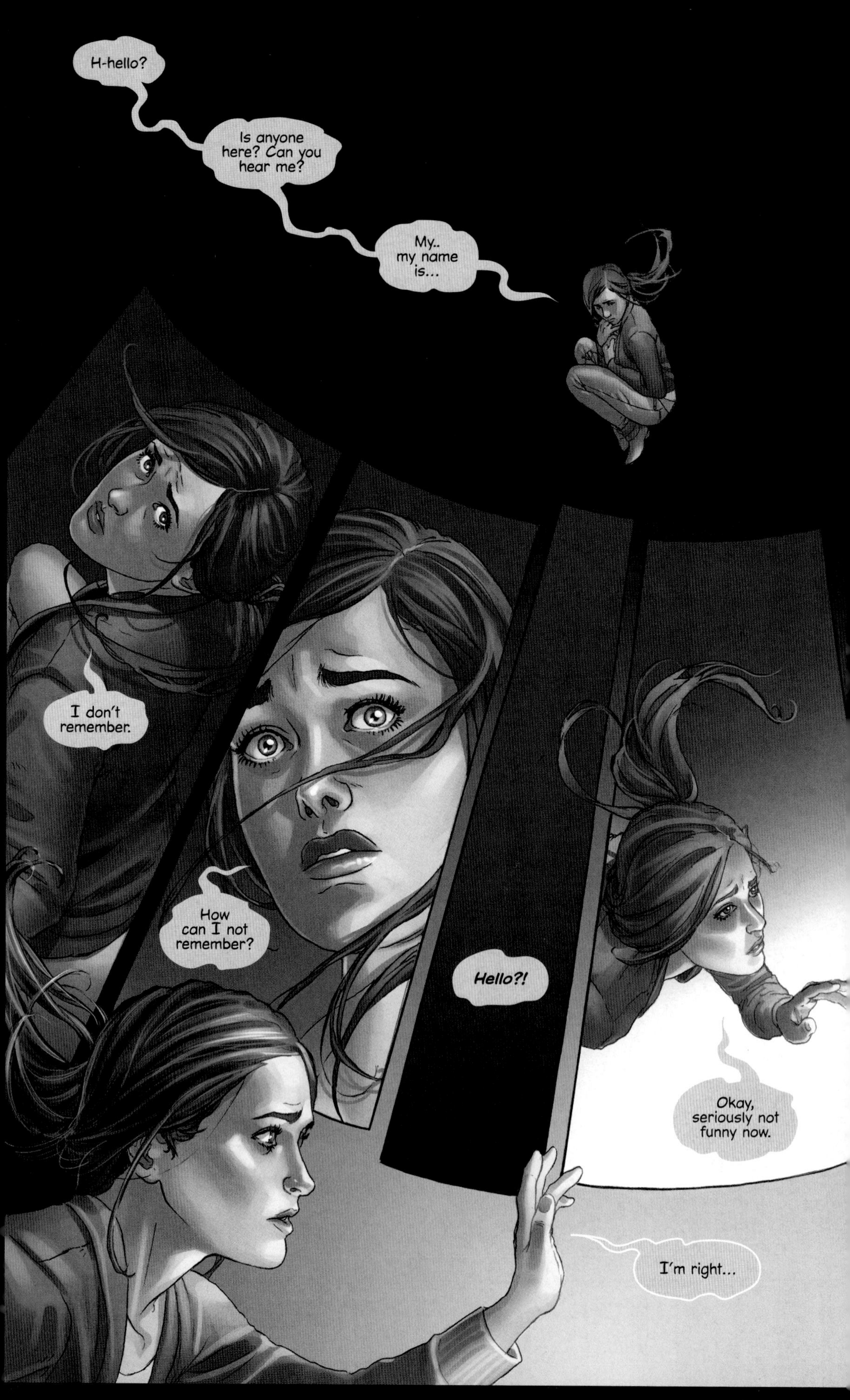
H-hello?
Is anyone here? Can you hear me?
My.. my name is...
I don't remember.
How can I not remember?
Hello?!
Okay, seriously not funny now.
I'm right...

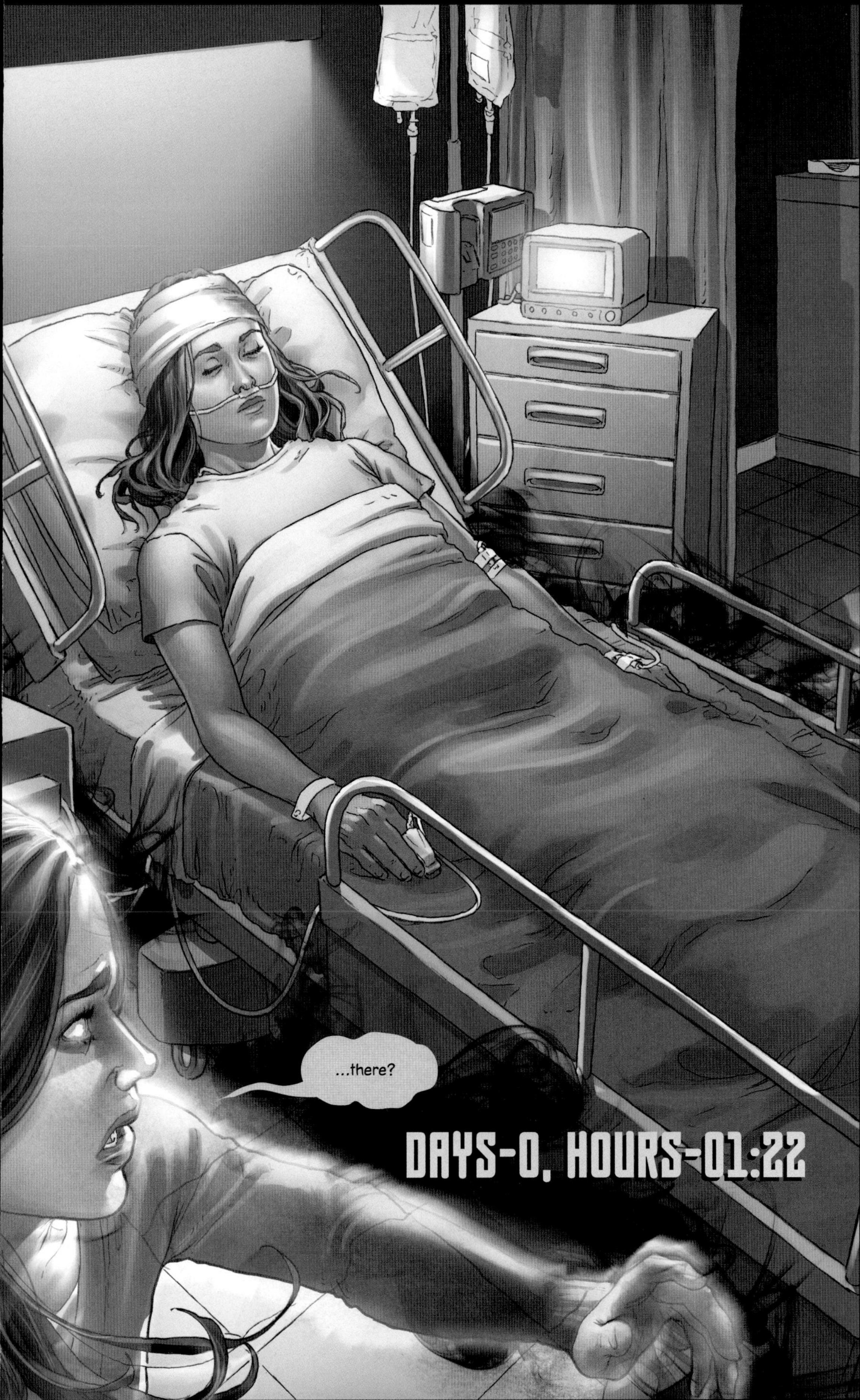
...there?
DAYS-0, HOURS-01:22

INTIMATE STRANGERS
PART I
"WELCOME TO THE NEIGHBORHOOD"

My life.

It's not sane.

I don't even know the "Hello My Name Is ___" that would label my life.

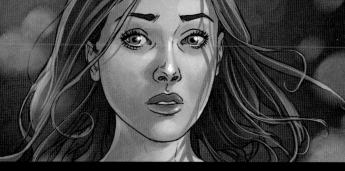But it's a great escape.

I don't--

Understand why I sleep all day.

I just--

Want someone to say to me...

I'll always be there when you wake.

That damn song.

Why is *that* song in my head? Is it special in some weird-ass way?

Oh crap. What if it's... what if I'm really...

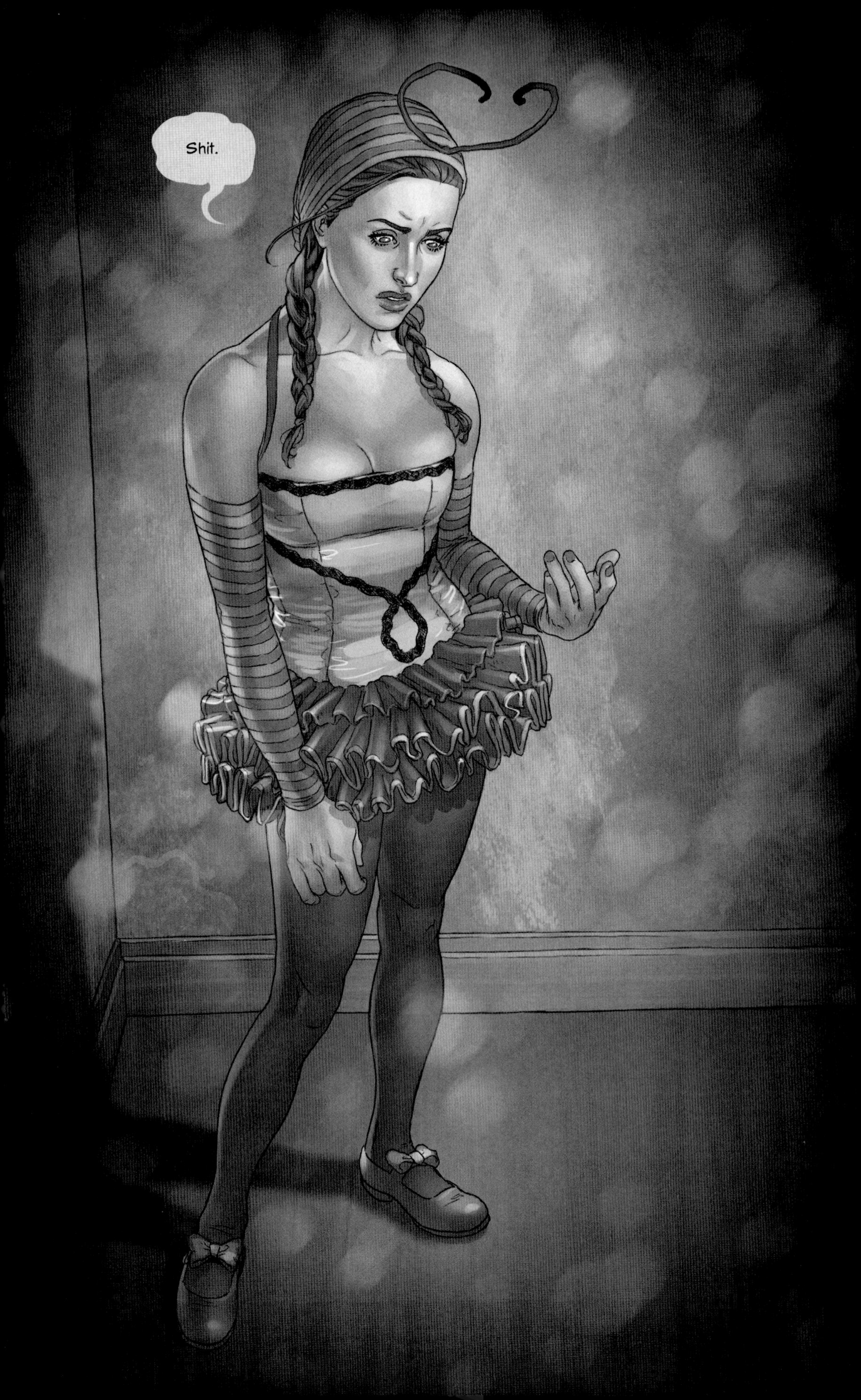
Shit.

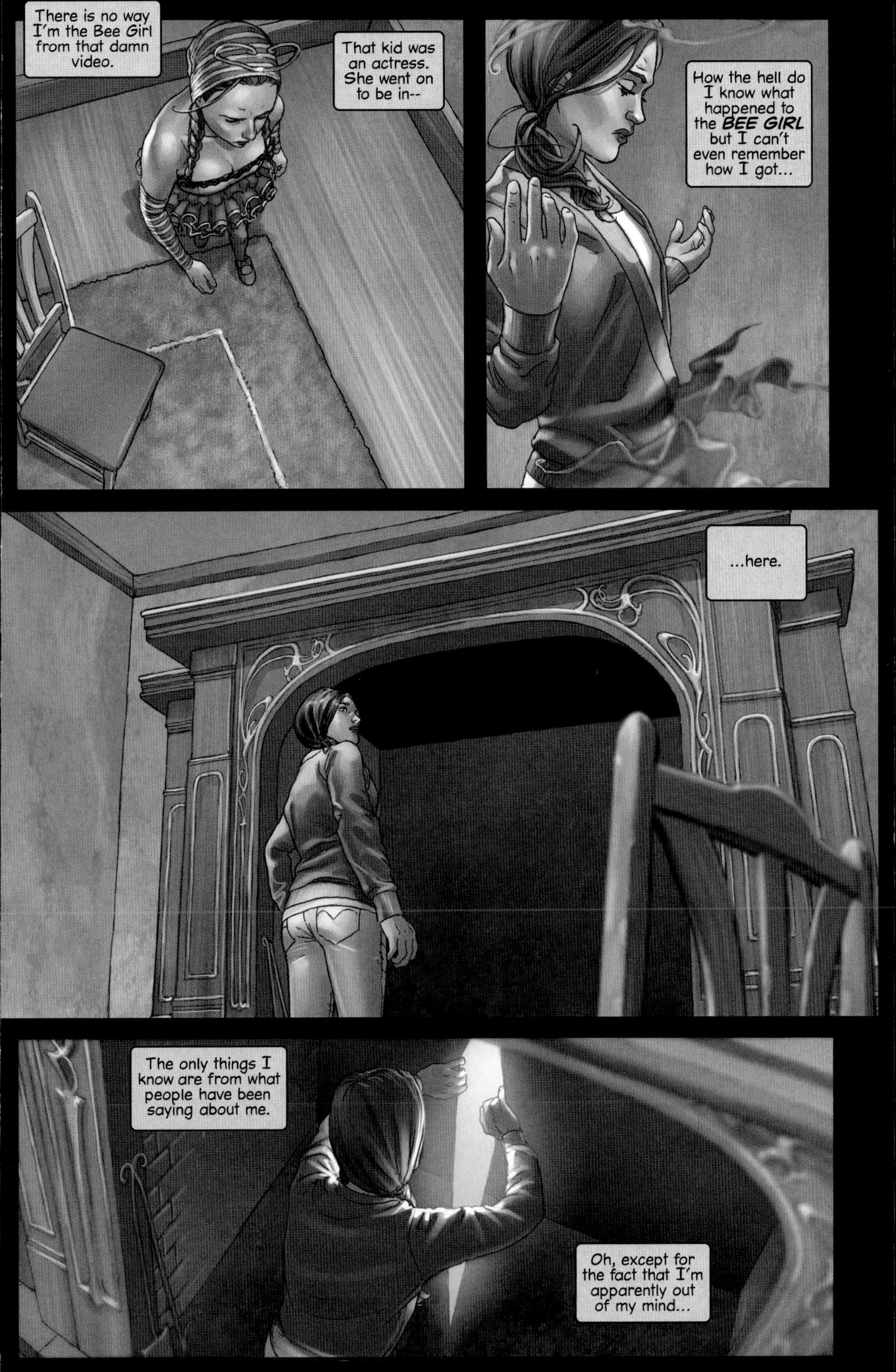

There is no way I'm the Bee Girl from that damn video.
That kid was an actress. She went on to be in--
How the hell do I know what happened to the BEE GIRL but I can't even remember how I got...
...here.
The only things I know are from what people have been saying about me.
Oh, except for the fact that I'm apparently out of my mind...

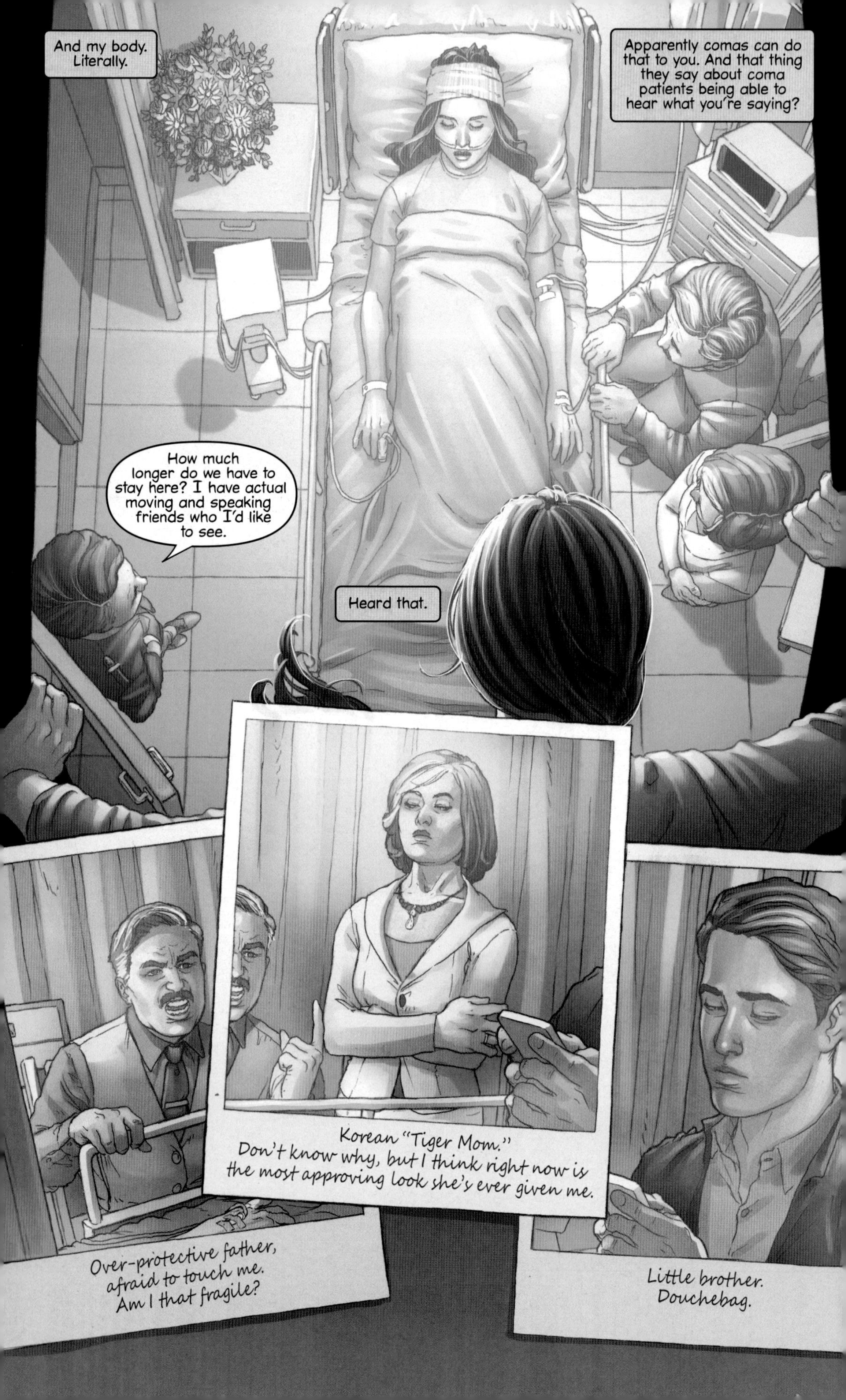
And my body. Literally.
Apparently comas can do that to you. And that thing they say about coma patients being able to hear what you're saying?
How much longer do we have to stay here? I have actual moving and speaking friends who I'd like to see.
Heard that.
Korean "Tiger Mom." Don't know why, but I think right now is the most approving look she's ever given me.
Over-protective father, afraid to touch me. Am I that fragile?
Little brother. Douchebag.

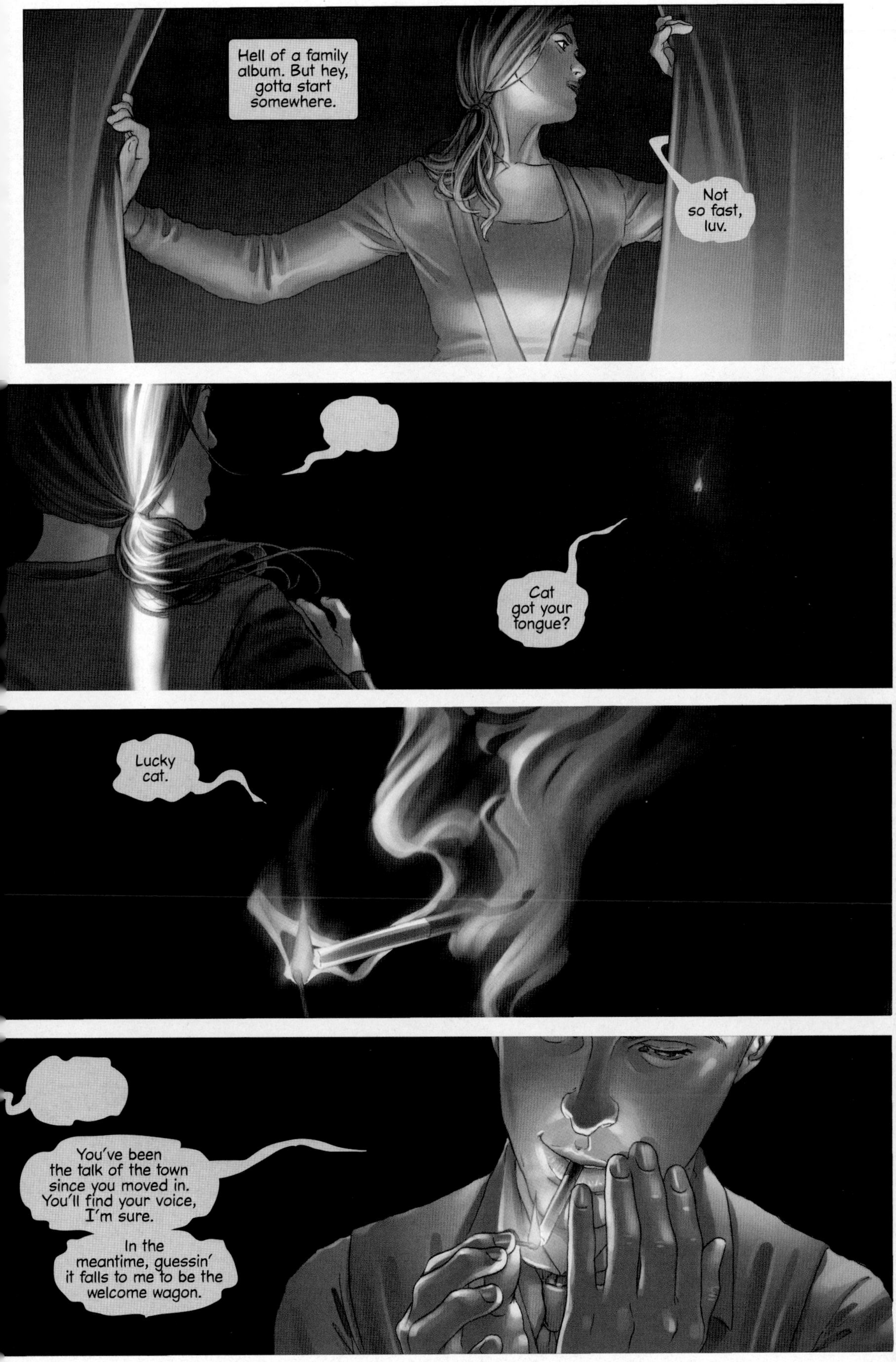
Hell of a family album. But hey, gotta start somewhere.
Not so fast, luv.
Cat got your tongue?
Lucky cat.
You've been the talk of the town since you moved in. You'll find your voice, I'm sure.
In the meantime, guessin' it falls to me to be the welcome wagon.

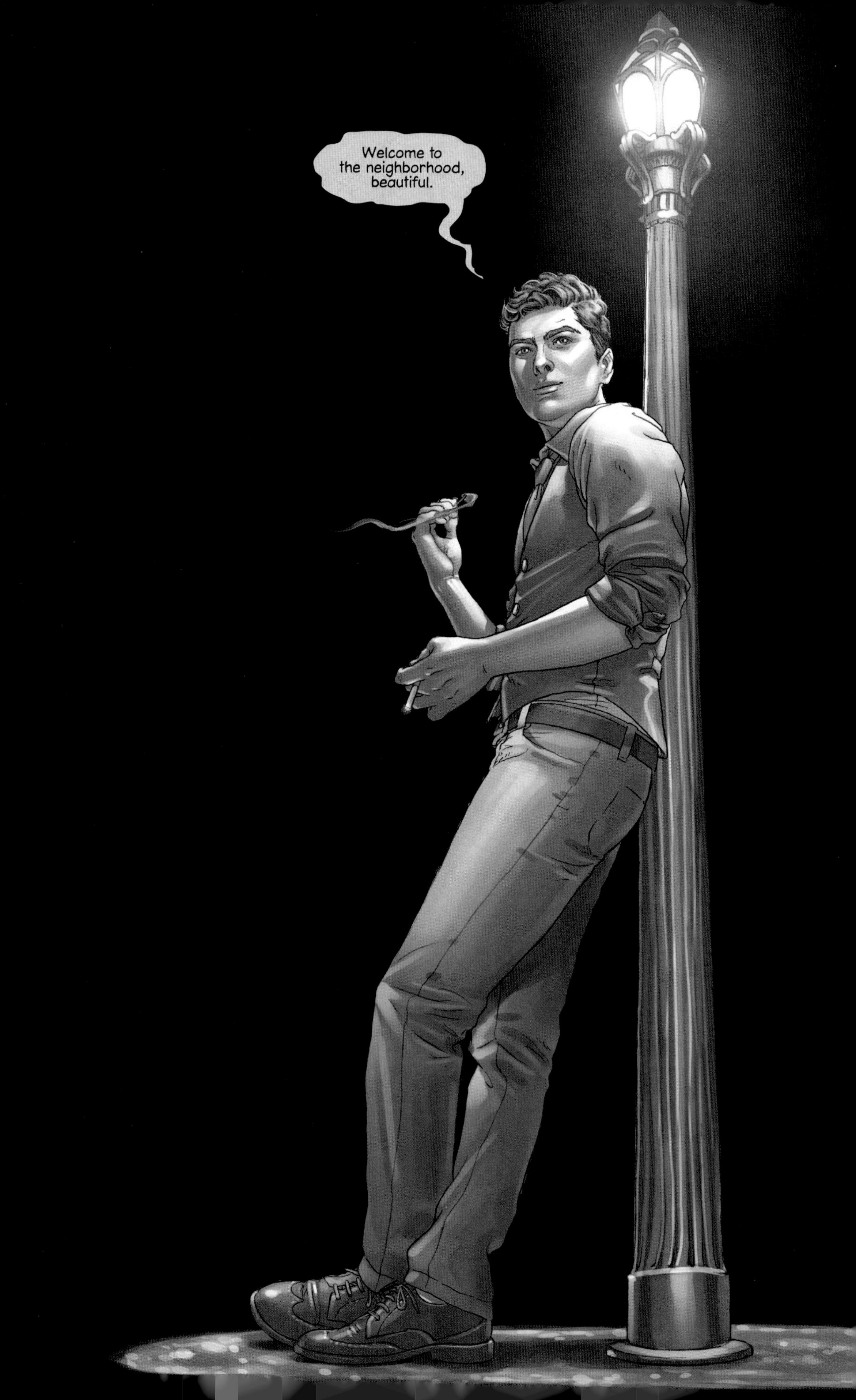
Welcome to the neighborhood, beautiful.

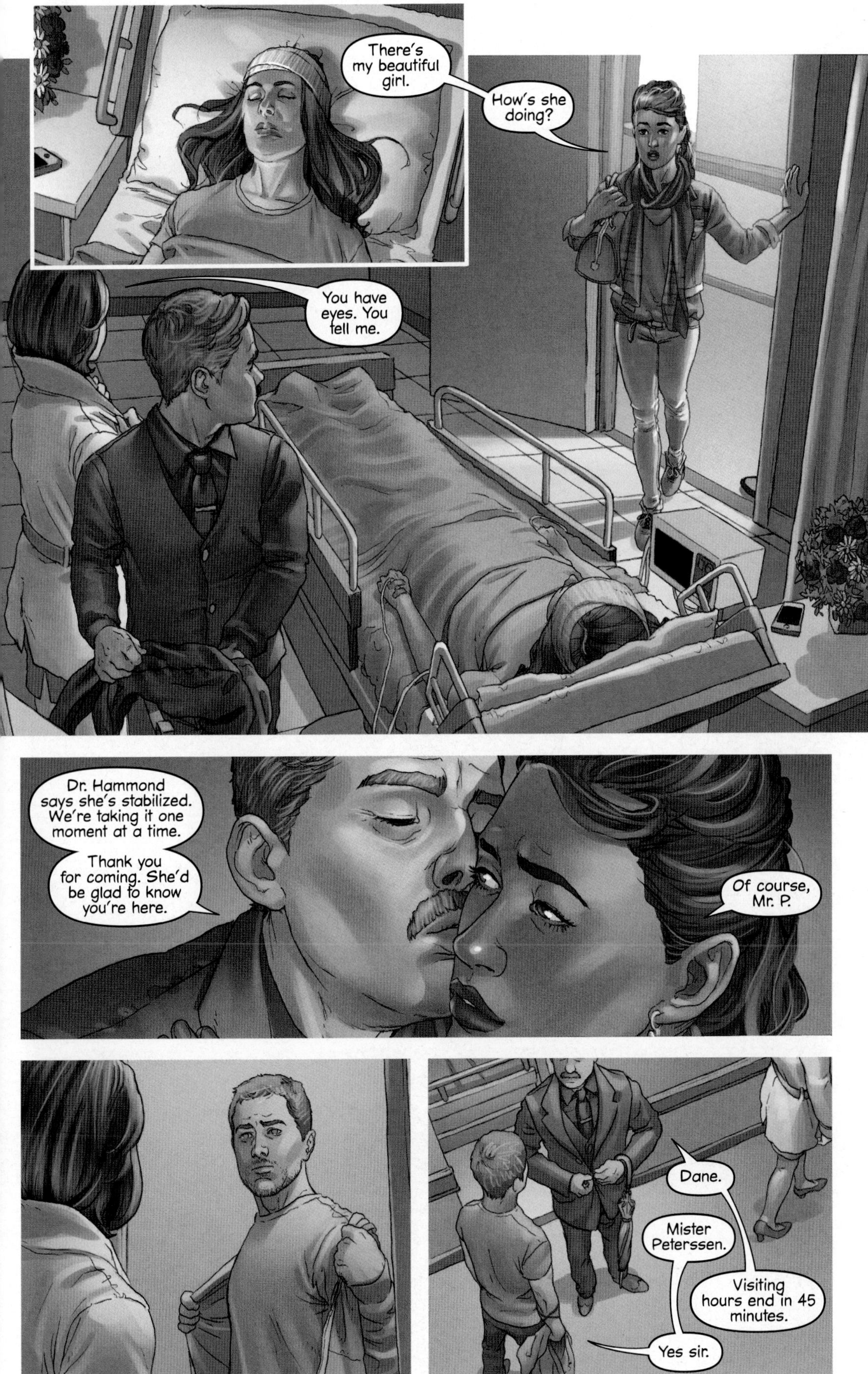
There's my beautiful girl.
How's she doing?
You have eyes. You tell me.
Dr. Hammond says she's stabilized. We're taking it one moment at a time.
Thank you for coming. She'd be glad to know you're here.
Of course, Mr. P.
Dane.
Mister Peterssen.
Visiting hours end in 45 minutes.
Yes sir.

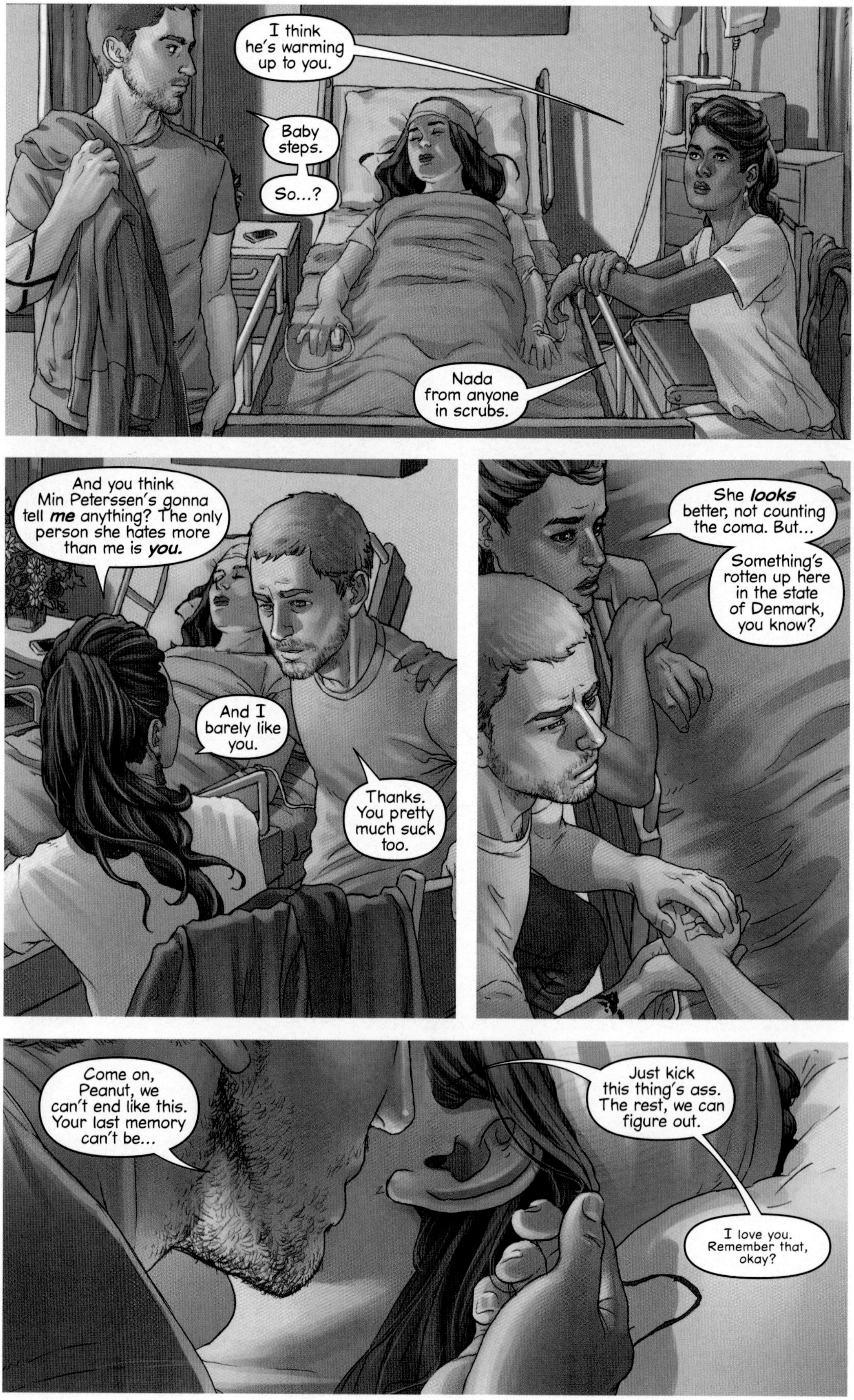

I think he's warming up to you.
Baby steps.
So...?
Nada from anyone in scrubs.
And you think Min Peterssen's gonna tell **me** anything? The only person she hates more than me is **you.**
And I barely like you.
Thanks. You pretty much suck too.
She **looks** better, not counting the coma. But...
Something's rotten up here in the state of Denmark, you know?
Come on, Peanut, we can't end like this. Your last memory can't be...
Just kick this thing's ass. The rest, we can figure out.
I love you. Remember that, okay?

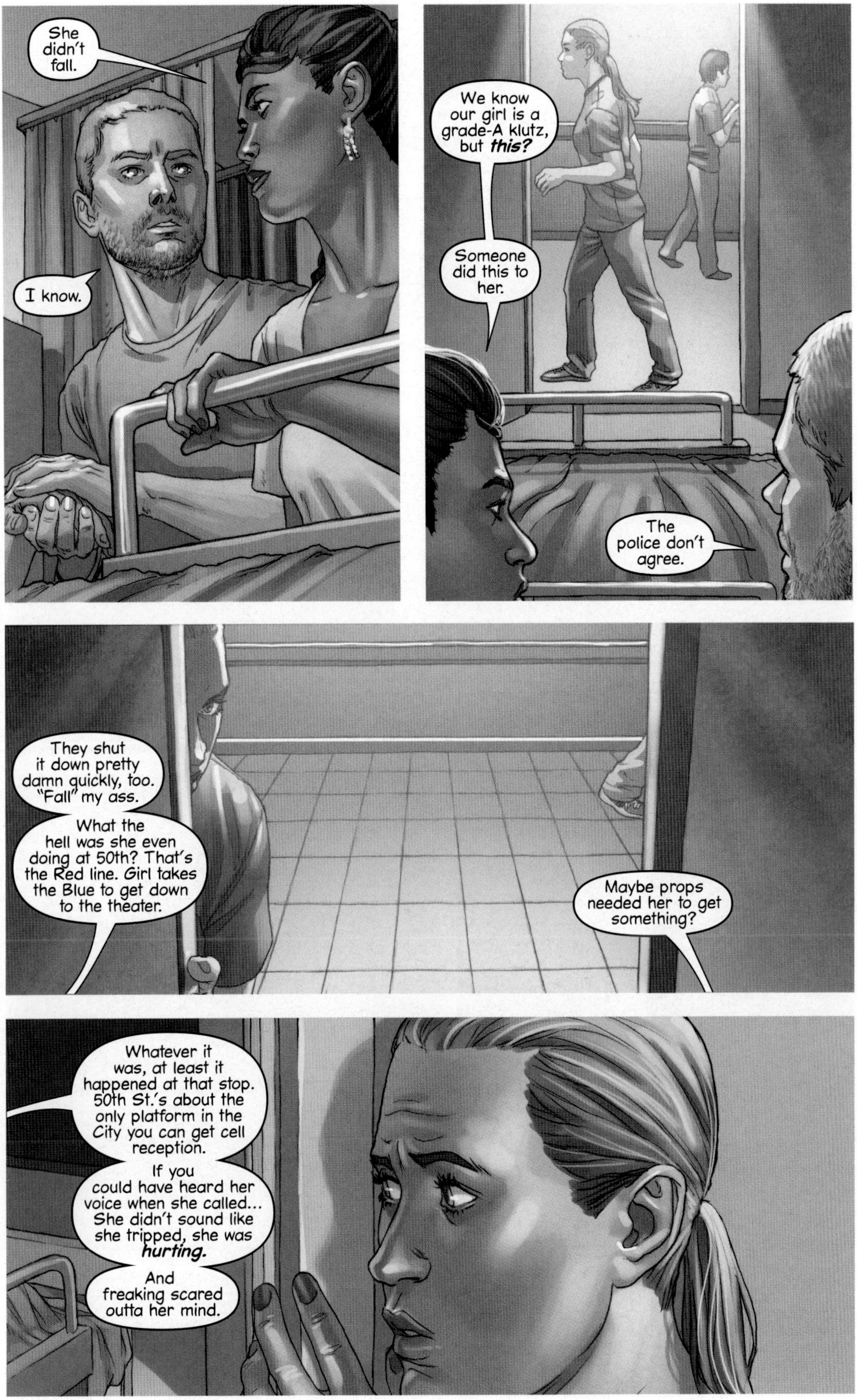
She didn't fall.
I know.
We know our girl is a grade-A klutz, but *this?*
Someone did this to her.
The police don't agree.
They shut it down pretty damn quickly, too. "Fall" my ass.
What the hell was she even doing at 50th? That's the Red line. Girl takes the Blue to get down to the theater.
Maybe props needed her to get something?
Whatever it was, at least it happened at that stop. 50th St.'s about the only platform in the City you can get cell reception.
If you could have heard her voice when she called... She didn't sound like she tripped, she was *hurting.*
And freaking scared outta her mind.

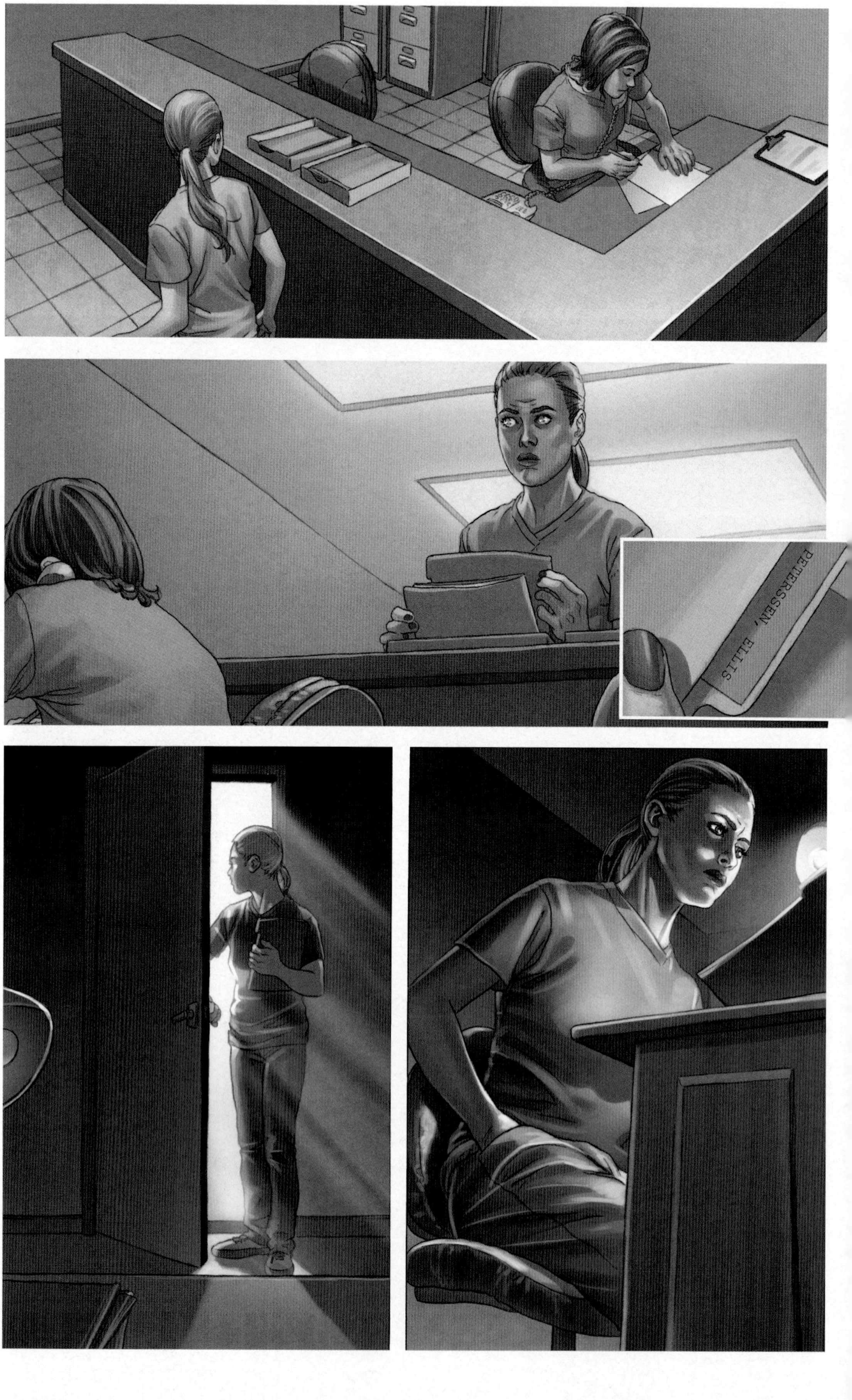
PETERSSEN, ELLIS

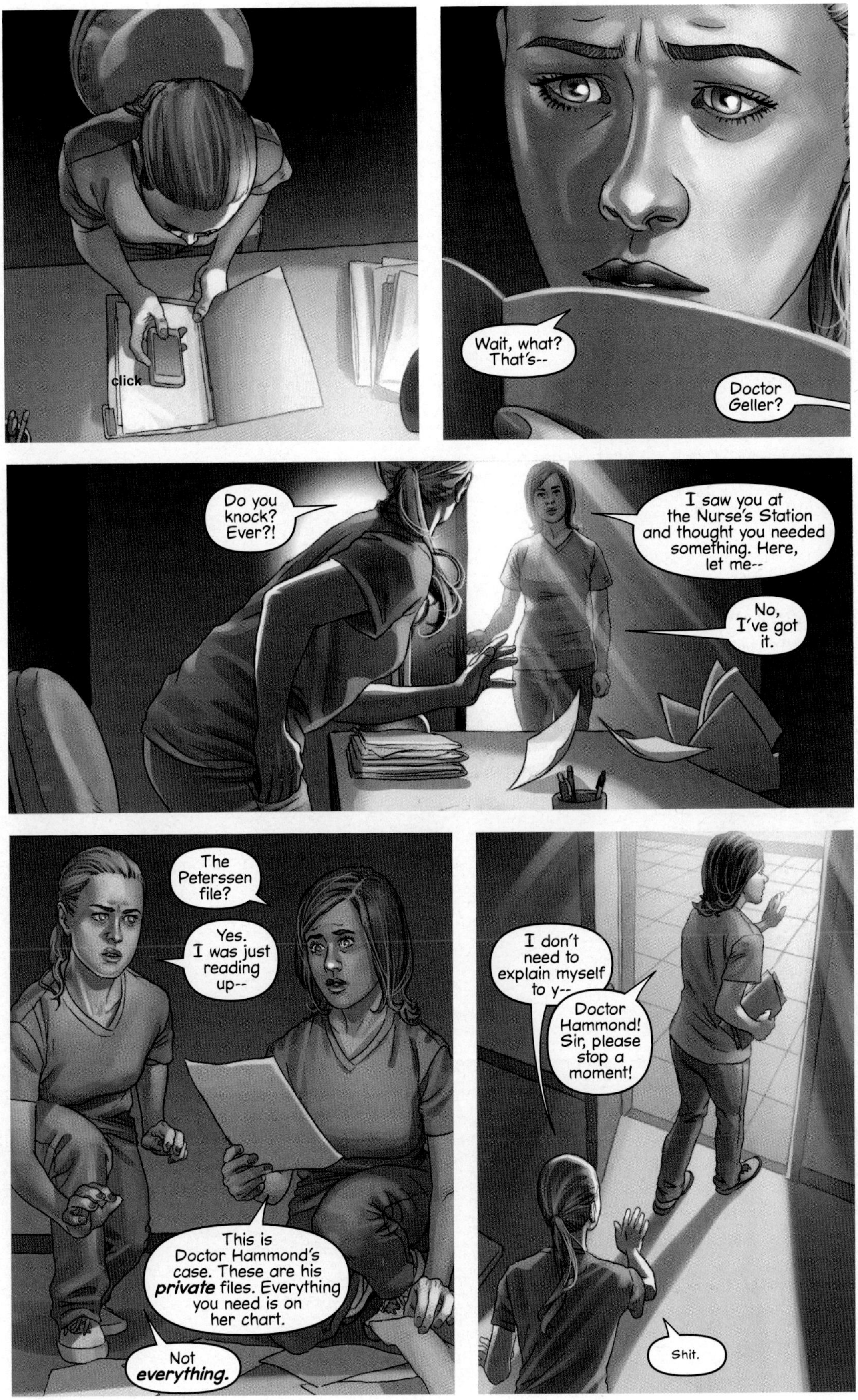
click
Wait, what? That's--
Doctor Geller?
Do you knock? Ever?!
I saw you at the Nurse's Station and thought you needed something. Here, let me--
No, I've got it.
The Peterssen file?
Yes. I was just reading up--
This is Doctor Hammond's case. These are his *private* files. Everything you need is on her chart.
Not *everything.*
I don't need to explain myself to y--
Doctor Hammond! Sir, please stop a moment!
Shit.

What the hell are you doing, Doctor Geller? Are those my *confidential* files?

For a patient that is also in *my* care while you're gone? Yes.

Everything you need is in her chart.

Really? You want to revise that statement, *Doctor?* Because from what I see, you've...

You see what you need to see, *Doctor.* I don't think I have to remind you that I am primary on this patient, not you.

And I need to know which patients are accurately showing progress and which are hopeless, living off our machines!

I don't know what you're insinuating, but I *highly* suggest...

How is it exactly that a patient who is *barely* a 4 on the Glasgow Scale is registering higher than normal brain activity? And how is it that she's at such a low level while the head trauma is so minor? Because that seems to only be present in *your* charts, not the general...

I think you're over-stepping here, Geller.

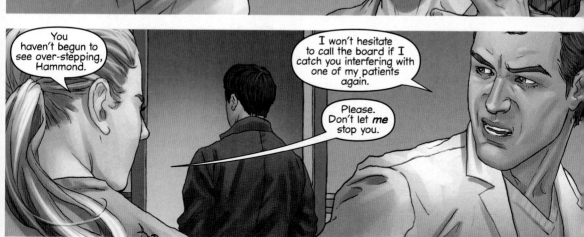

You haven't begun to see over-stepping, Hammond.

I won't hesitate to call the board if I catch you interfering with one of my patients again.

Please. Don't let *me* stop you.

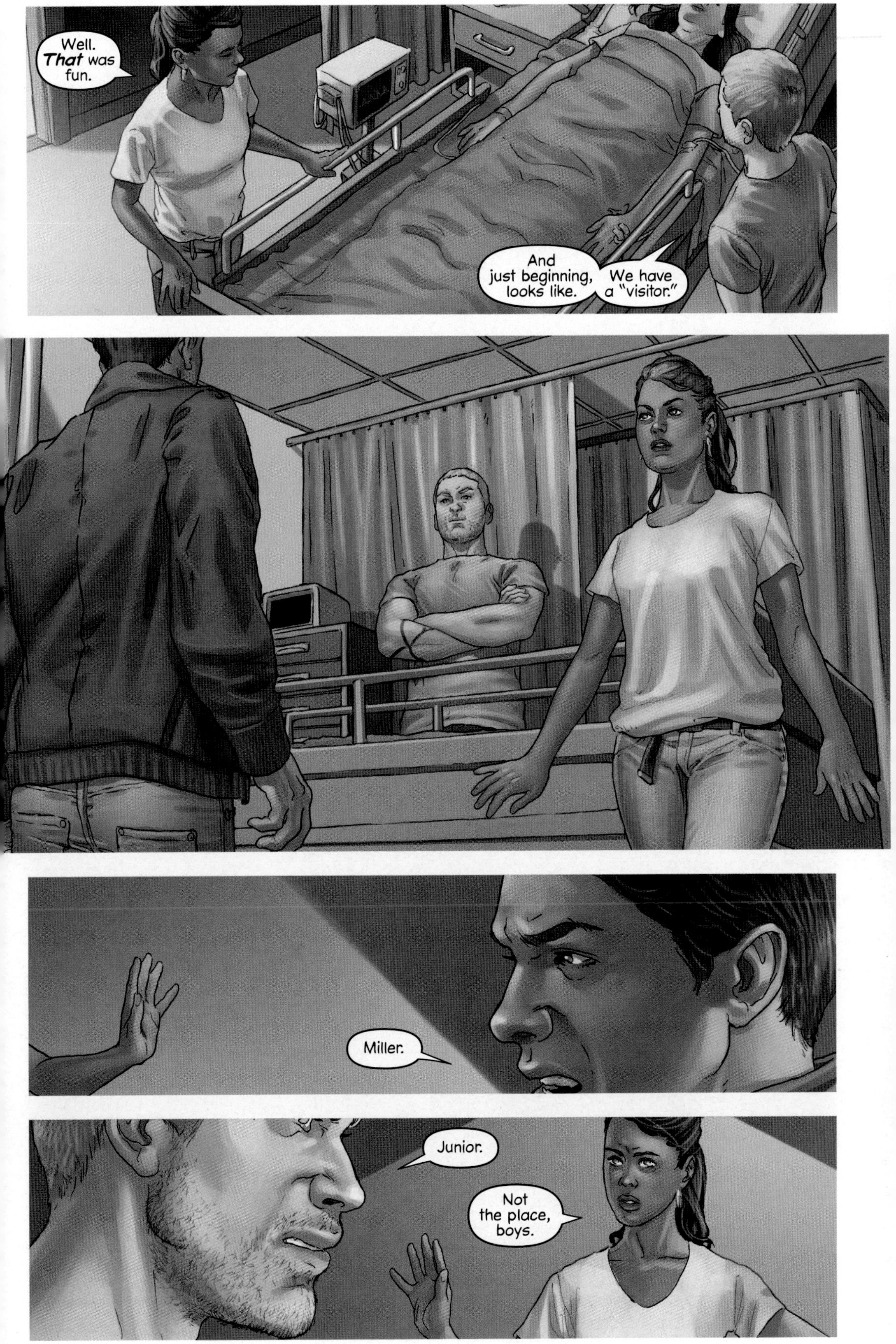

Well. **That** was fun.
And just beginning, looks like.
We have a "visitor."
Miller.
Junior.
Not the place, boys.

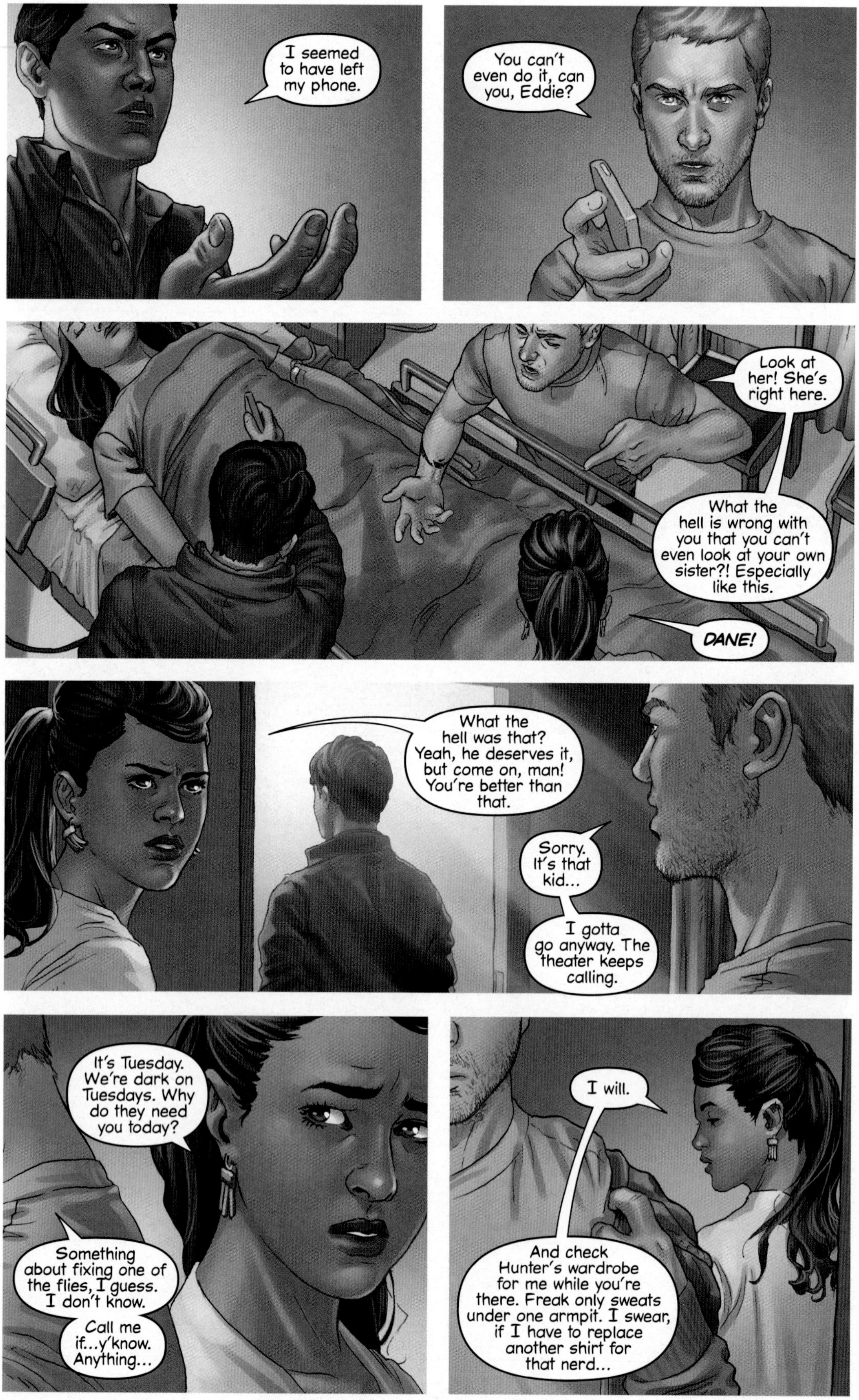

I seemed to have left my phone.
You can't even do it, can you, Eddie?
Look at her! She's right here.
What the hell is wrong with you that you can't even look at your own sister?! Especially like this.
DANE!
What the hell was that? Yeah, he deserves it, but come on, man! You're better than that.
Sorry. It's that kid...
I gotta go anyway. The theater keeps calling.
It's Tuesday. We're dark on Tuesdays. Why do they need you today?
Something about fixing one of the flies, I guess. I don't know.
Call me if...y'know. Anything...
I will.
And check Hunter's wardrobe for me while you're there. Freak only sweats under one armpit. I swear, if I have to replace another shirt for that nerd...

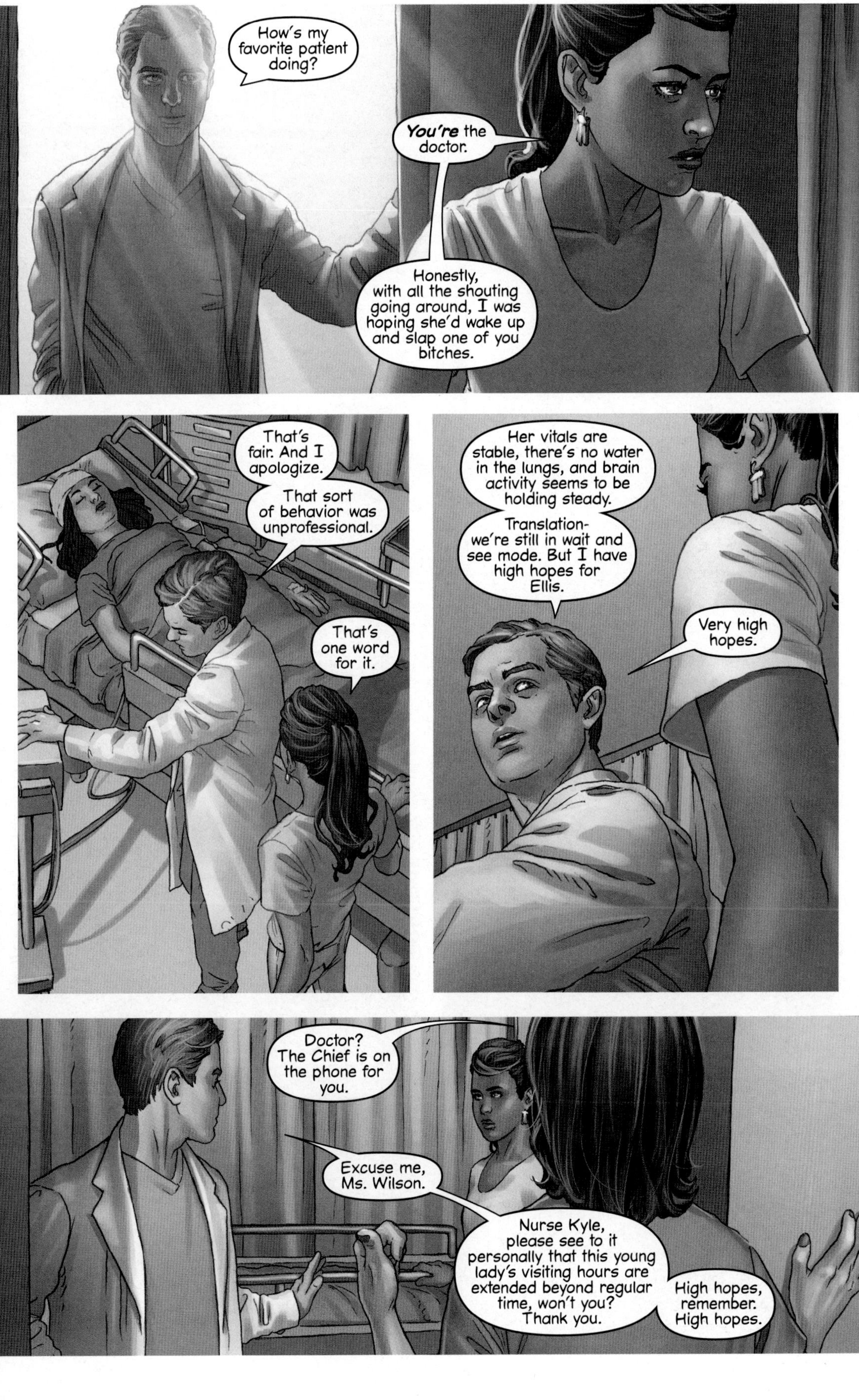

How's my favorite patient doing?
You're the doctor.
Honestly, with all the shouting going around, I was hoping she'd wake up and slap one of you bitches.
That's fair. And I apologize.
That sort of behavior was unprofessional.
That's one word for it.
Her vitals are stable, there's no water in the lungs, and brain activity seems to be holding steady.
Translation- we're still in wait and see mode. But I have high hopes for Ellis.
Very high hopes.
Doctor? The Chief is on the phone for you.
Excuse me, Ms. Wilson.
Nurse Kyle, please see to it personally that this young lady's visiting hours are extended beyond regular time, won't you? Thank you.
High hopes, remember. High hopes.

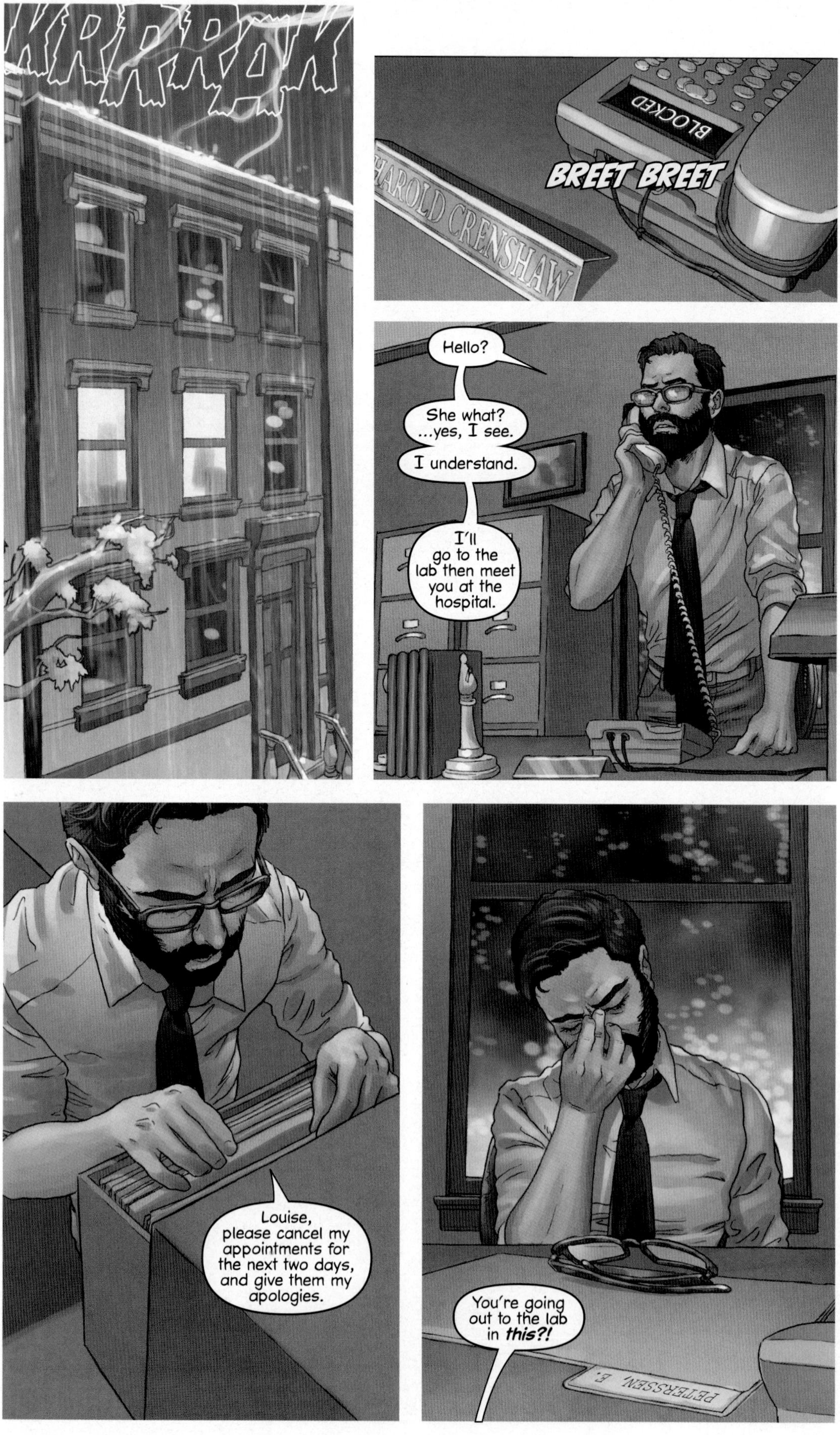
KRRRAK
BLOCKED
BREET BREET
Hello?
She what? ...yes, I see.
I understand.
I'll go to the lab then meet you at the hospital.
Louise, please cancel my appointments for the next two days, and give them my apologies.
You're going out to the lab in ***this?!***
PETERSSEN, E.

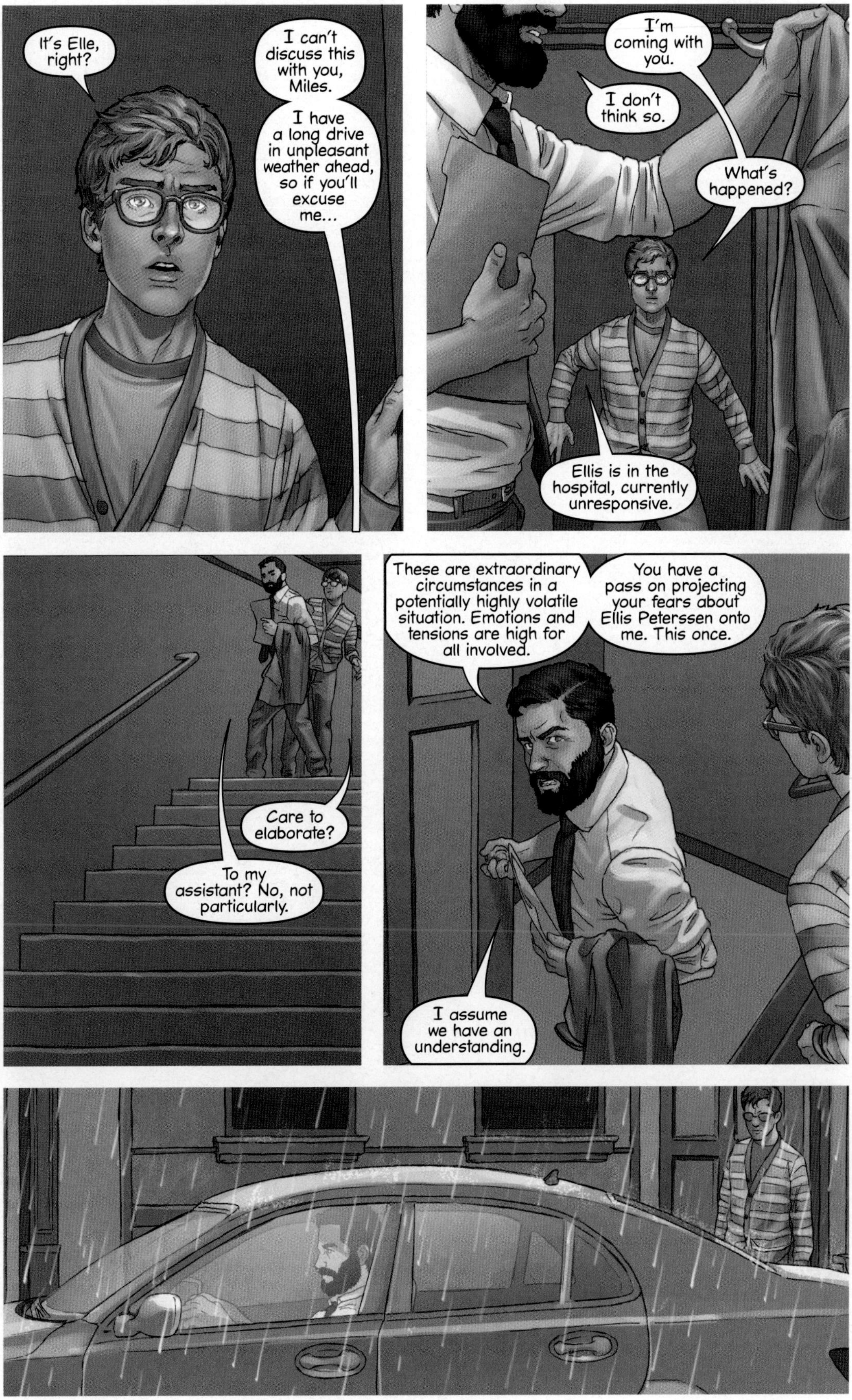

It's Elle, right?
I can't discuss this with you, Miles.
I have a long drive in unpleasant weather ahead, so if you'll excuse me...
I'm coming with you.
I don't think so.
What's happened?
Ellis is in the hospital, currently unresponsive.
Care to elaborate?
To my assistant? No, not particularly.
These are extraordinary circumstances in a potentially highly volatile situation. Emotions and tensions are high for all involved.
You have a pass on projecting your fears about Ellis Peterssen onto me. This once.
I assume we have an understanding.

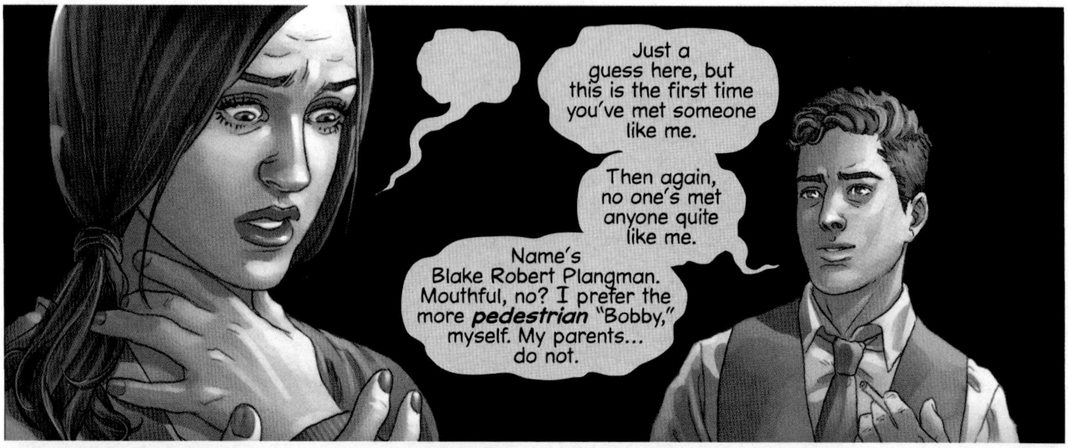
Just a guess here, but this is the first time you've met someone like me.
Then again, no one's met anyone quite like me.
Name's Blake Robert Plangman. Mouthful, no? I prefer the more **pedestrian** "Bobby," myself. My parents... do not.

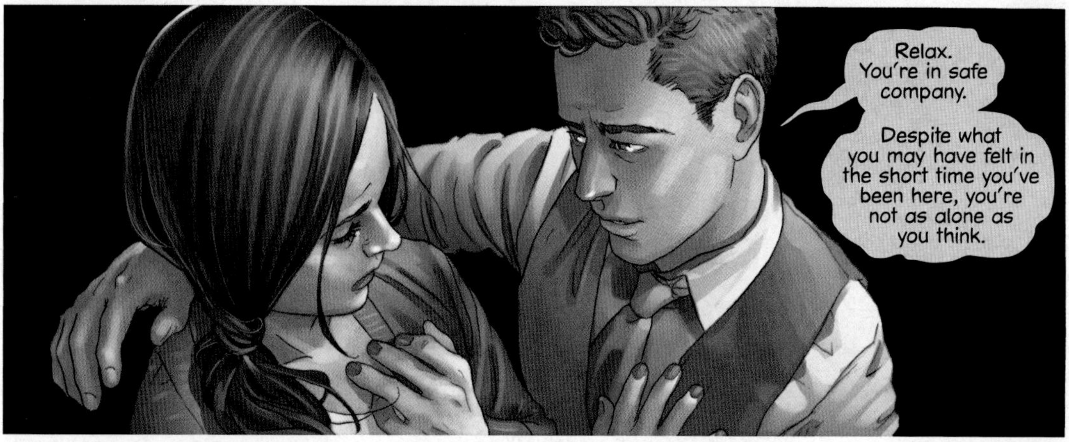
Relax. You're in safe company.
Despite what you may have felt in the short time you've been here, you're not as alone as you think.

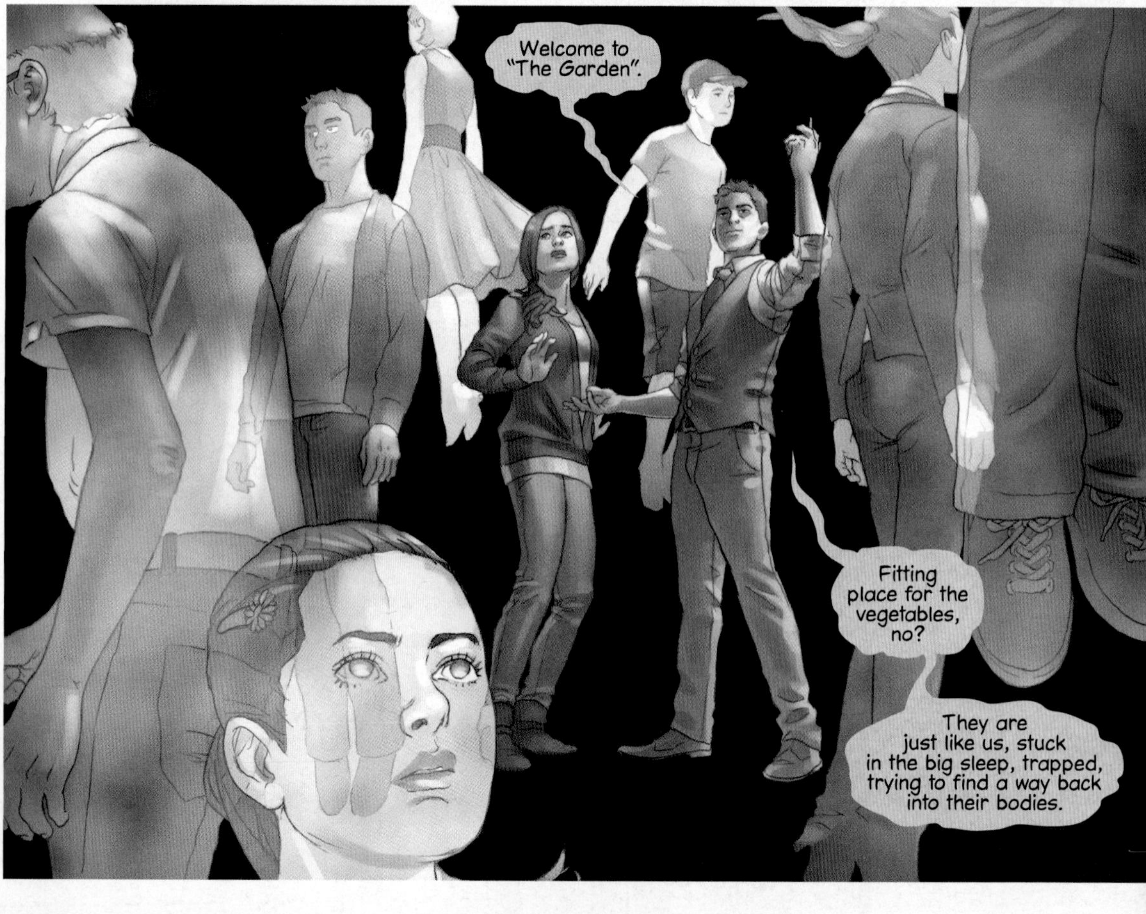
Welcome to "The Garden".
Fitting place for the vegetables, no?
They are just like us, stuck in the big sleep, trapped, trying to find a way back into their bodies.

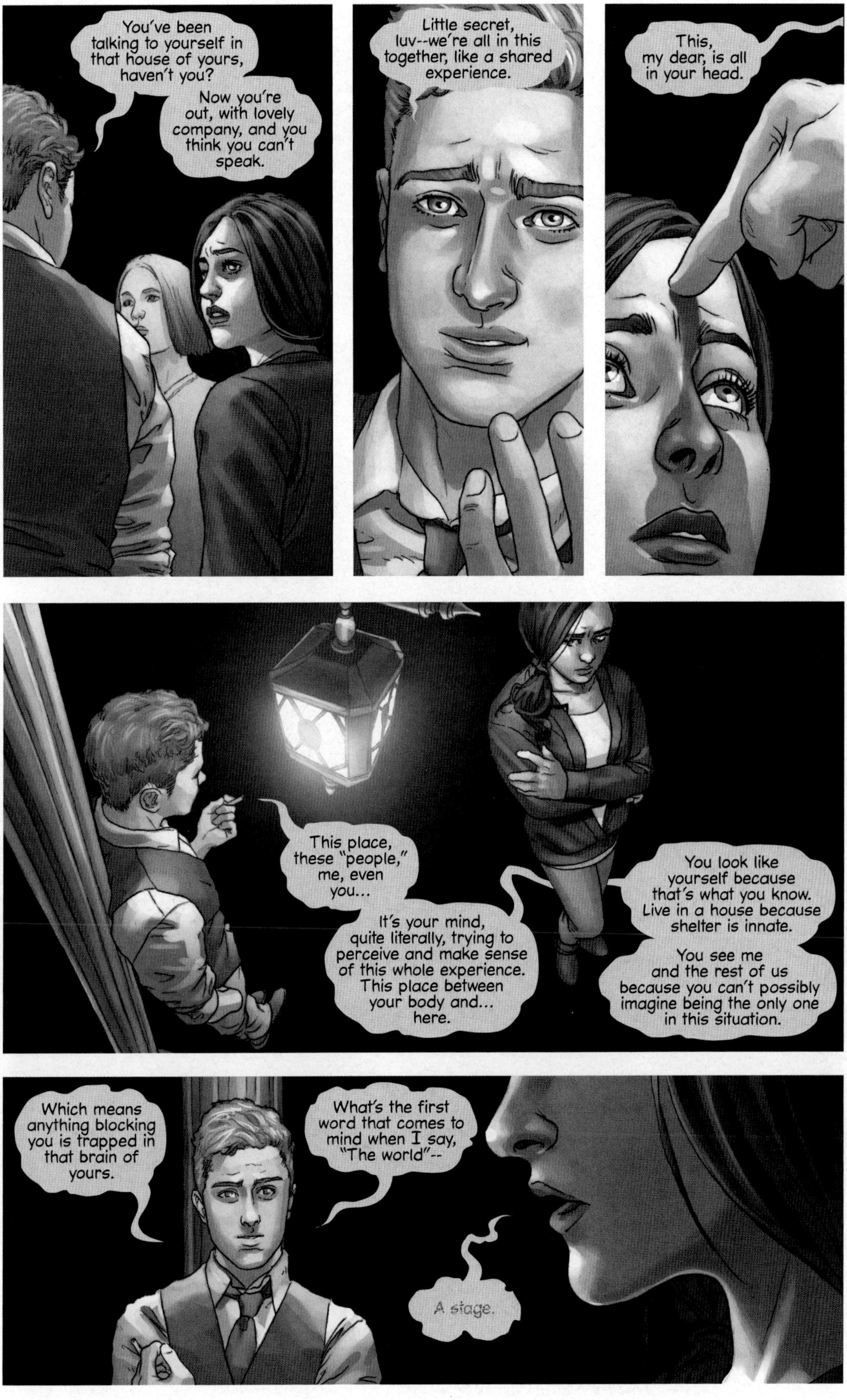
You've been talking to yourself in that house of yours, haven't you?
Now you're out, with lovely company, and you think you can't speak.
Little secret, luv--we're all in this together, like a shared experience.
This, my dear, is all in your head.
This place, these "people," me, even you...
It's your mind, quite literally, trying to perceive and make sense of this whole experience. This place between your body and... here.
You look like yourself because that's what you know. Live in a house because shelter is innate.
You see me and the rest of us because you can't possibly imagine being the only one in this situation.
Which means anything blocking you is trapped in that brain of yours.
What's the first word that comes to mind when I say, "The world"--
A stage.

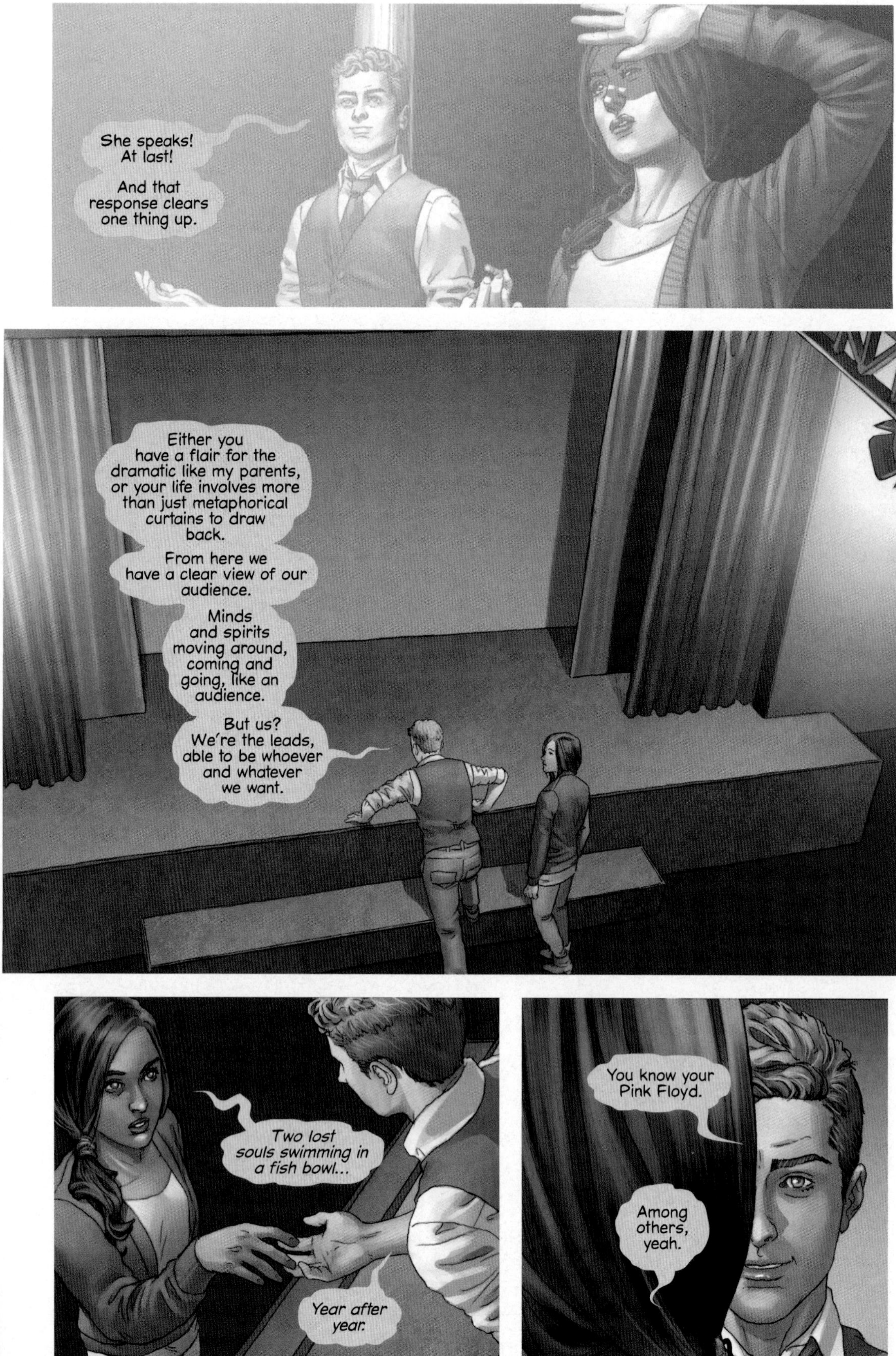
She speaks! At last!
And that response clears one thing up.
Either you have a flair for the dramatic like my parents, or your life involves more than just metaphorical curtains to draw back.
From here we have a clear view of our audience.
Minds and spirits moving around, coming and going, like an audience.
But us? We're the leads, able to be whoever and whatever we want.
Two lost souls swimming in a fish bowl...
Year after year.
You know your Pink Floyd.
Among others, yeah.

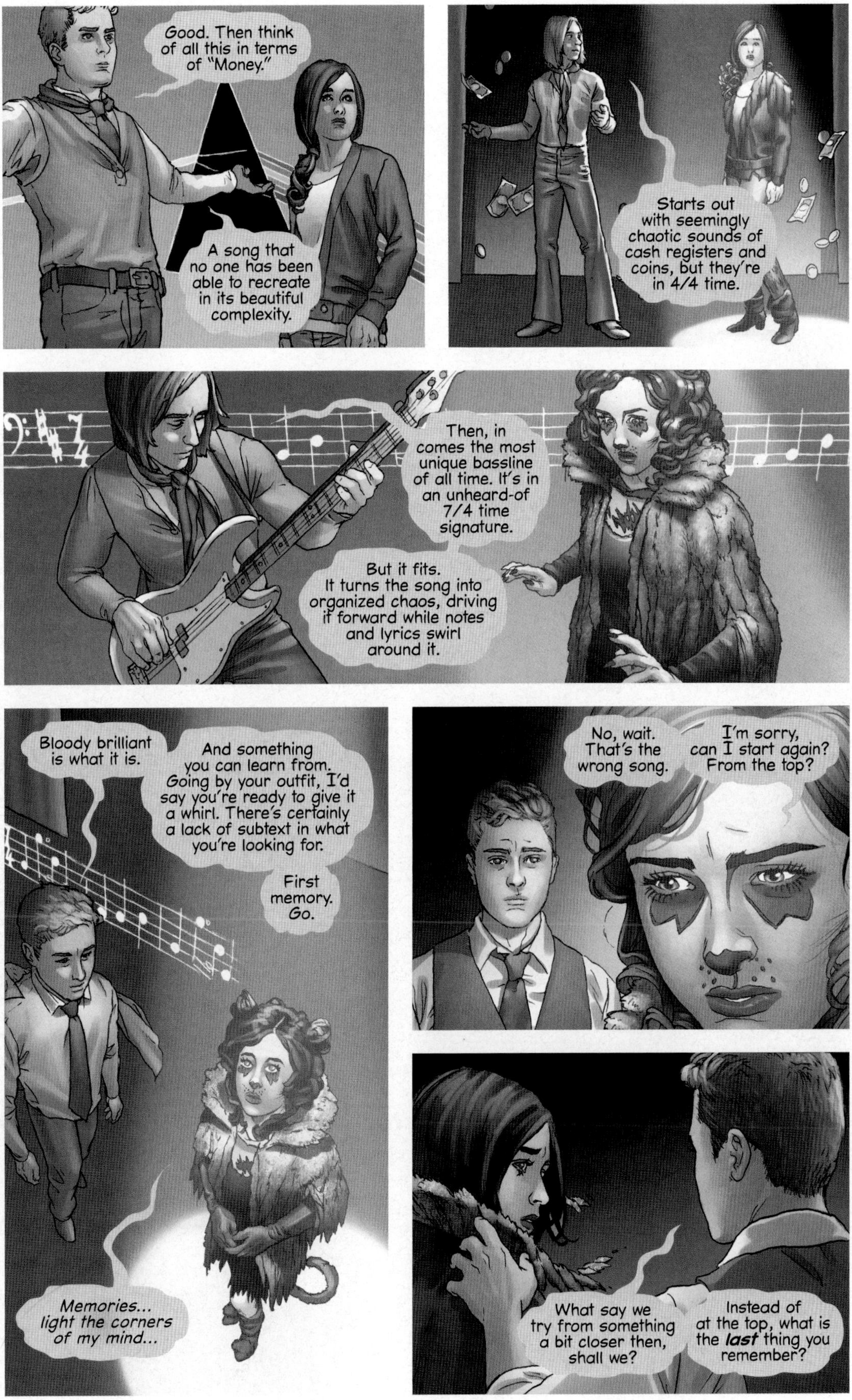

Good. Then think of all this in terms of "Money."
A song that no one has been able to recreate in its beautiful complexity.
Starts out with seemingly chaotic sounds of cash registers and coins, but they're in 4/4 time.
Then, in comes the most unique bassline of all time. It's in an unheard-of 7/4 time signature.
But it fits. It turns the song into organized chaos, driving it forward while notes and lyrics swirl around it.
Bloody brilliant is what it is.
And something you can learn from. Going by your outfit, I'd say you're ready to give it a whirl. There's certainly a lack of subtext in what you're looking for.
First memory. Go.
Memories... light the corners of my mind...
No, wait. That's the wrong song.
I'm sorry, can I start again? From the top?
What say we try from something a bit closer then, shall we?
Instead of at the top, what is the *last* thing you remember?

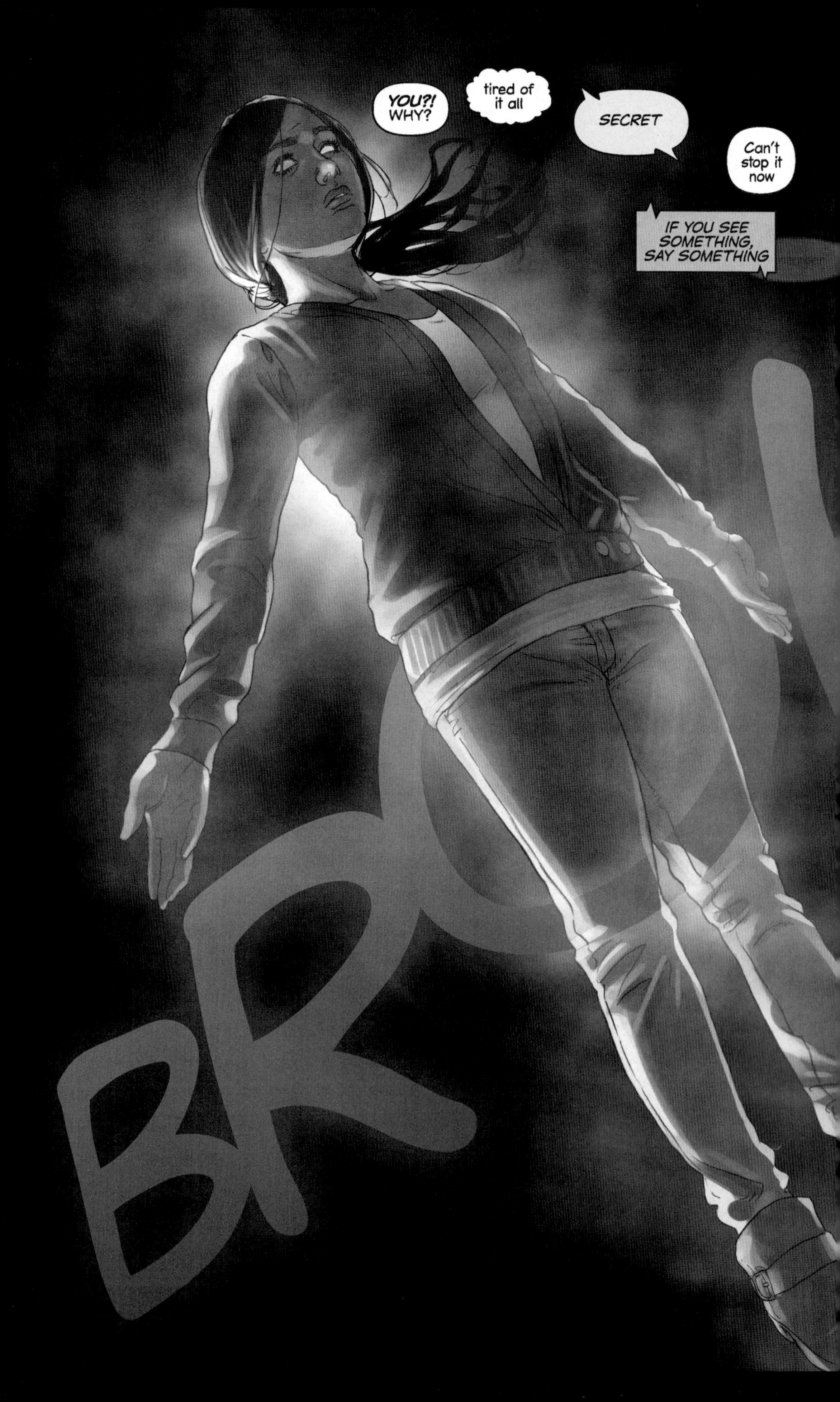

YOU?! WHY?
tired of it all
SECRET
Can't stop it now
IF YOU SEE SOMETHING, SAY SOMETHING
BR

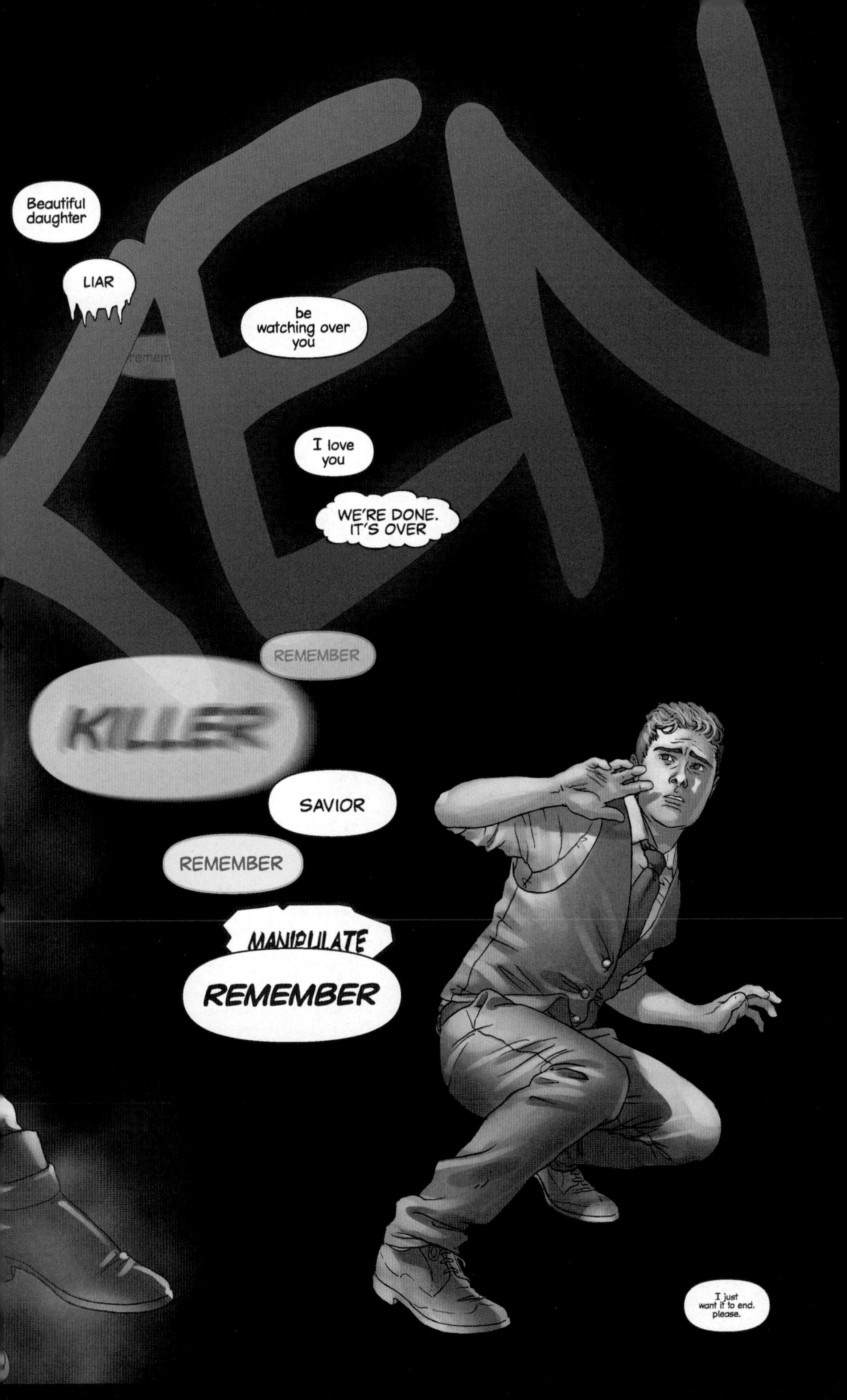
Beautiful daughter
LIAR
be watching over you
I love you
WE'RE DONE. IT'S OVER
REMEMBER
KILLER
SAVIOR
REMEMBER
MANIPULATE
REMEMBER
I just want it to end. please.

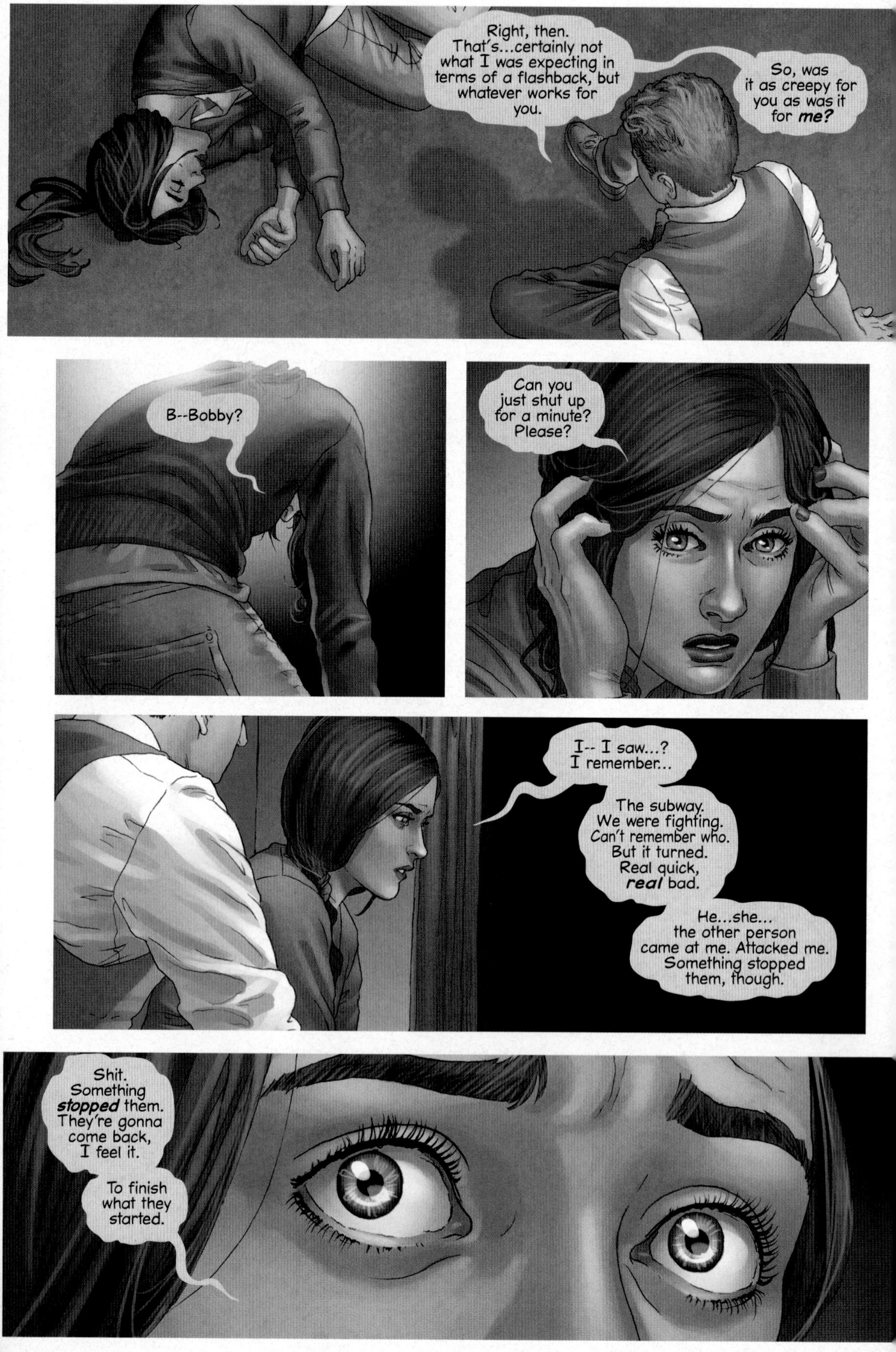
Right, then. That's...certainly not what I was expecting in terms of a flashback, but whatever works for you.
So, was it as creepy for you as was it for **me?**
B--Bobby?
Can you just shut up for a minute? Please?
I-- I saw...? I remember...
The subway. We were fighting. Can't remember who. But it turned. Real quick, ***real*** bad.
He...she... the other person came at me. Attacked me. Something stopped them, though.
Shit. Something ***stopped*** them. They're gonna come back, I feel it.
To finish what they started.

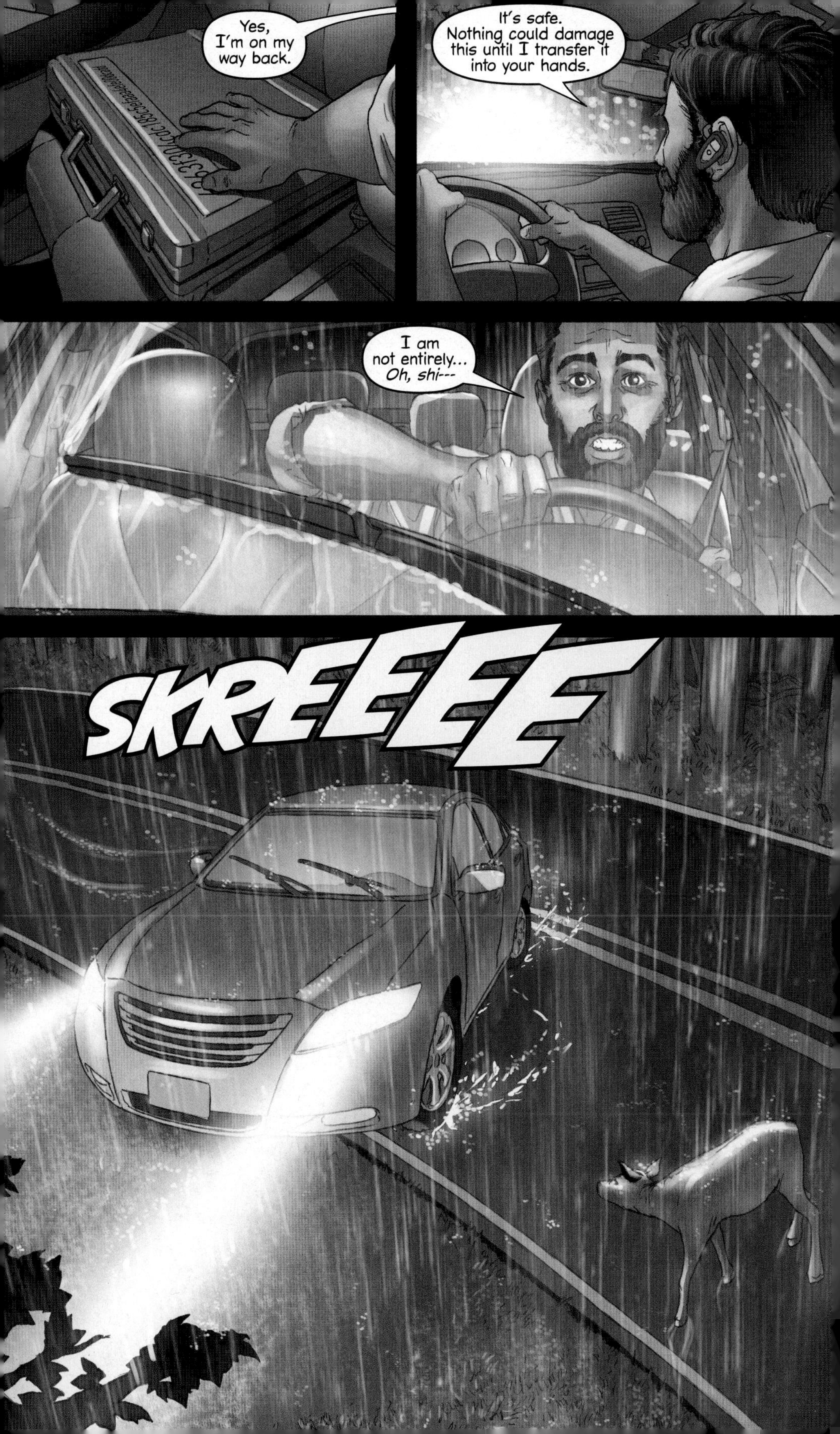
Yes, I'm on my way back.
It's safe. Nothing could damage this until I transfer it into your hands.
I am not entirely... Oh, shi---
SKREEEE

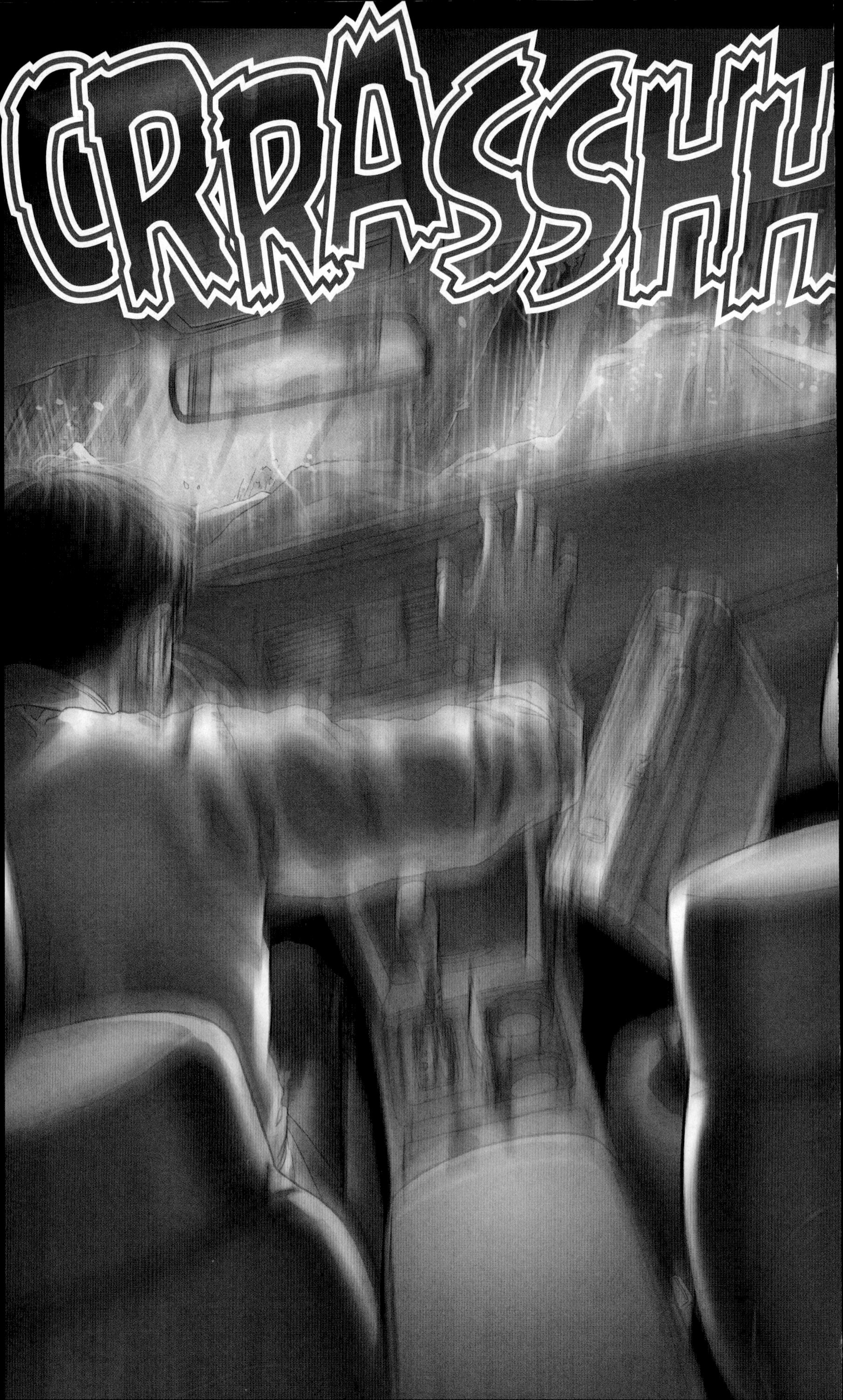
CRRASSHH

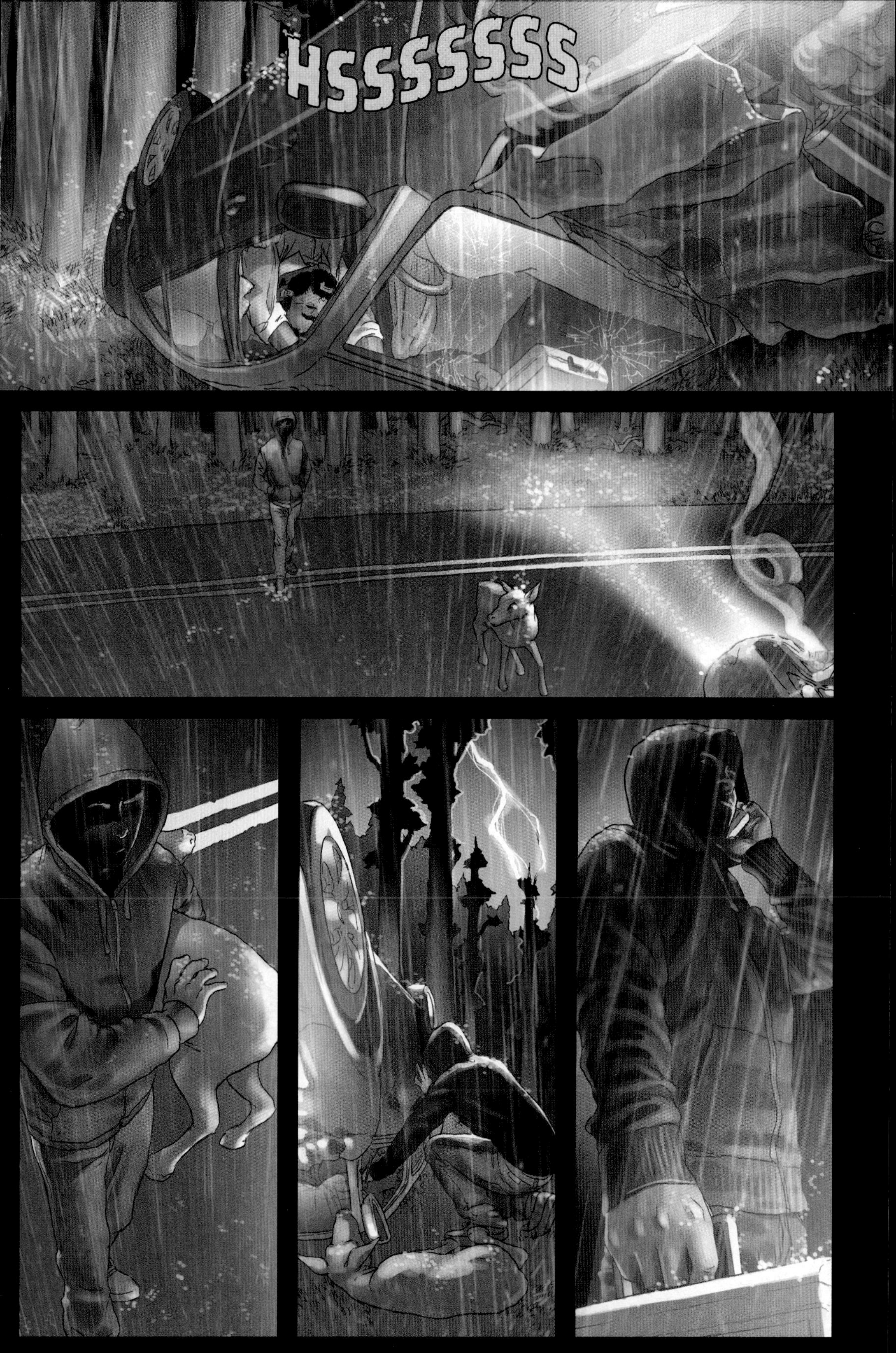
HSSSSSSS

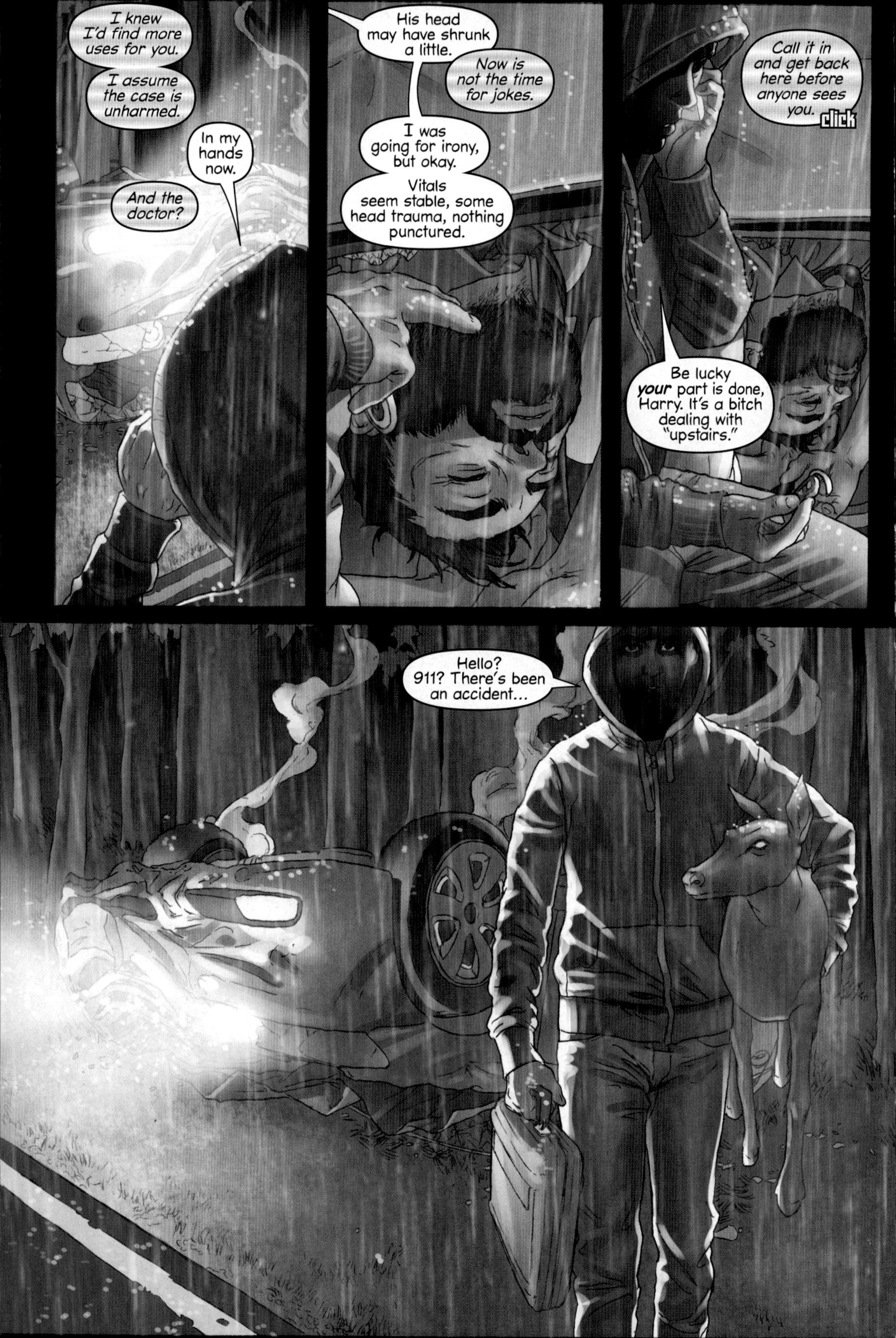
I knew I'd find more uses for you.
I assume the case is unharmed.
In my hands now.
And the doctor?
His head may have shrunk a little.
Now is not the time for jokes.
I was going for irony, but okay.
Vitals seem stable, some head trauma, nothing punctured.
Call it in and get back here before anyone sees you.
click
Be lucky *your* part is done, Harry. It's a bitch dealing with "upstairs."
Hello? 911? There's been an accident...

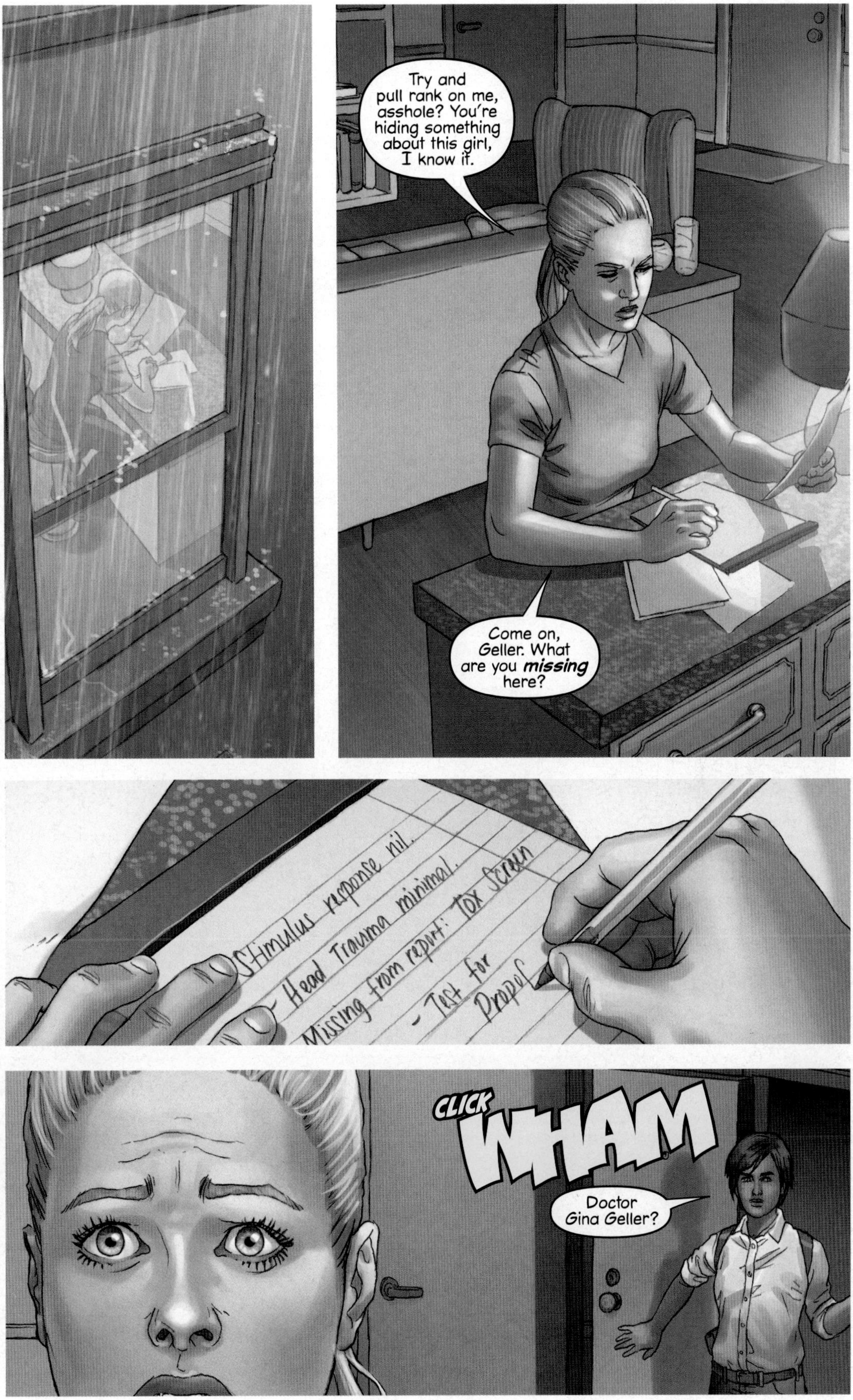

Try and pull rank on me, asshole? You're hiding something about this girl, I know it.
Come on, Geller. What are you *missing* here?
Stimulus response nil.
- Head Trauma minimal.
Missing from report: Tox Screen
- Test for Propof
CLICK
WHAM
Doctor Gina Geller?

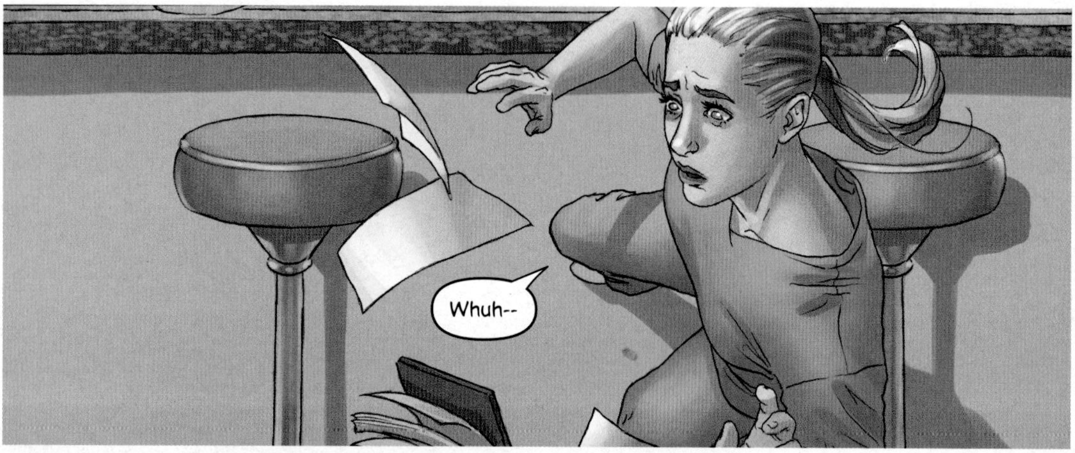
Whuh--

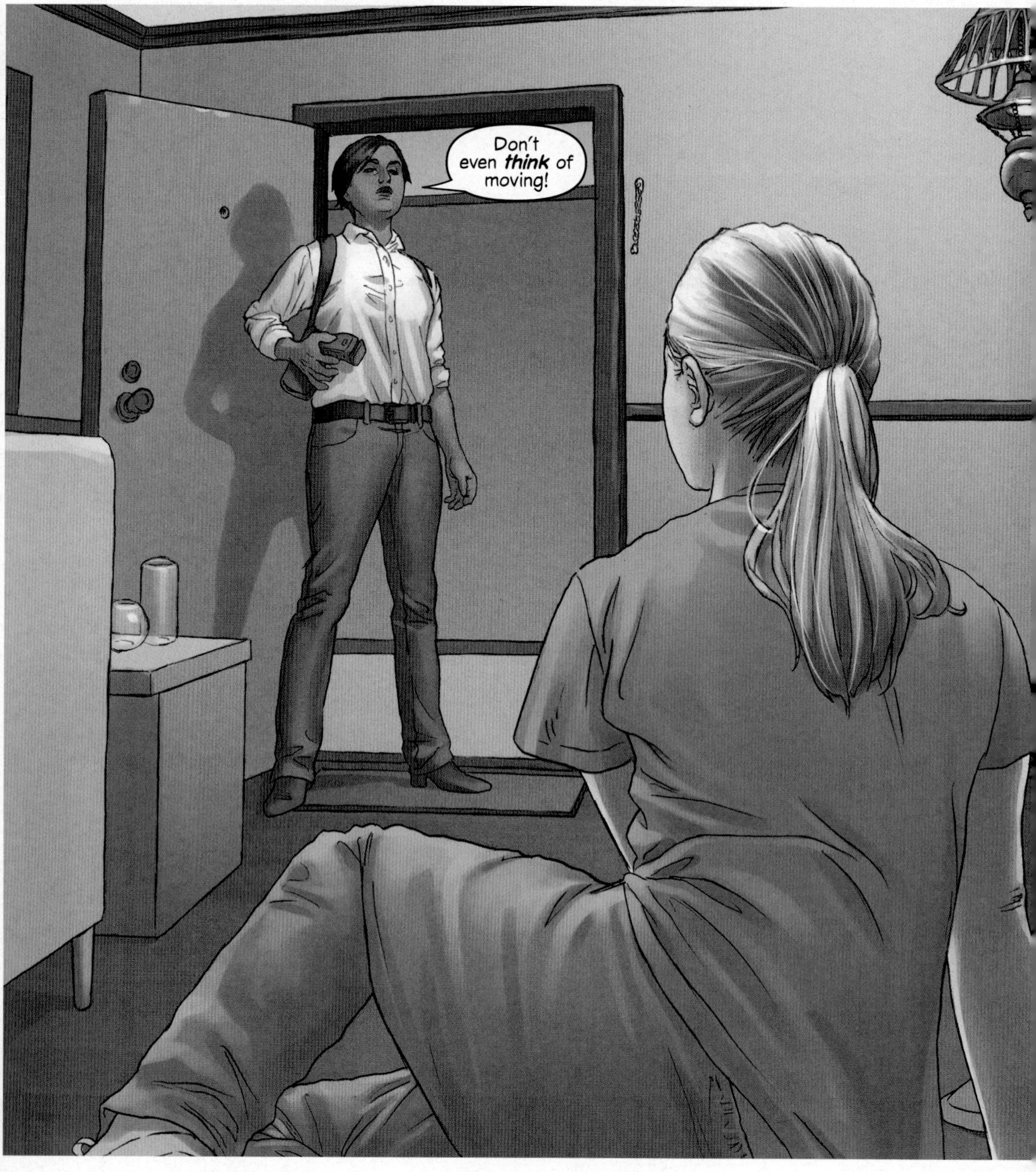
Don't even *think* of moving!

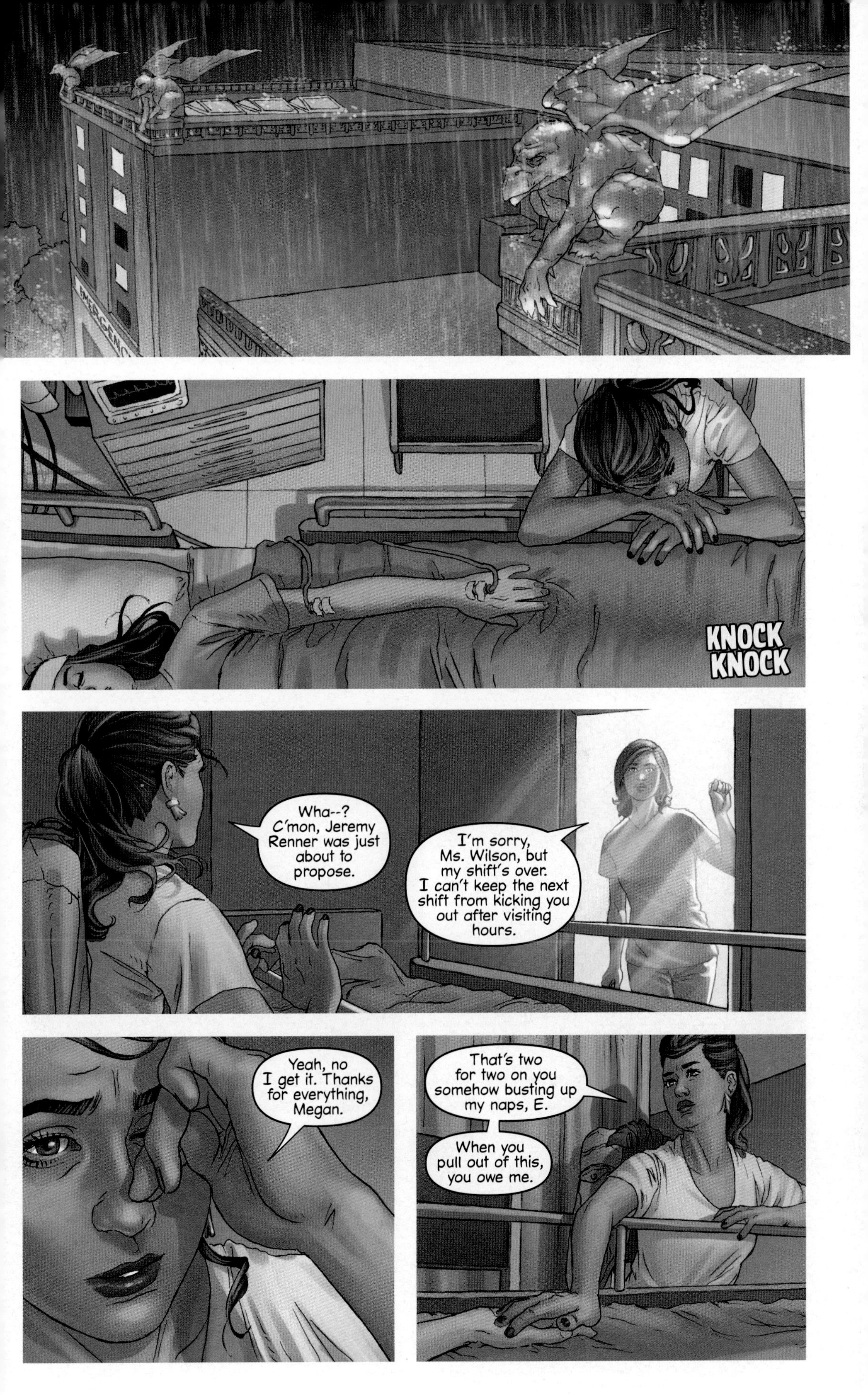

EMERGENCY
KNOCK KNOCK
Wha--? C'mon, Jeremy Renner was just about to propose.
I'm sorry, Ms. Wilson, but my shift's over. I can't keep the next shift from kicking you out after visiting hours.
Yeah, no I get it. Thanks for everything, Megan.
That's two for two on you somehow busting up my naps, E.
When you pull out of this, you owe me.

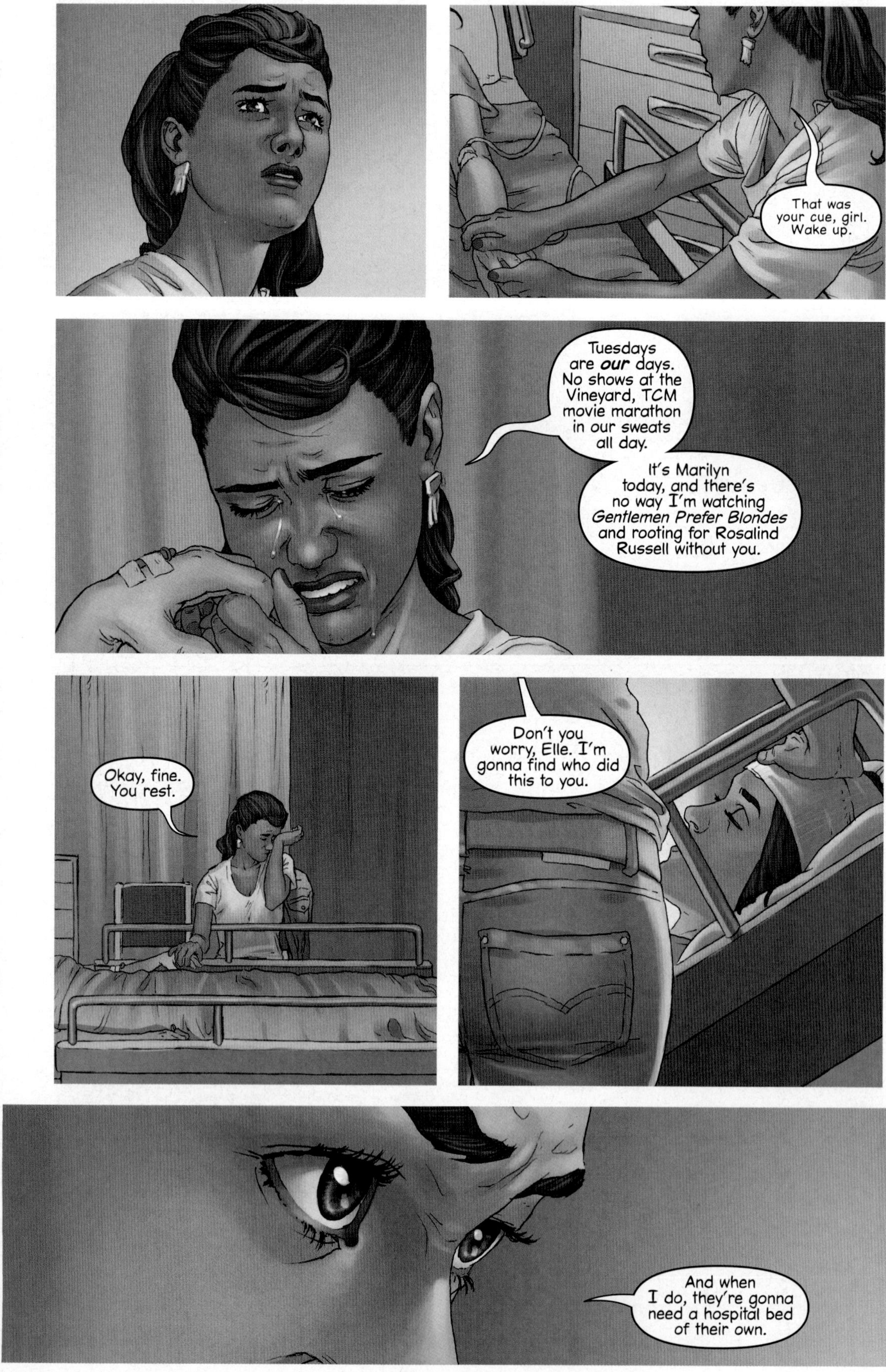
That was your cue, girl. Wake up.
Tuesdays are *our* days. No shows at the Vineyard, TCM movie marathon in our sweats all day.
It's Marilyn today, and there's no way I'm watching *Gentlemen Prefer Blondes* and rooting for Rosalind Russell without you.
Okay, fine. You rest.
Don't you worry, Elle. I'm gonna find who did this to you.
And when I do, they're gonna need a hospital bed of their own.

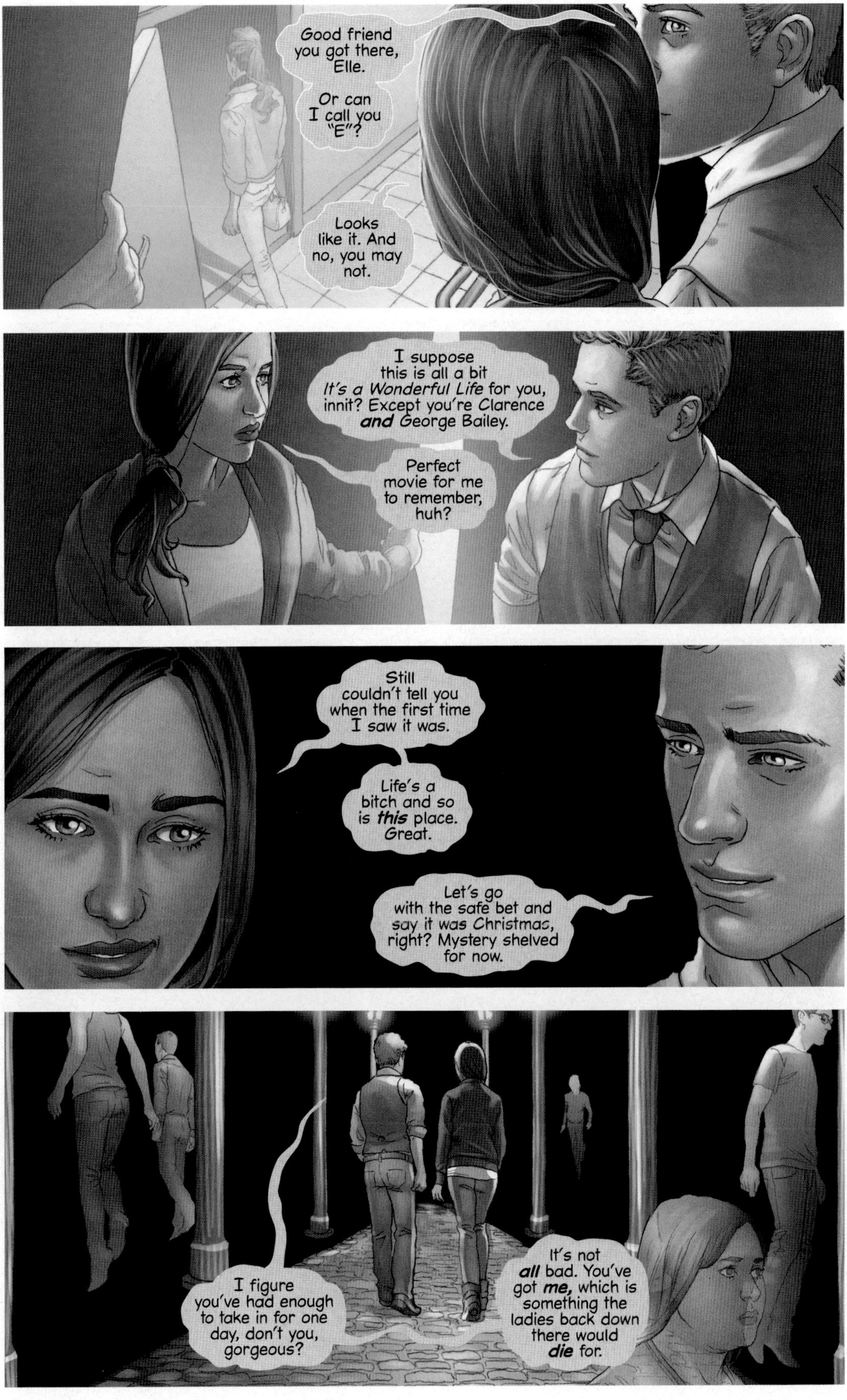

Good friend you got there, Elle.
Or can I call you "E"?
Looks like it. And no, you may not.
I suppose this is all a bit *It's a Wonderful Life* for you, innit? Except you're Clarence **and** George Bailey.
Perfect movie for me to remember, huh?
Still couldn't tell you when the first time I saw it was.
Life's a bitch and so is ***this*** place. Great.
Let's go with the safe bet and say it was Christmas, right? Mystery shelved for now.
I figure you've had enough to take in for one day, don't you, gorgeous?
It's not ***all*** bad. You've got ***me,*** which is something the ladies back down there would ***die*** for.

Apparently I have a boyfriend, so watch it with the pet names, Blake Robert "Bobby" Plangman.

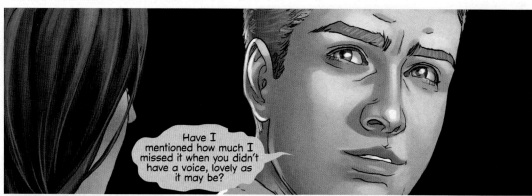

Have I mentioned how much I missed it when you didn't have a voice, lovely as it may be?

Crap!

Sorry, no offense but I seriously doubt I will ever get used to that.

Está bien. I'm one less to worry about, *bonita.*

Wait a minute, Esteban. I know that look.

You're leaving.

Sí. El Dios calls, my friend.

Sylvia and your *bambinos...?*

In God's hands now. I have faith it is my time and they will be cared for.

I only wish we could have had a proper goodbye.

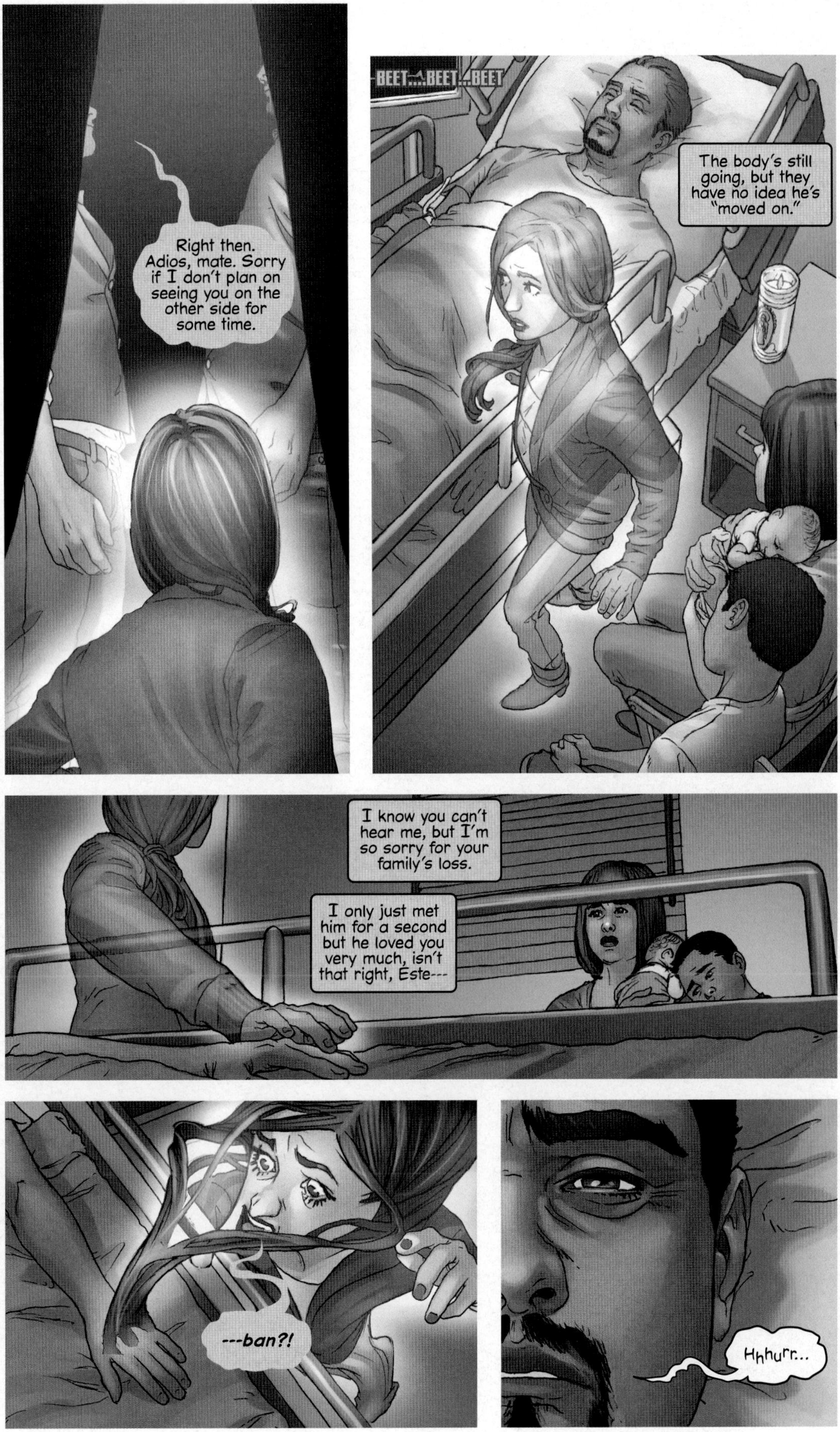
Right then. Adios, mate. Sorry if I don't plan on seeing you on the other side for some time.
BEET...BEET...BEET
The body's still going, but they have no idea he's "moved on."
I know you can't hear me, but I'm so sorry for your family's loss.
I only just met him for a second but he loved you very much, isn't that right, Este---
---ban?!
Hhhurr...

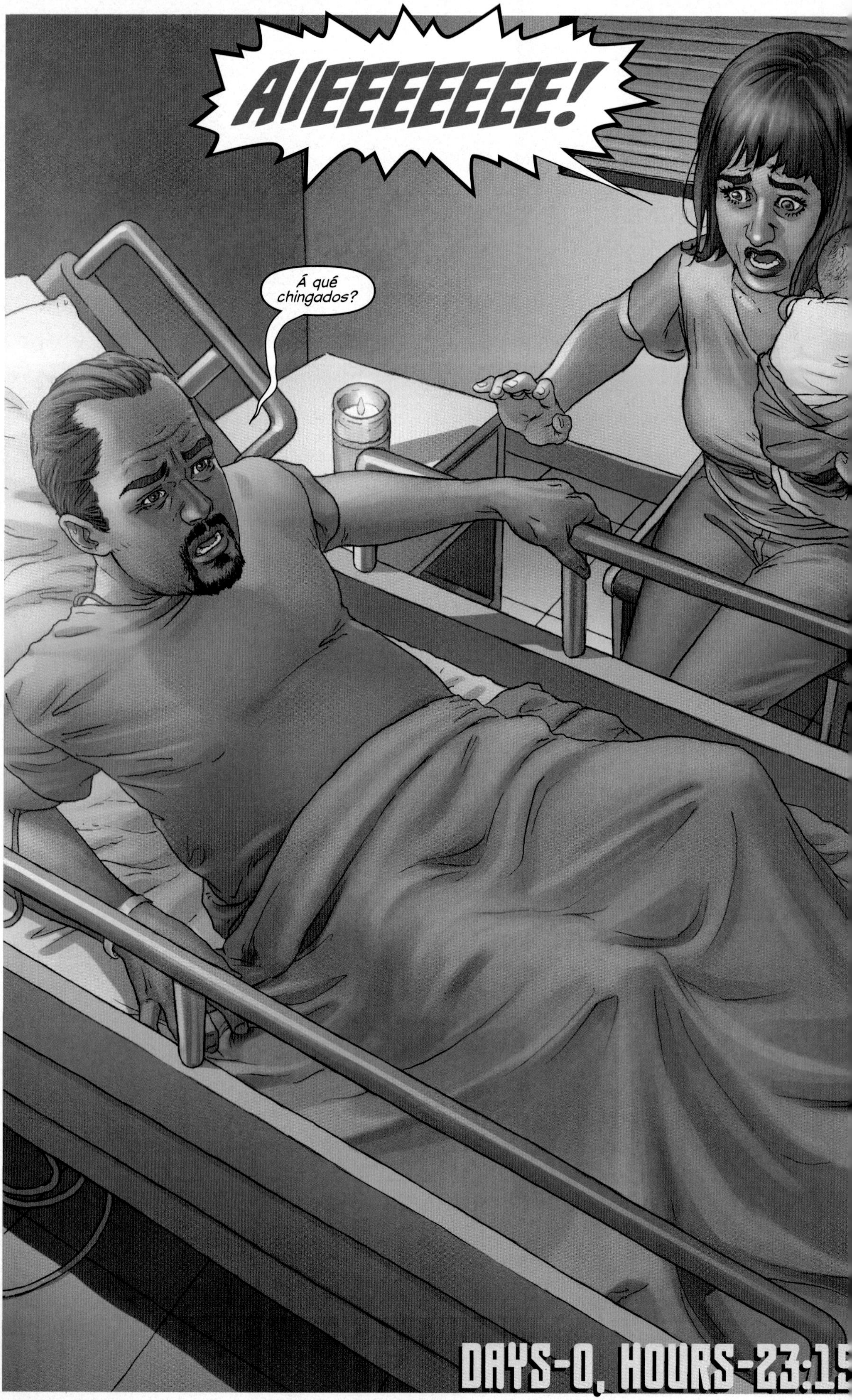
AIEEEEEEEE!
Á qué chingados?
DAYS-0, HOURS-23:15

existence. They may beli̶ . . . . . . one is around but is now transmitting signals, like radio or TV that we in our limited physical world can't pick up. And yet we long to. We may try to contact the dead, to speak to them and pierce the veil between life and death. It is futile to debate the reality of this, for it is beyond our knowing. In loss we are looking and longing for connection. The longing for that exploration should be stopped and questioned only if you believe it is being exploi̶ . . . .

-Elisabeth Kübler-Ross, *On Grief and Grieving*

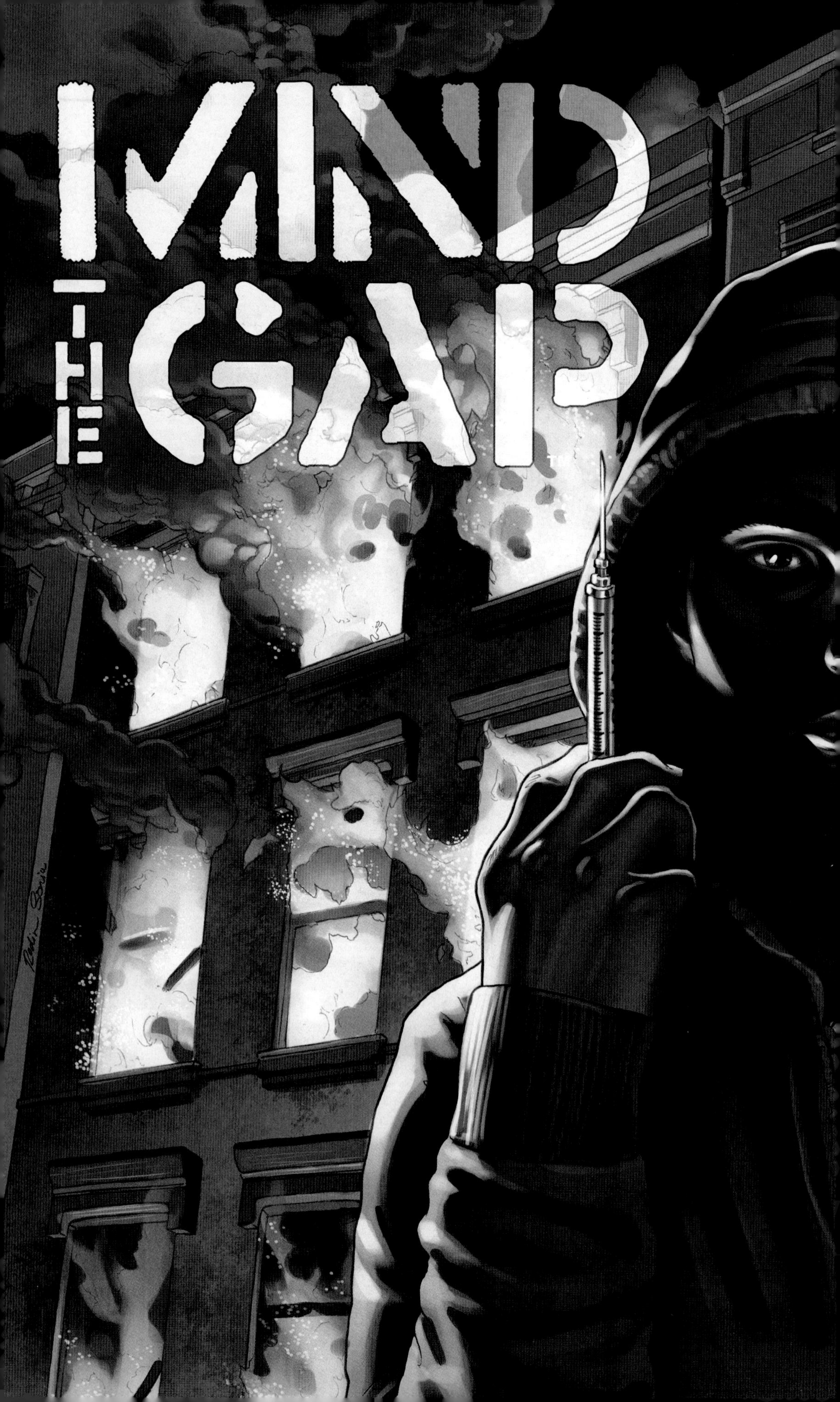
MIND
THE
GAP™

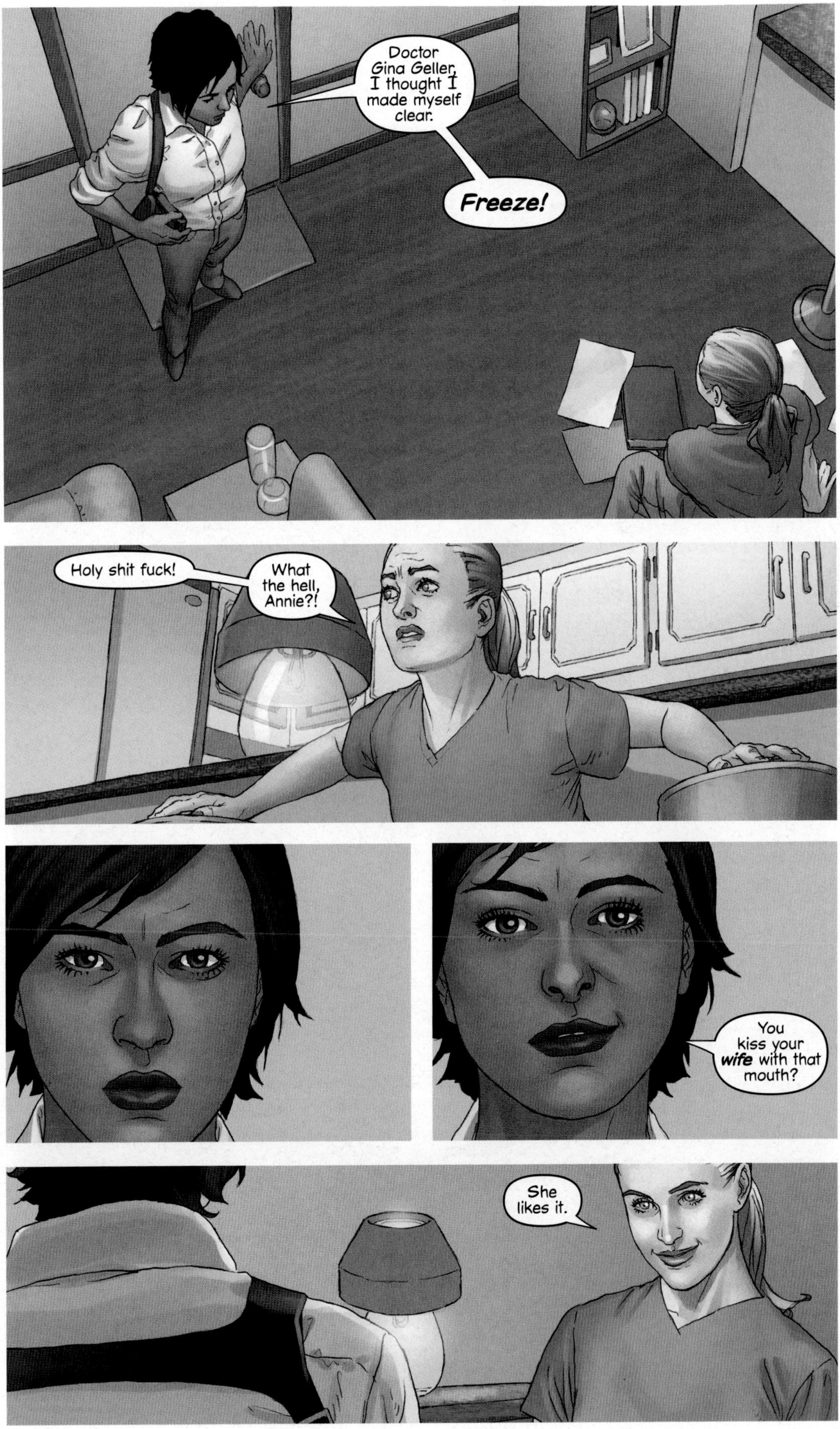

Doctor Gina Geller, I thought I made myself clear.
Freeze!
Holy shit fuck!
What the hell, Annie?!
You kiss your wife with that mouth?
She likes it.

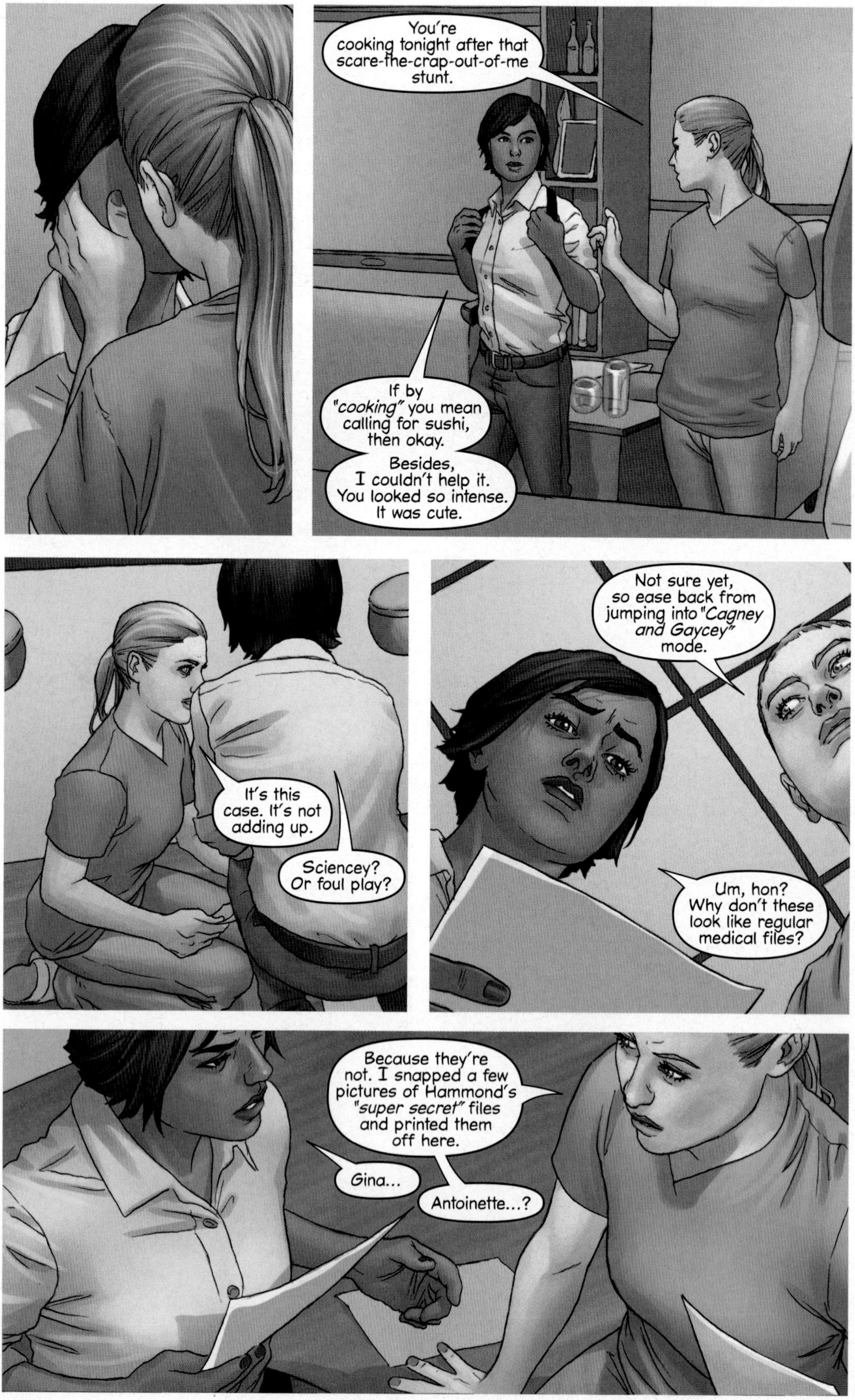
You're cooking tonight after that scare-the-crap-out-of-me stunt.
If by "cooking" you mean calling for sushi, then okay.
Besides, I couldn't help it. You looked so intense. It was cute.
It's this case. It's not adding up.
Sciencey? Or foul play?
Not sure yet, so ease back from jumping into "Cagney and Gaycey" mode.
Um, hon? Why don't these look like regular medical files?
Because they're not. I snapped a few pictures of Hammond's "super secret" files and printed them off here.
Gina...
Antoinette...?

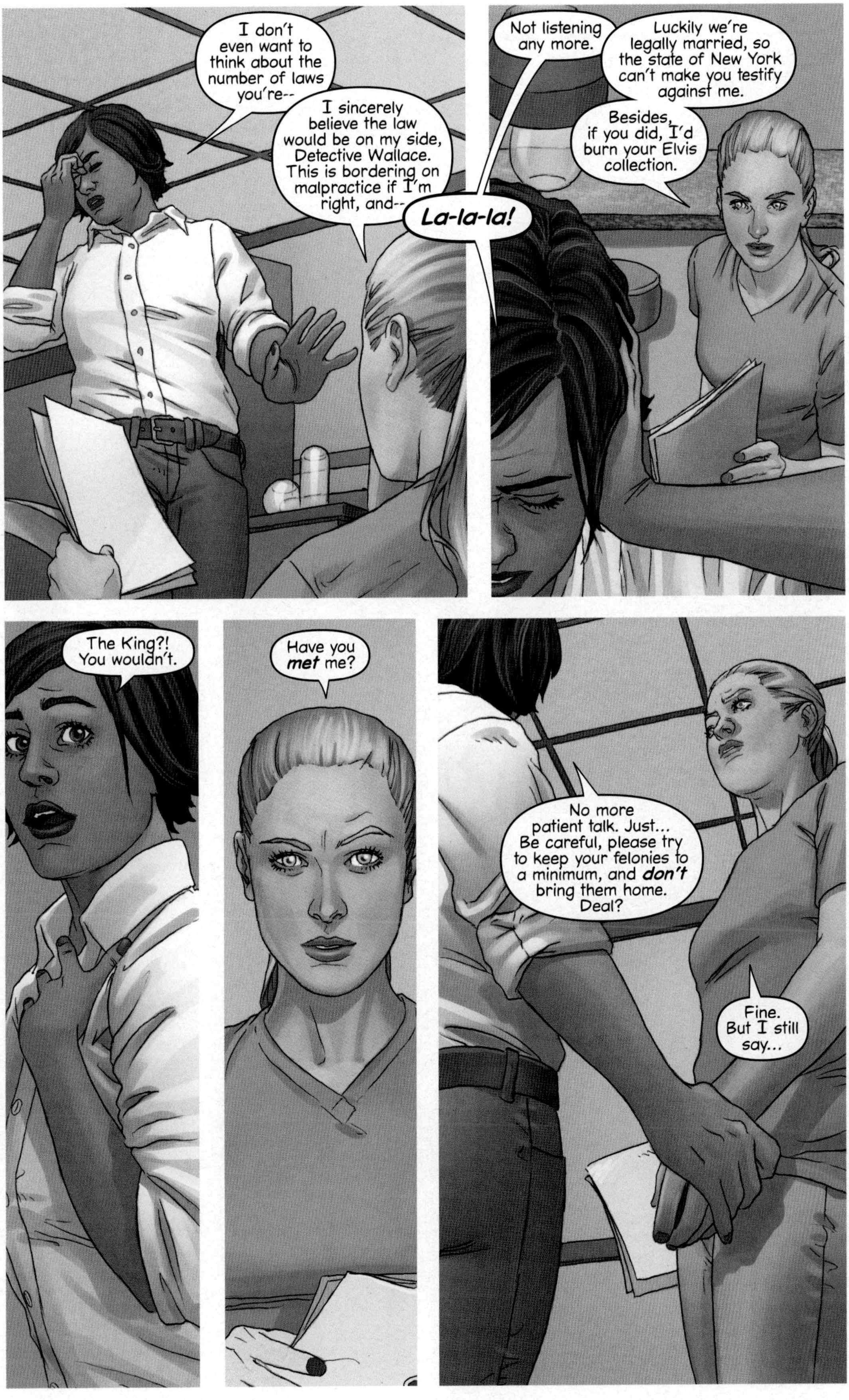
I don't even want to think about the number of laws you're--
I sincerely believe the law would be on my side, Detective Wallace. This is bordering on malpractice if I'm right, and--
La-la-la!
Not listening any more.
Luckily we're legally married, so the state of New York can't make you testify against me.
Besides, if you did, I'd burn your Elvis collection.
The King?! You wouldn't.
Have you *met* me?
No more patient talk. Just... Be careful, please try to keep your felonies to a minimum, and *don't* bring them home. Deal?
Fine. But I still say...

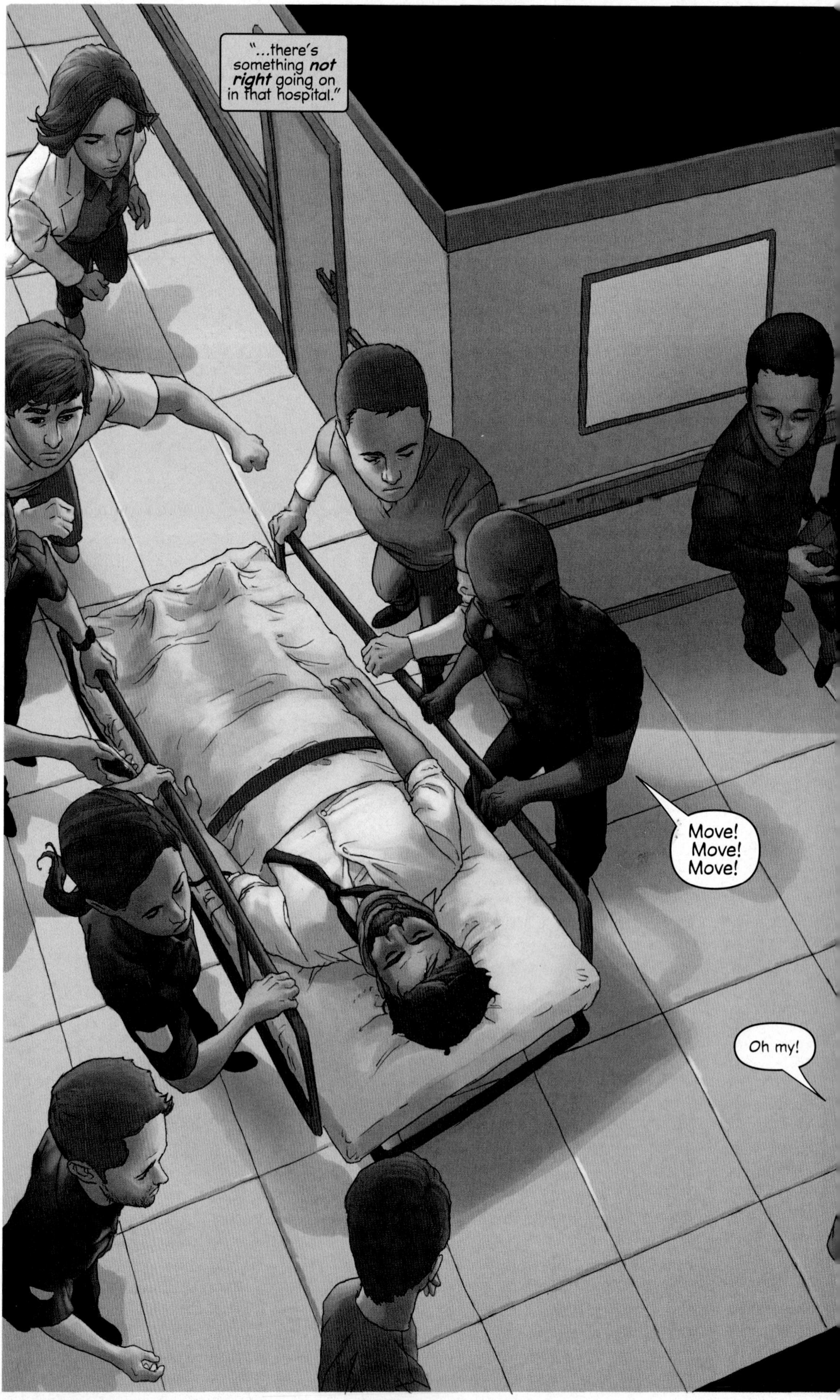
"...there's something **not right** going on in that hospital."
Move! Move! Move!
Oh my!

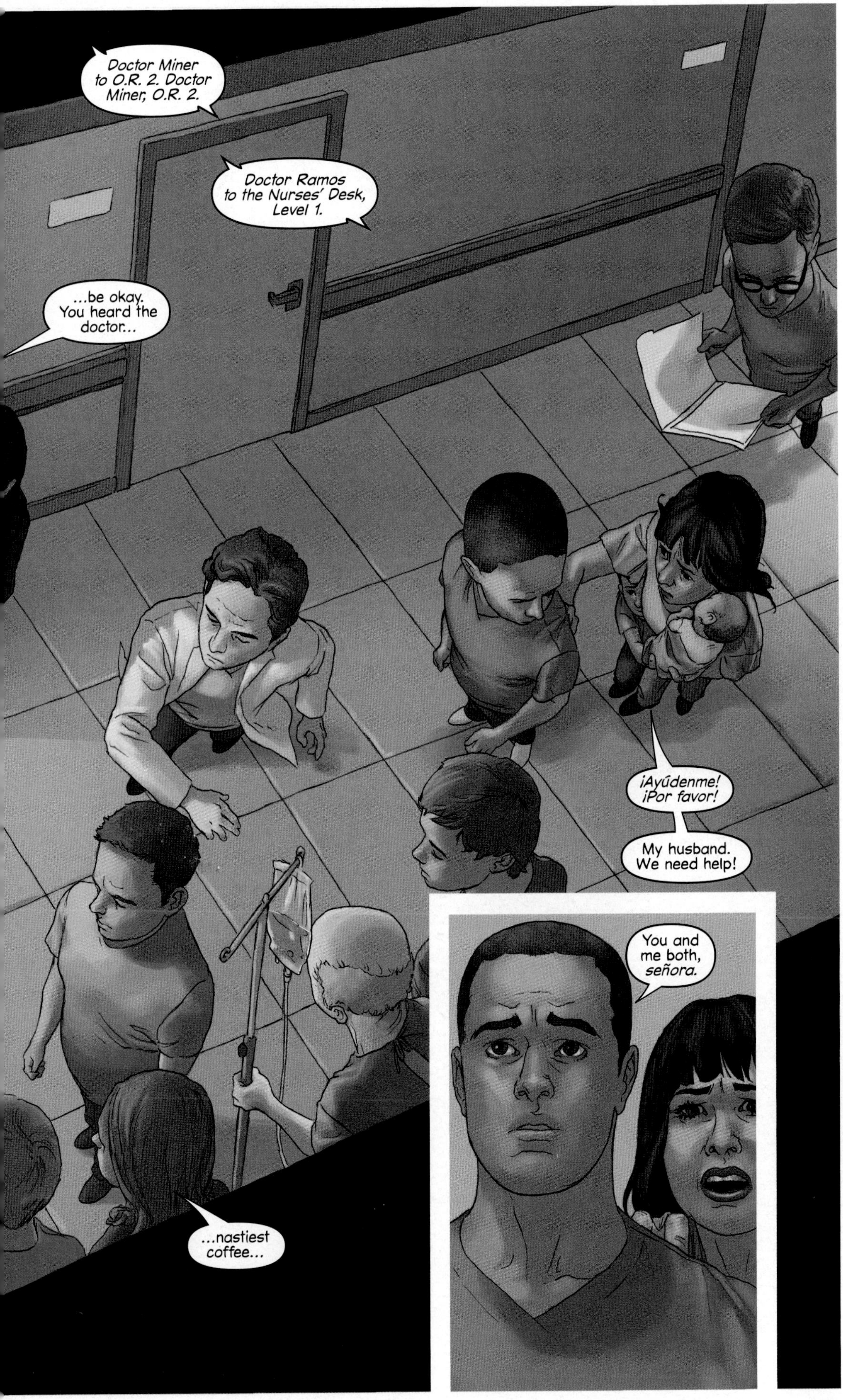
Doctor Miner to O.R. 2. Doctor Miner, O.R. 2.
Doctor Ramos to the Nurses' Desk, Level 1.
...be okay. You heard the doctor...
¡Ayúdenme! ¡Por favor!
My husband. We need help!
...nastiest coffee...
You and me both, *señora.*

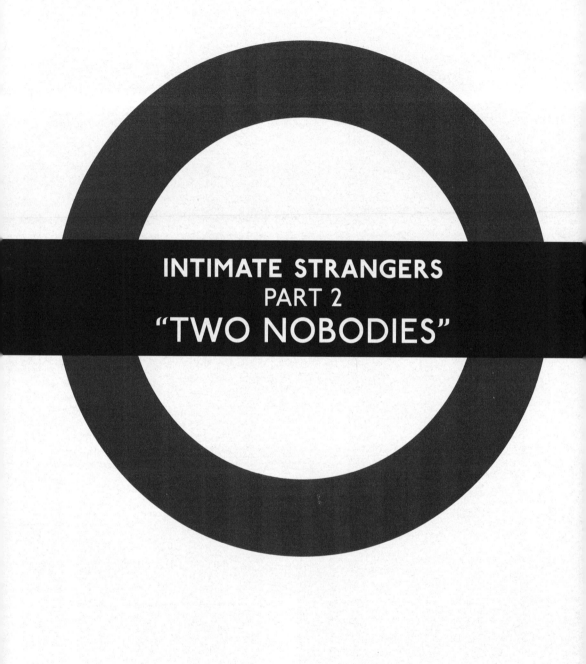

INTIMATE STRANGERS
PART 2
"TWO NOBODIES"

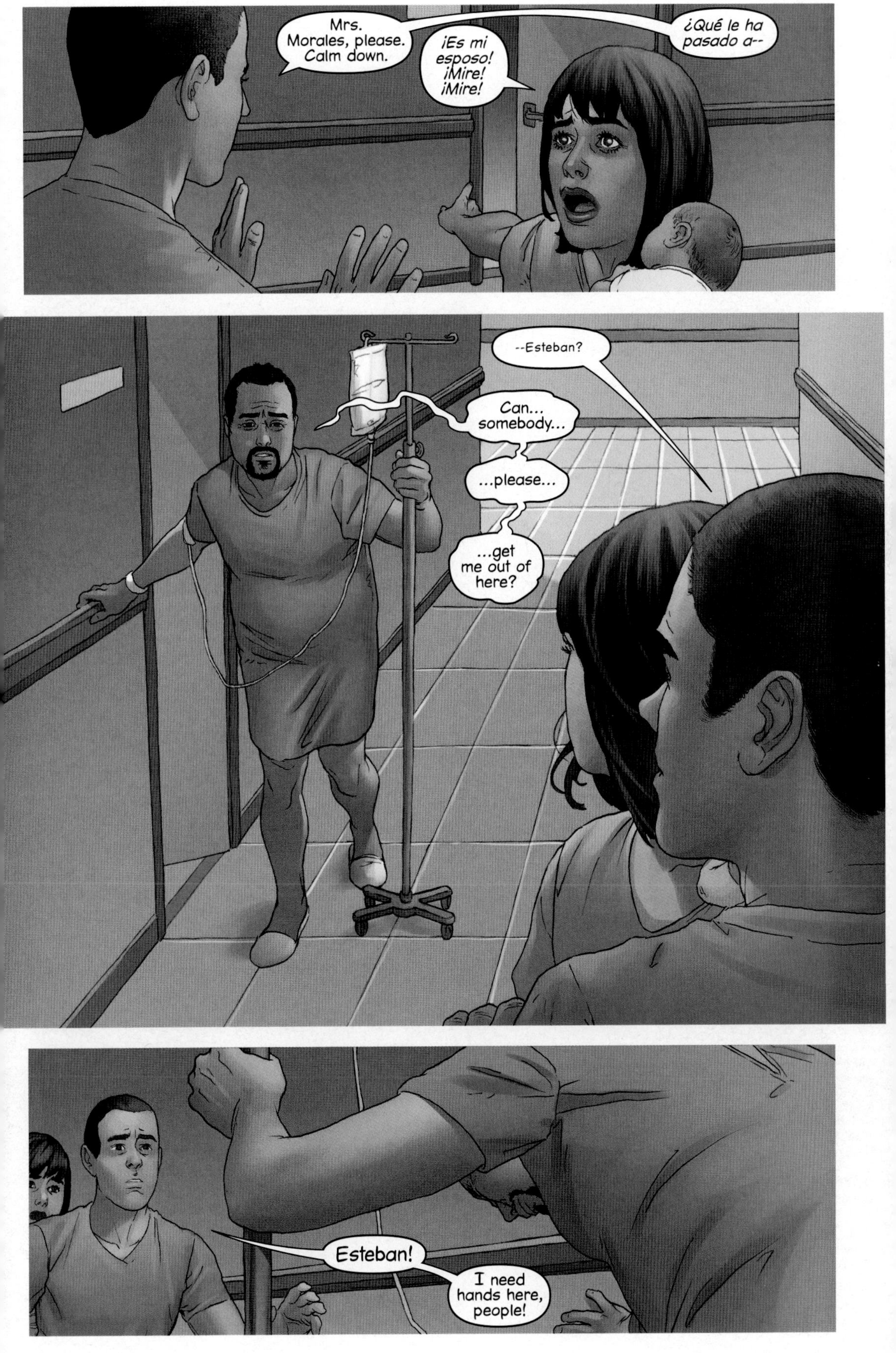
Mrs. Morales, please. Calm down.
¿Qué le ha pasado a--
¡Es mi esposo! ¡Mire! ¡Mire!
--Esteban?
Can... somebody...
...please...
...get me out of here?
Esteban!
I need hands here, people!

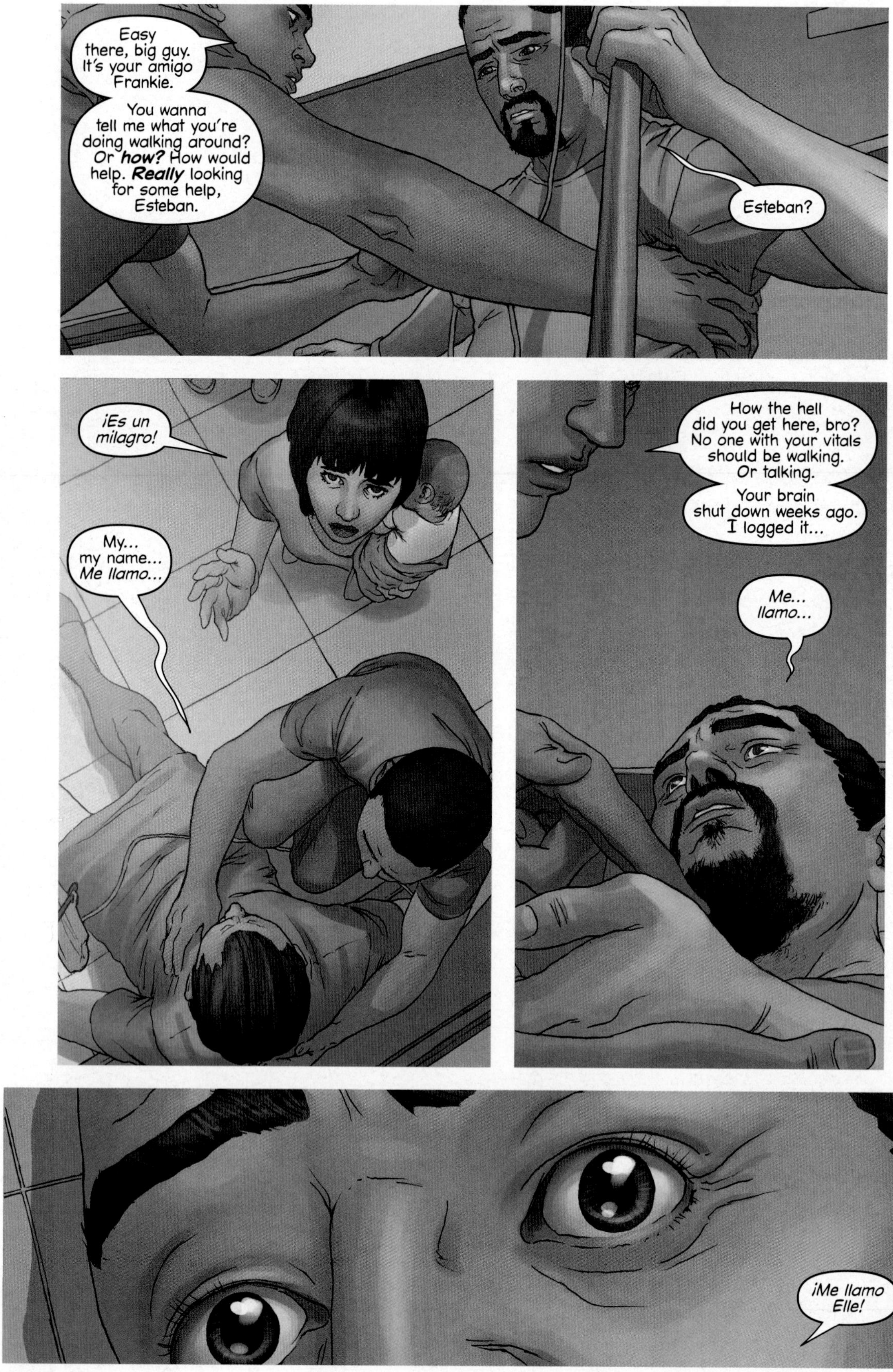

Easy there, big guy. It's your amigo Frankie.
You wanna tell me what you're doing walking around? Or *how?* How would help. *Really* looking for some help, Esteban.
Esteban?
¡Es un milagro!
My... my name... *Me llamo...*
How the hell did you get here, bro? No one with your vitals should be walking. Or talking.
Your brain shut down weeks ago. I logged it...
Me... llamo...
¡Me llamo Elle!

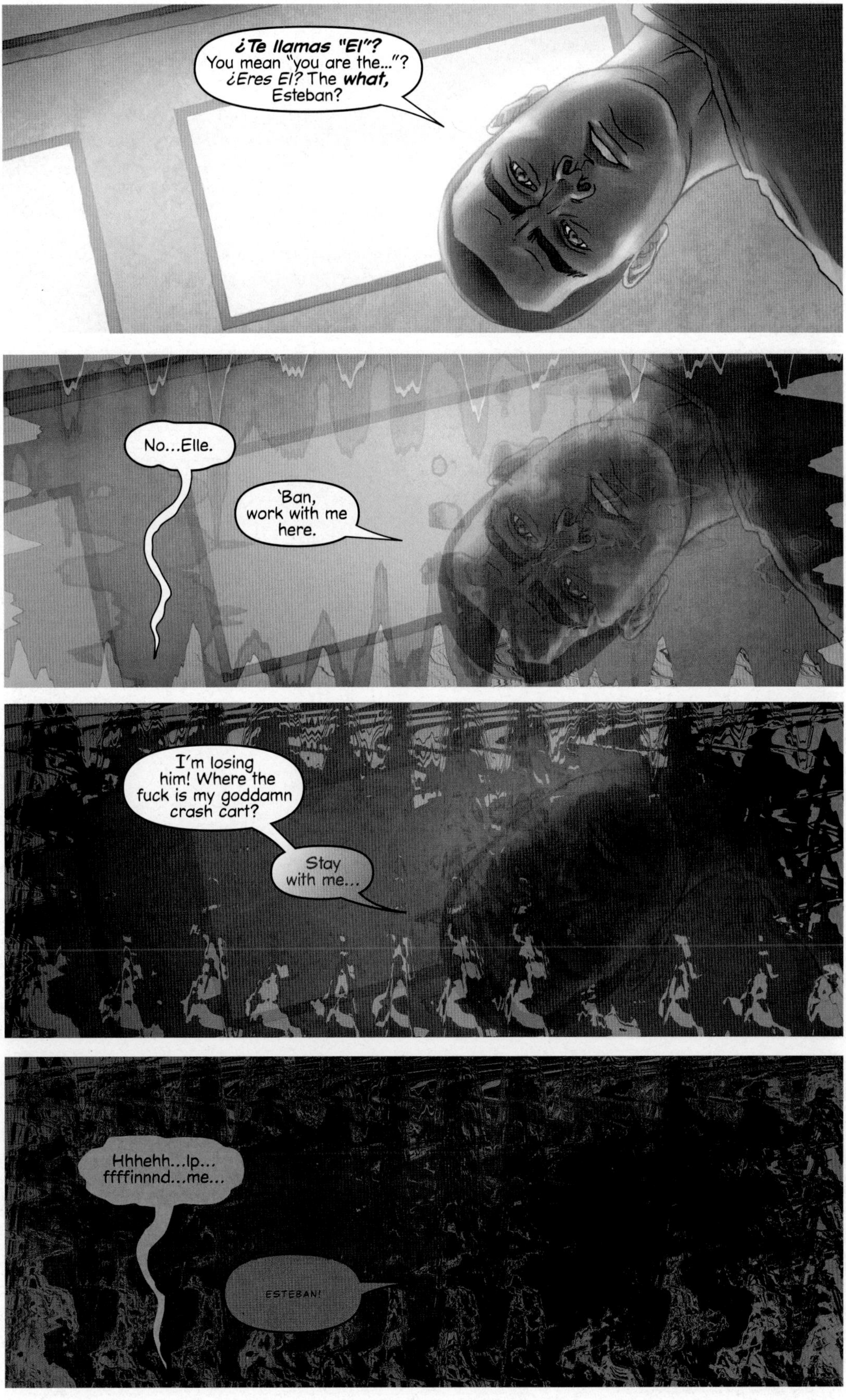
¿Te llamas "El"? You mean "you are the..."? ¿Eres El? The what, Esteban?
No...Elle.
'Ban, work with me here.
I'm losing him! Where the fuck is my goddamn crash cart?
Stay with me...
Hhhehh...lp... ffffinnnd...me...
ESTEBAN!

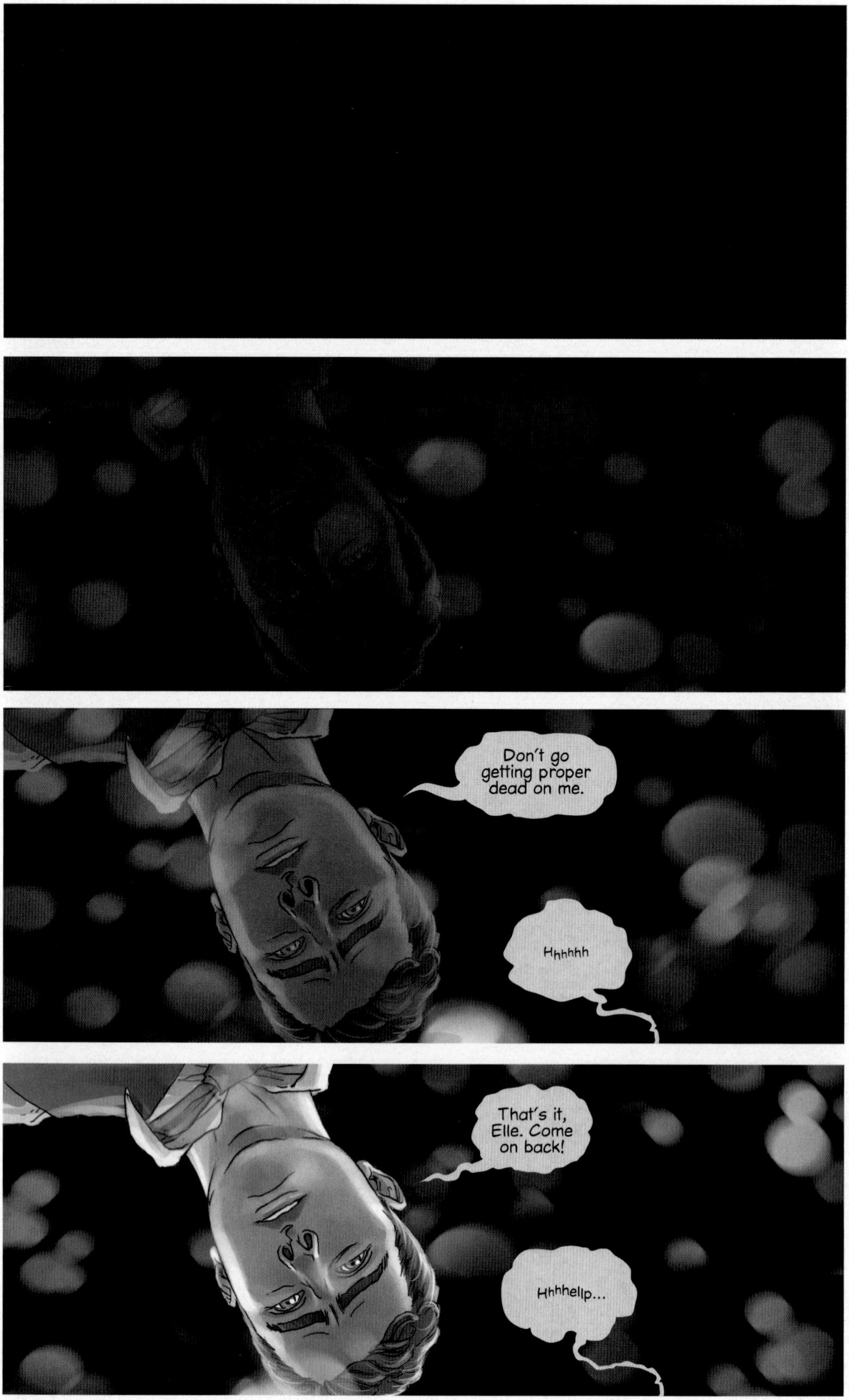
Don't go getting proper dead on me.
Hhhhhh
That's it, Elle. Come on back!
Hhhhellp...

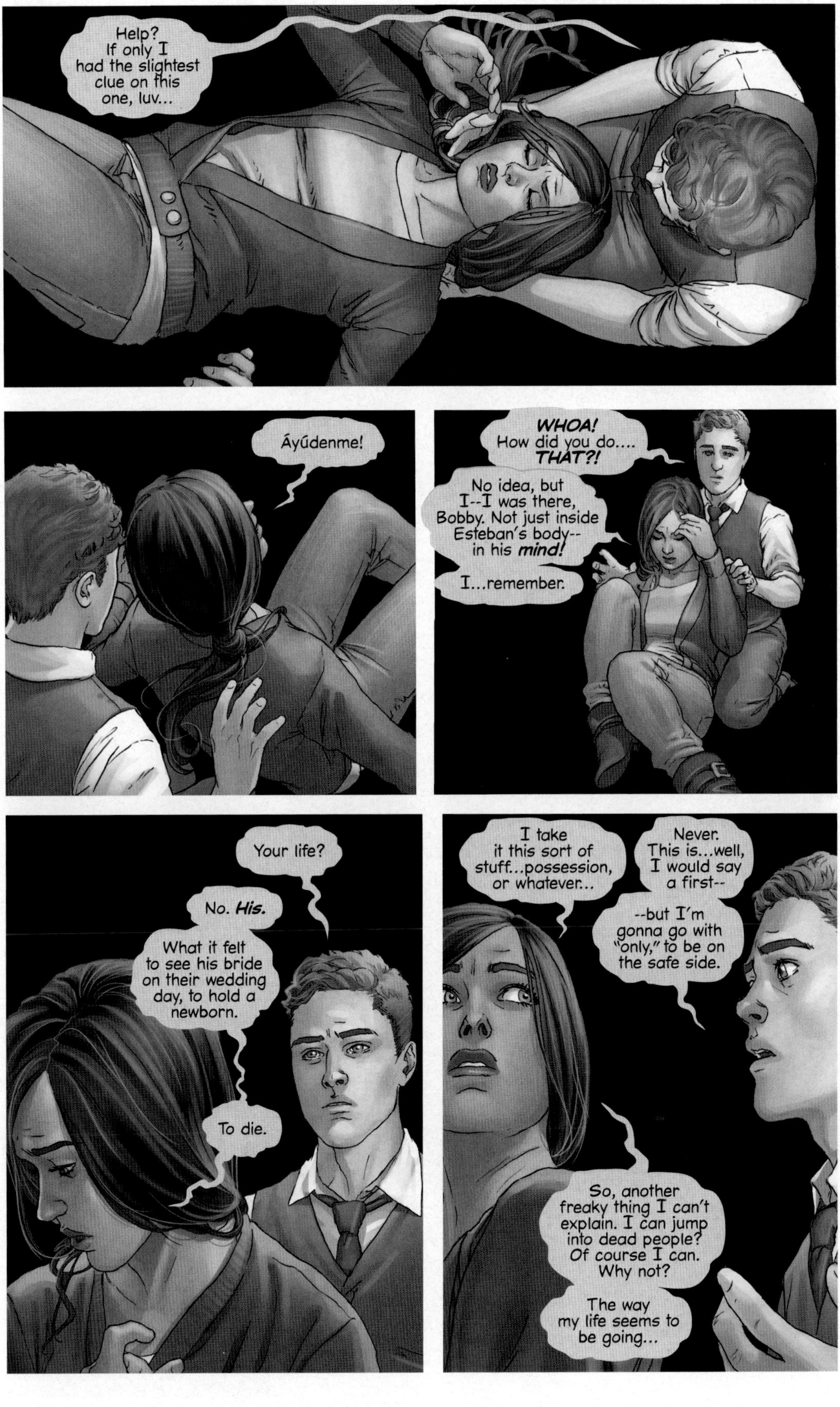

Help? If only I had the slightest clue on this one, luv...
Áyúdenme!
WHOA! How did you do.... THAT?!
No idea, but I--I was there, Bobby. Not just inside Esteban's body-- in his mind!
I...remember.
Your life?
No. His.
What it felt to see his bride on their wedding day, to hold a newborn.
To die.
I take it this sort of stuff...possession, or whatever...
Never. This is...well, I would say a first--
--but I'm gonna go with "only," to be on the safe side.
So, another freaky thing I can't explain. I can jump into dead people? Of course I can. Why not?
The way my life seems to be going...

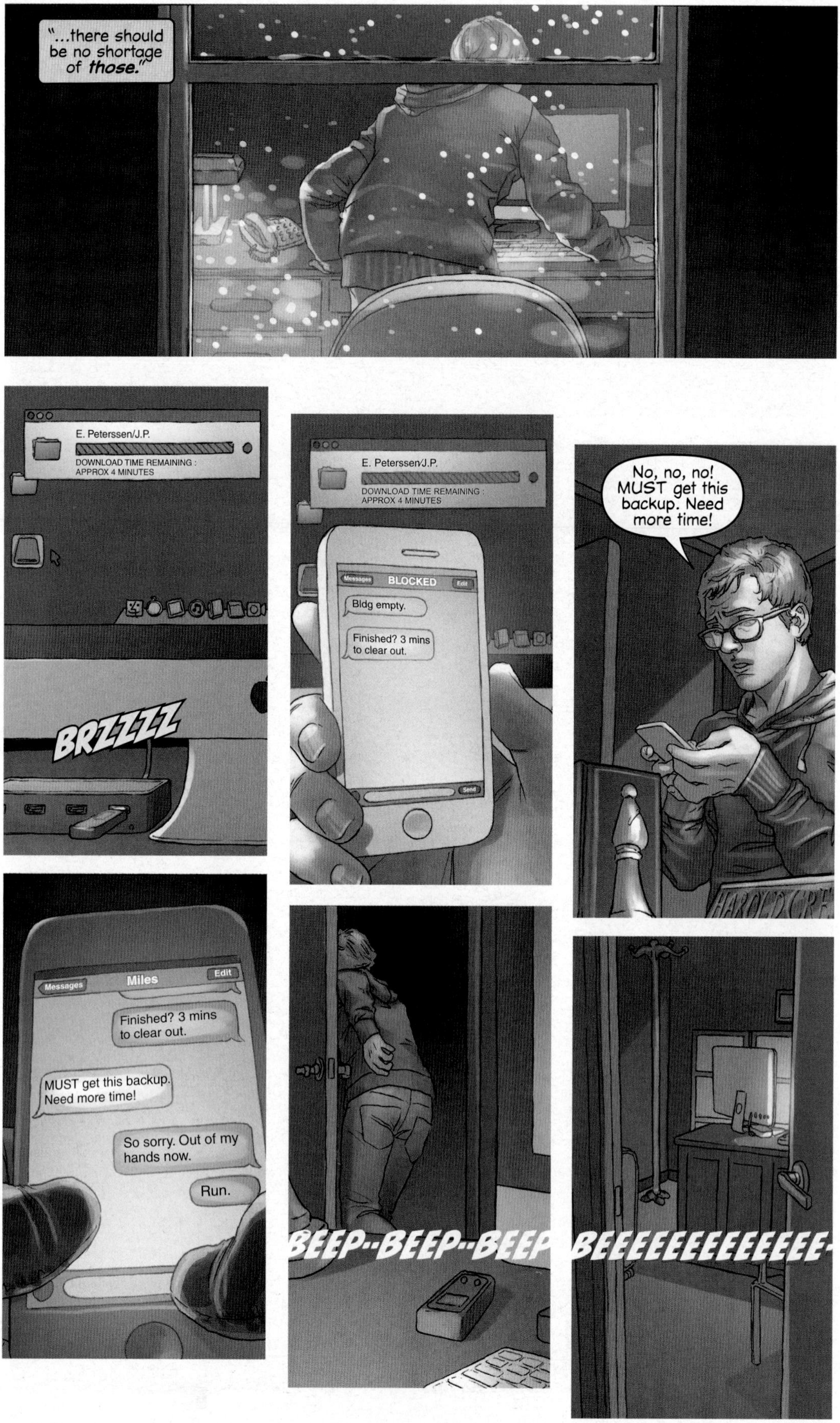
"...there should be no shortage of *those.*"
E. Peterssen/J.P.
DOWNLOAD TIME REMAINING : APPROX 4 MINUTES
BRZZZZ
E. Peterssen/J.P.
DOWNLOAD TIME REMAINING : APPROX 4 MINUTES
Messages BLOCKED Edit
Bldg empty.
Finished? 3 mins to clear out.
Send
No, no, no! MUST get this backup. Need more time!
Messages Miles Edit
Finished? 3 mins to clear out.
MUST get this backup. Need more time!
So sorry. Out of my hands now.
Run.
BEEP--BEEP--BEEP
BEEEEEEEEEEEEE-

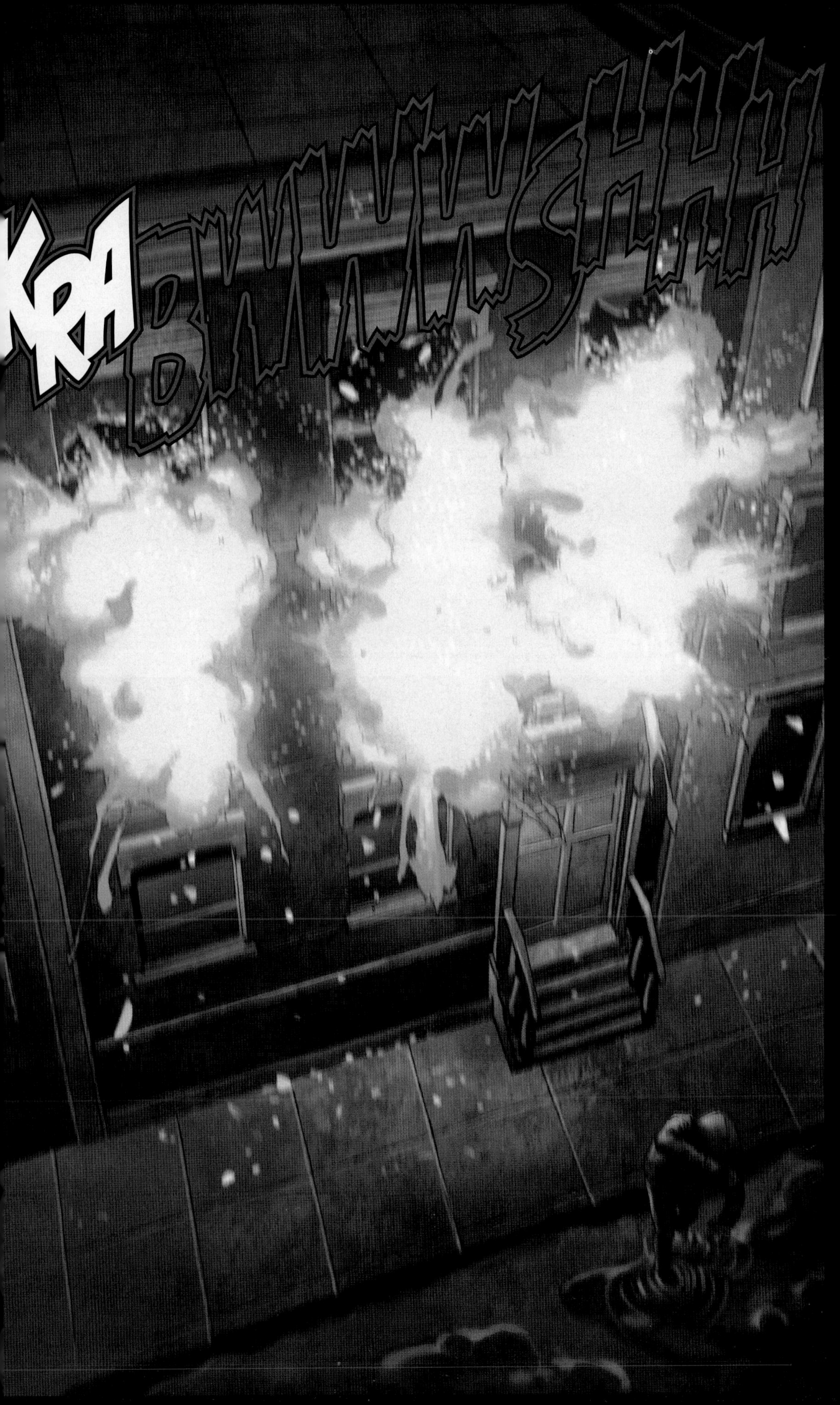
KRA

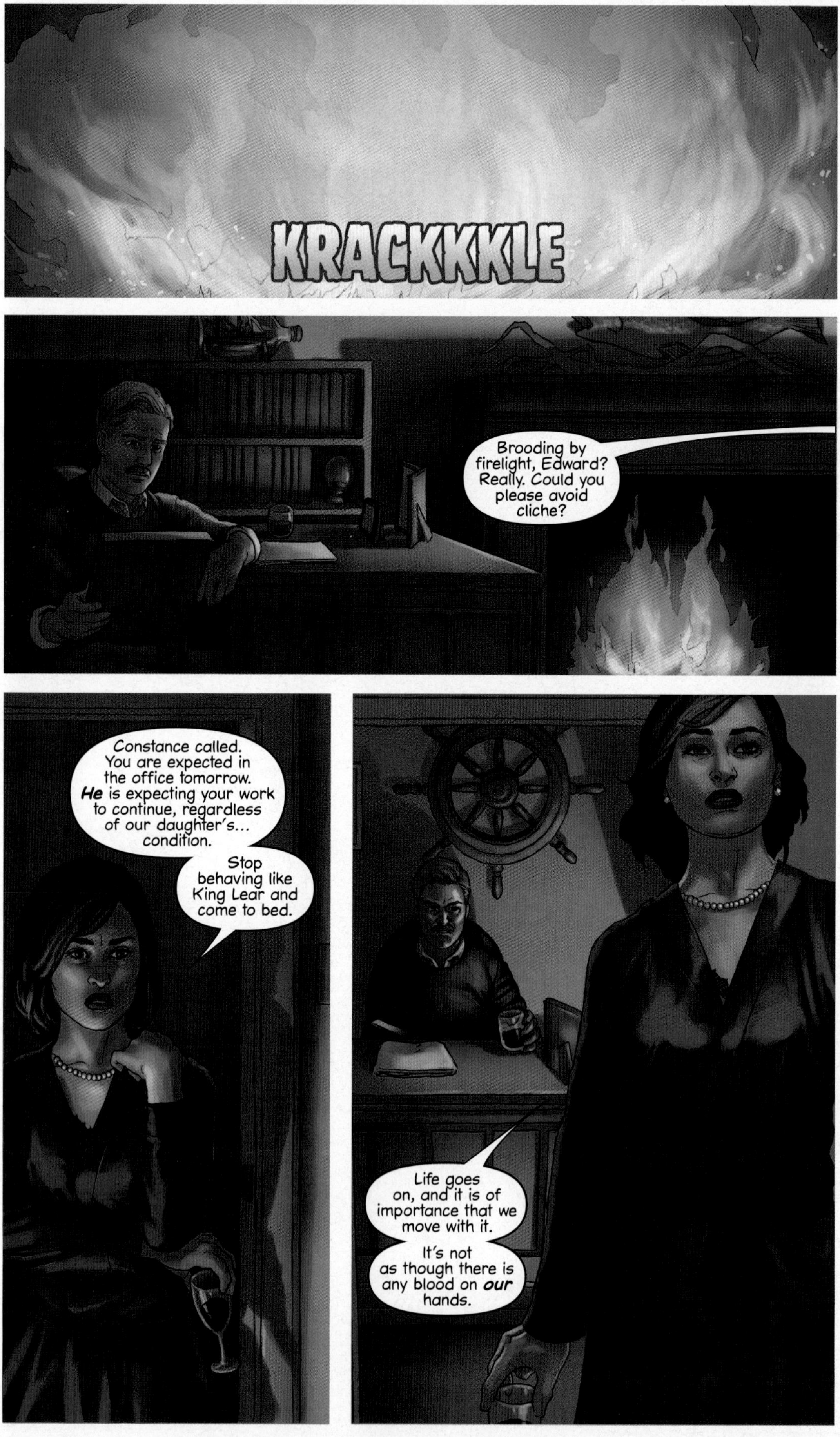
KRACKKKLE
Brooding by firelight, Edward? Really. Could you please avoid cliche?
Constance called. You are expected in the office tomorrow. ***He*** is expecting your work to continue, regardless of our daughter's... condition.
Stop behaving like King Lear and come to bed.
Life goes on, and it is of importance that we move with it.
It's not as though there is any blood on ***our*** hands.

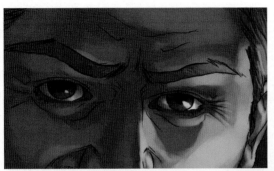

KRACKK

God help me...

What have I done...?

IT'S A GIRL!!!

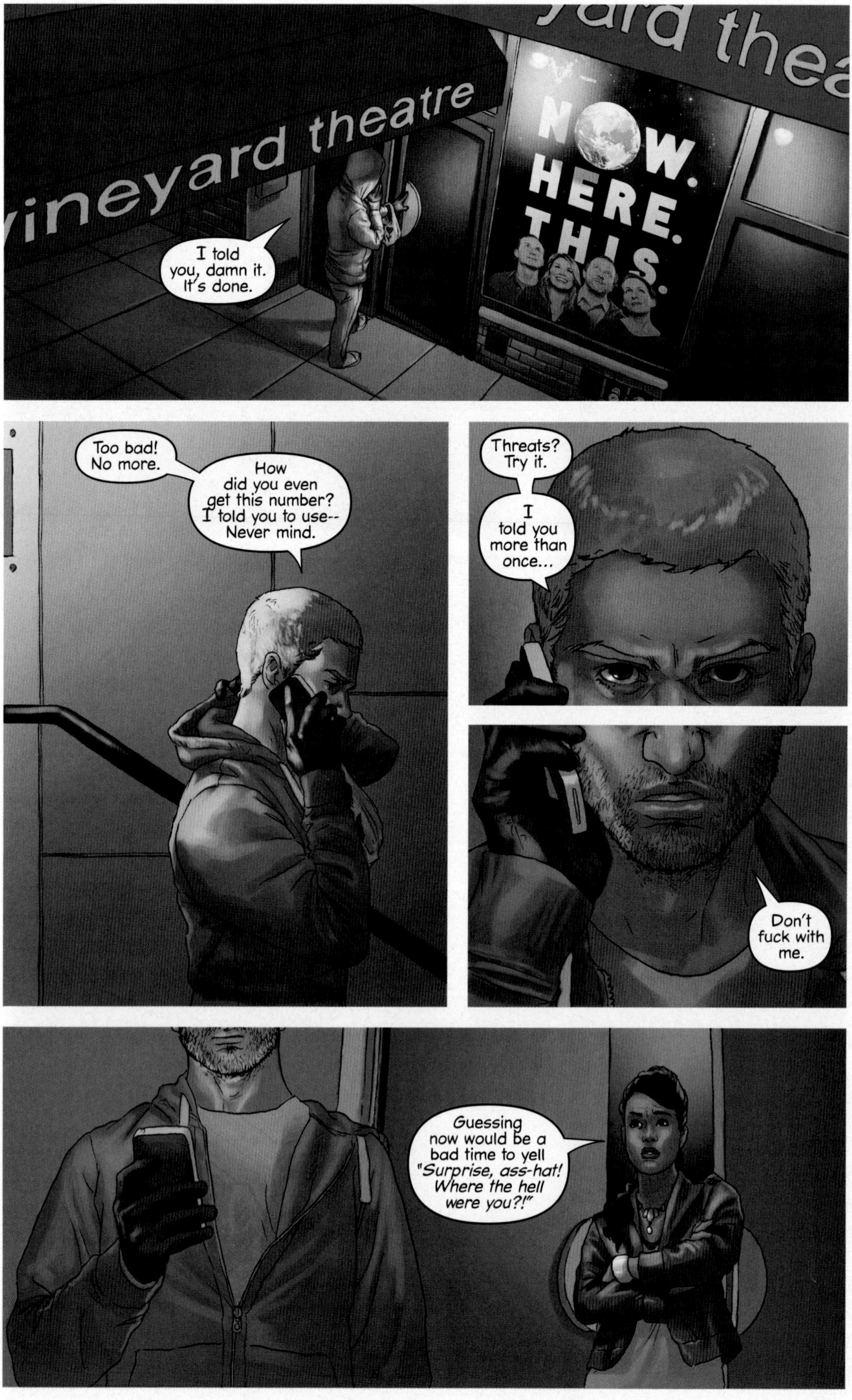
vineyard theatre
NOW. HERE. THIS.
I told you, damn it. It's done.
Too bad! No more.
How did you even get this number? I told you to use-- Never mind.
Threats? Try it.
I told you more than once...
Don't fuck with me.
Guessing now would be a bad time to yell "Surprise, ass-hat! Where the hell were you?!"

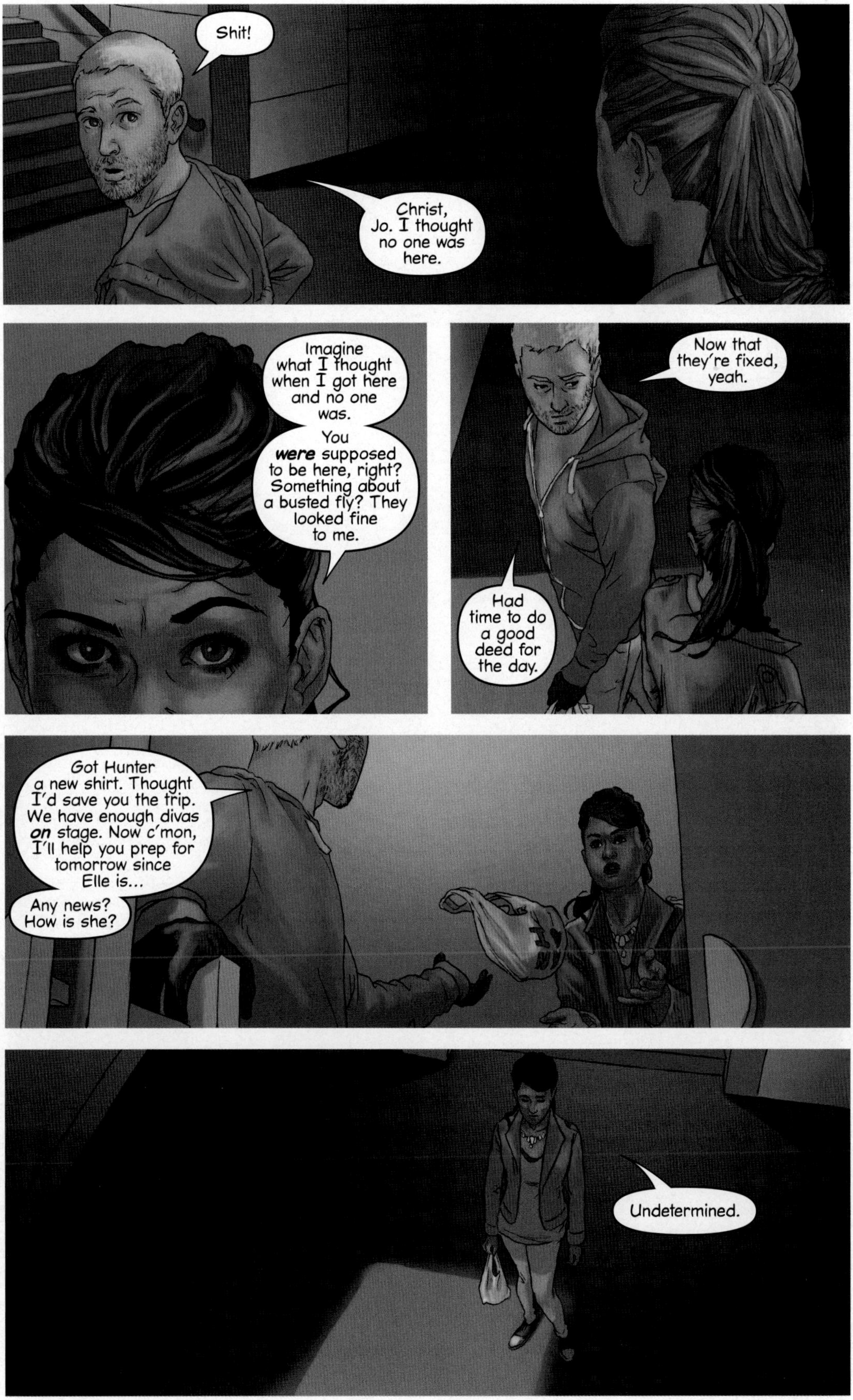
Shit!
Christ, Jo. I thought no one was here.
Imagine what I thought when I got here and no one was.
You *were* supposed to be here, right? Something about a busted fly? They looked fine to me.
Now that they're fixed, yeah.
Had time to do a good deed for the day.
Got Hunter a new shirt. Thought I'd save you the trip. We have enough divas *on* stage. Now c'mon, I'll help you prep for tomorrow since Elle is...
Any news? How is she?
Undetermined.

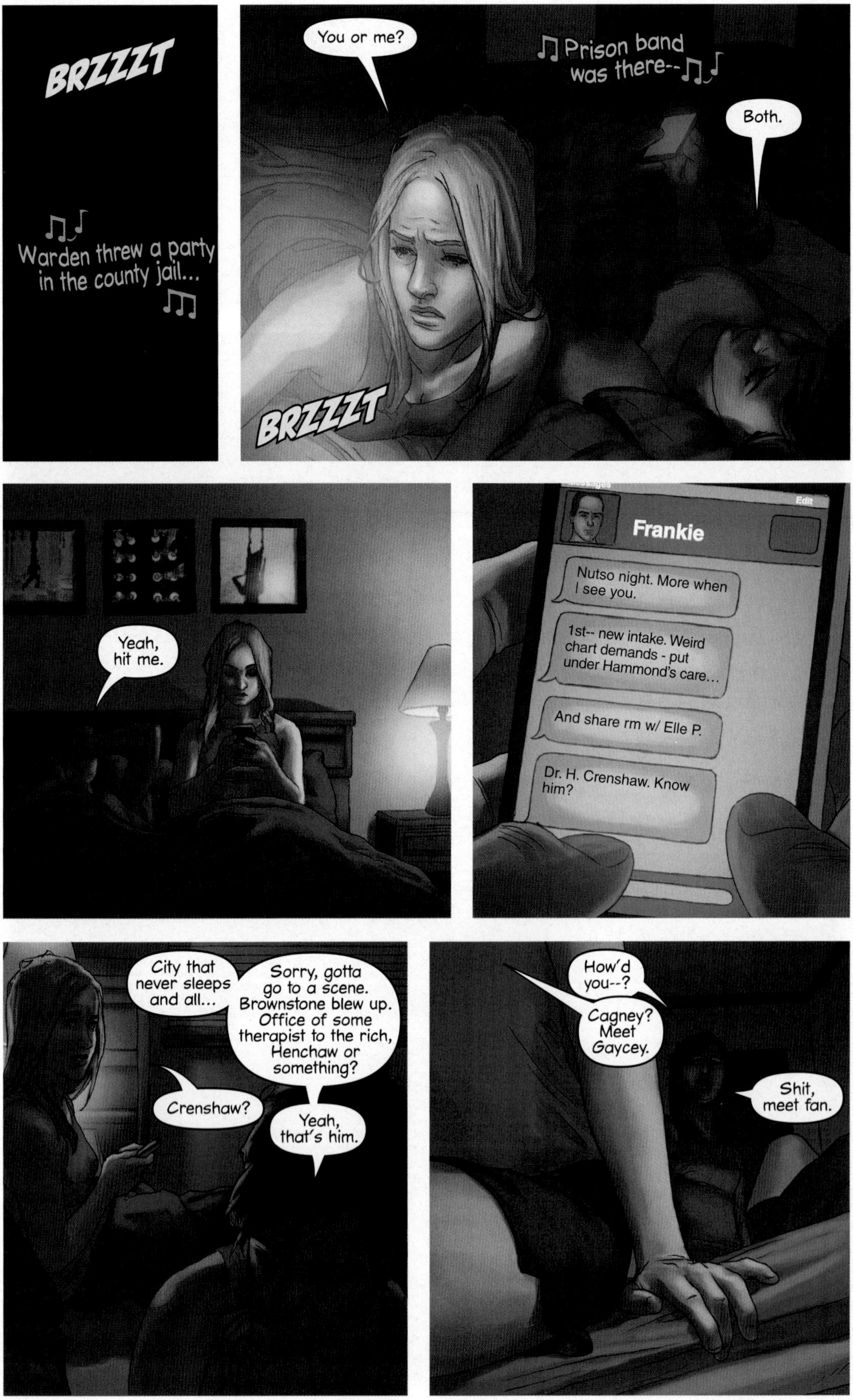
BRZZZT
♫ Warden threw a party in the county jail... ♫
You or me?
♫ Prison band was there-- ♫
Both.
BRZZZT
Yeah, hit me.
Edit
Frankie
Nutso night. More when I see you.
1st-- new intake. Weird chart demands - put under Hammond's care...
And share rm w/ Elle P.
Dr. H. Crenshaw. Know him?
City that never sleeps and all...
Sorry, gotta go to a scene. Brownstone blew up. Office of some therapist to the rich, Henchaw or something?
Crenshaw?
Yeah, that's him.
How'd you--?
Cagney? Meet Gaycey.
Shit, meet fan.

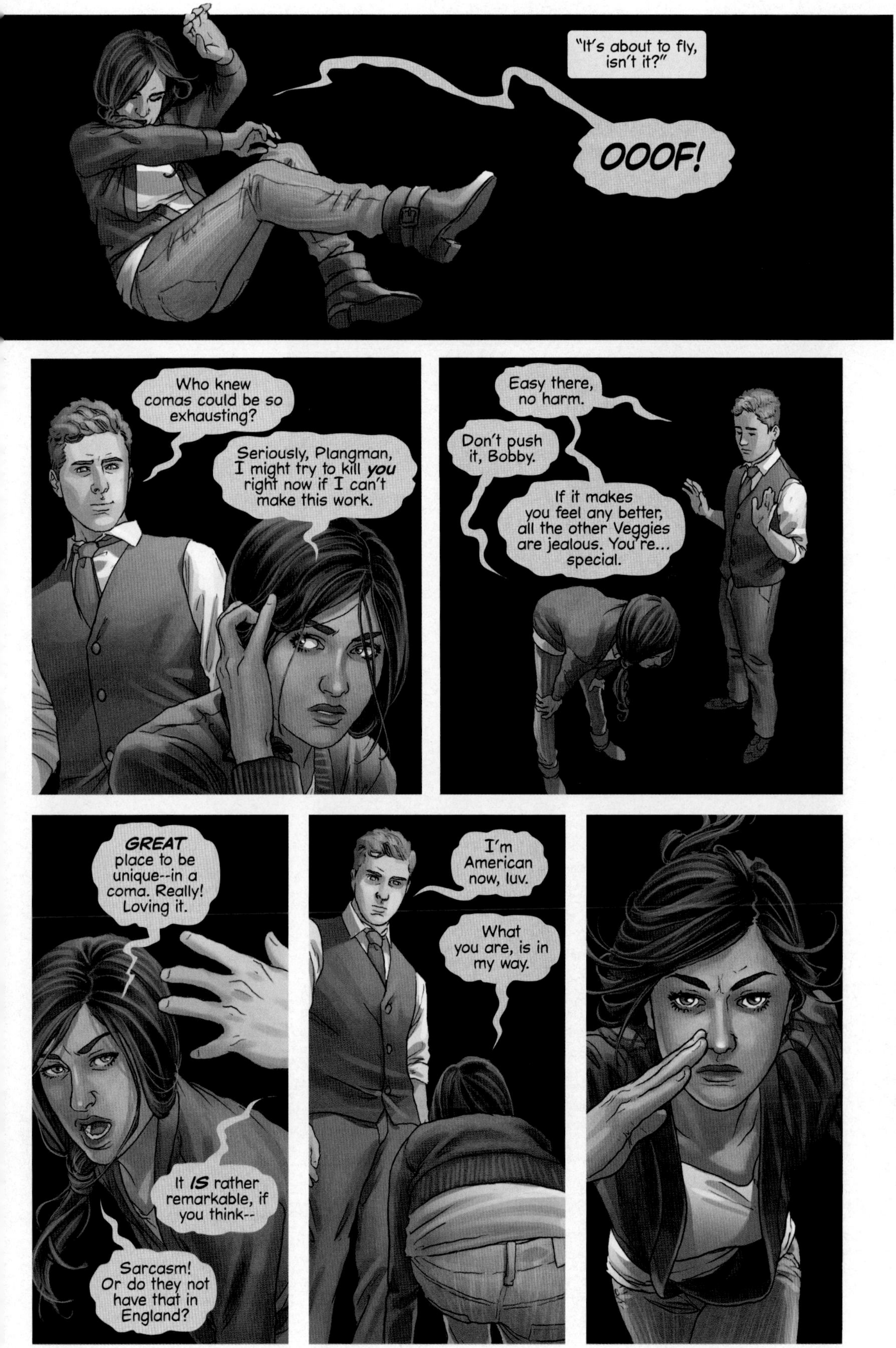
"It's about to fly, isn't it?"
OOOF!
Who knew comas could be so exhausting?
Seriously, Plangman, I might try to kill *you* right now if I can't make this work.
Easy there, no harm.
Don't push it, Bobby.
If it makes you feel any better, all the other Veggies are jealous. You're... special.
GREAT place to be unique--in a coma. Really! Loving it.
It *IS* rather remarkable, if you think--
Sarcasm! Or do they not have that in England?
I'm American now, luv.
What you are, is in my way.

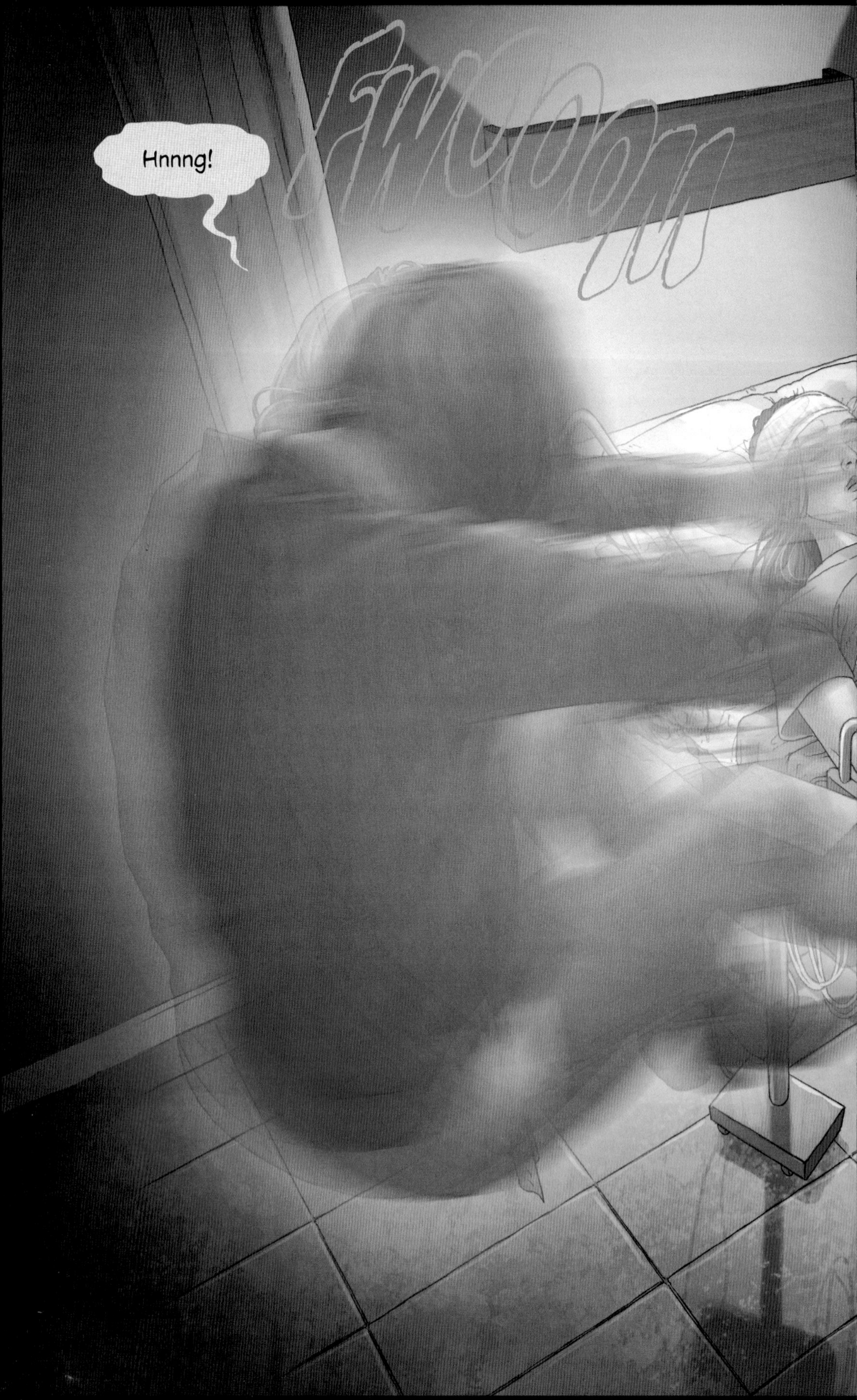
Hnnng!

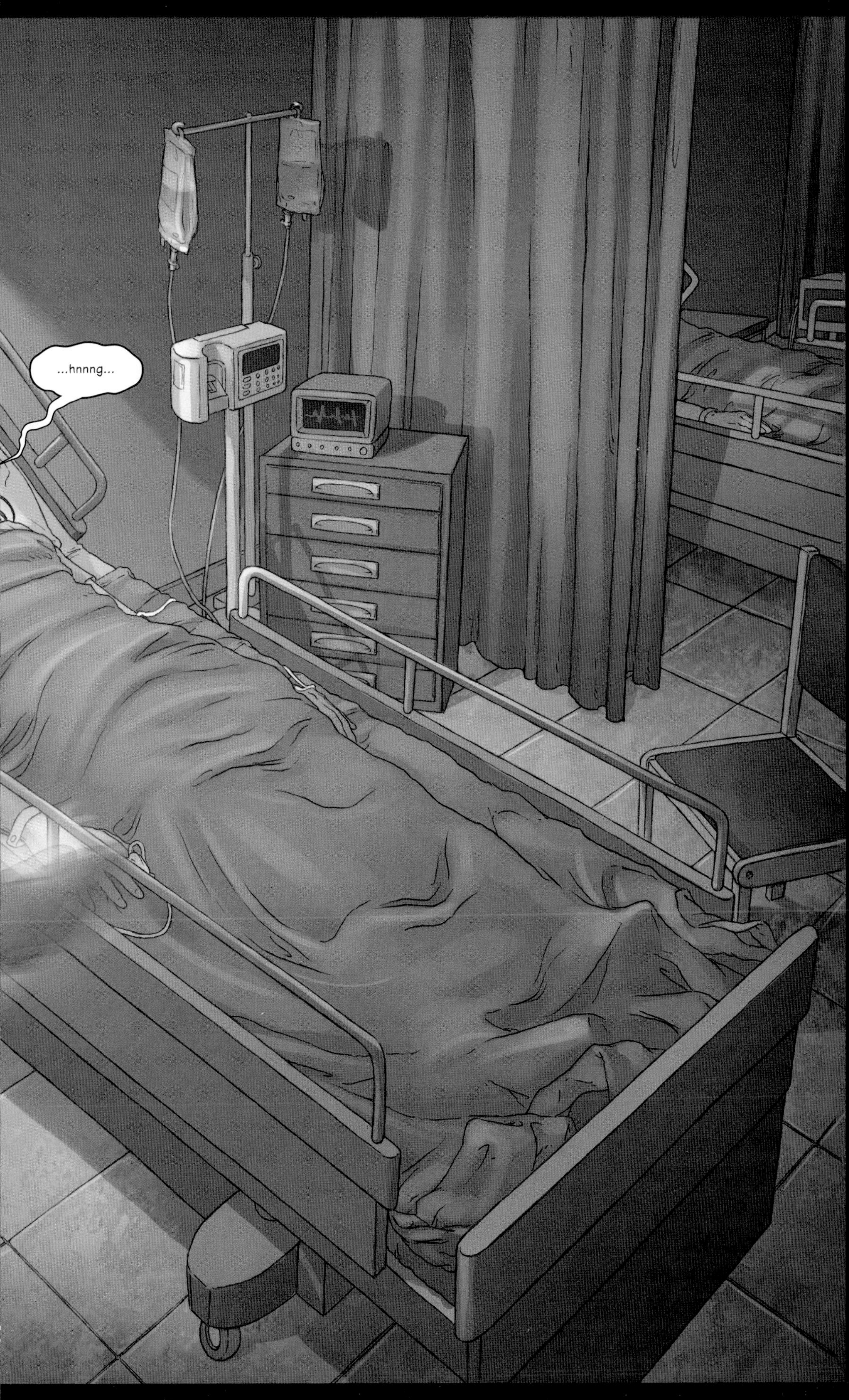
...hnnng...

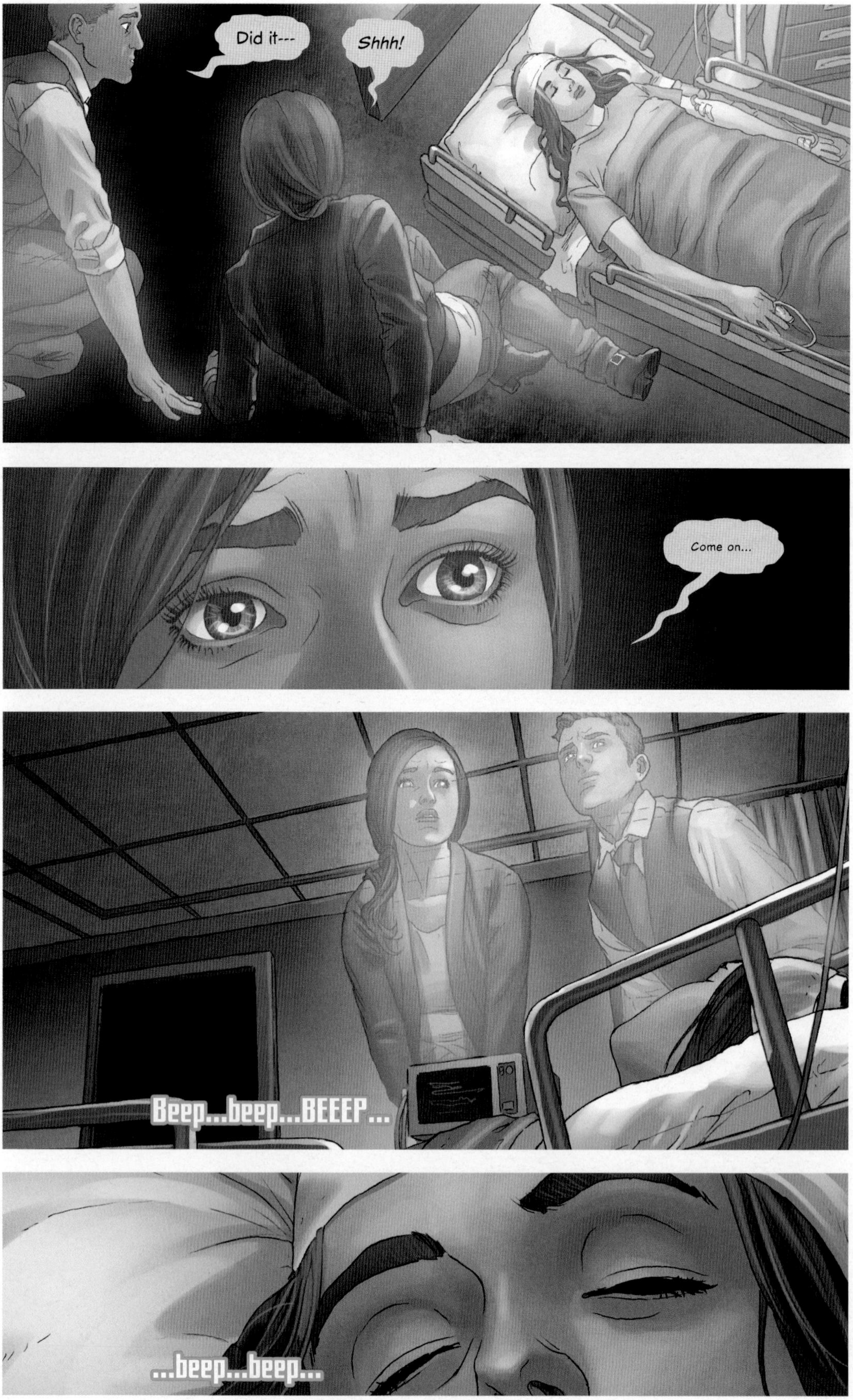

Did it---
Shhh!
Come on...
Beep...beep...BEEEP...
...beep...beep...

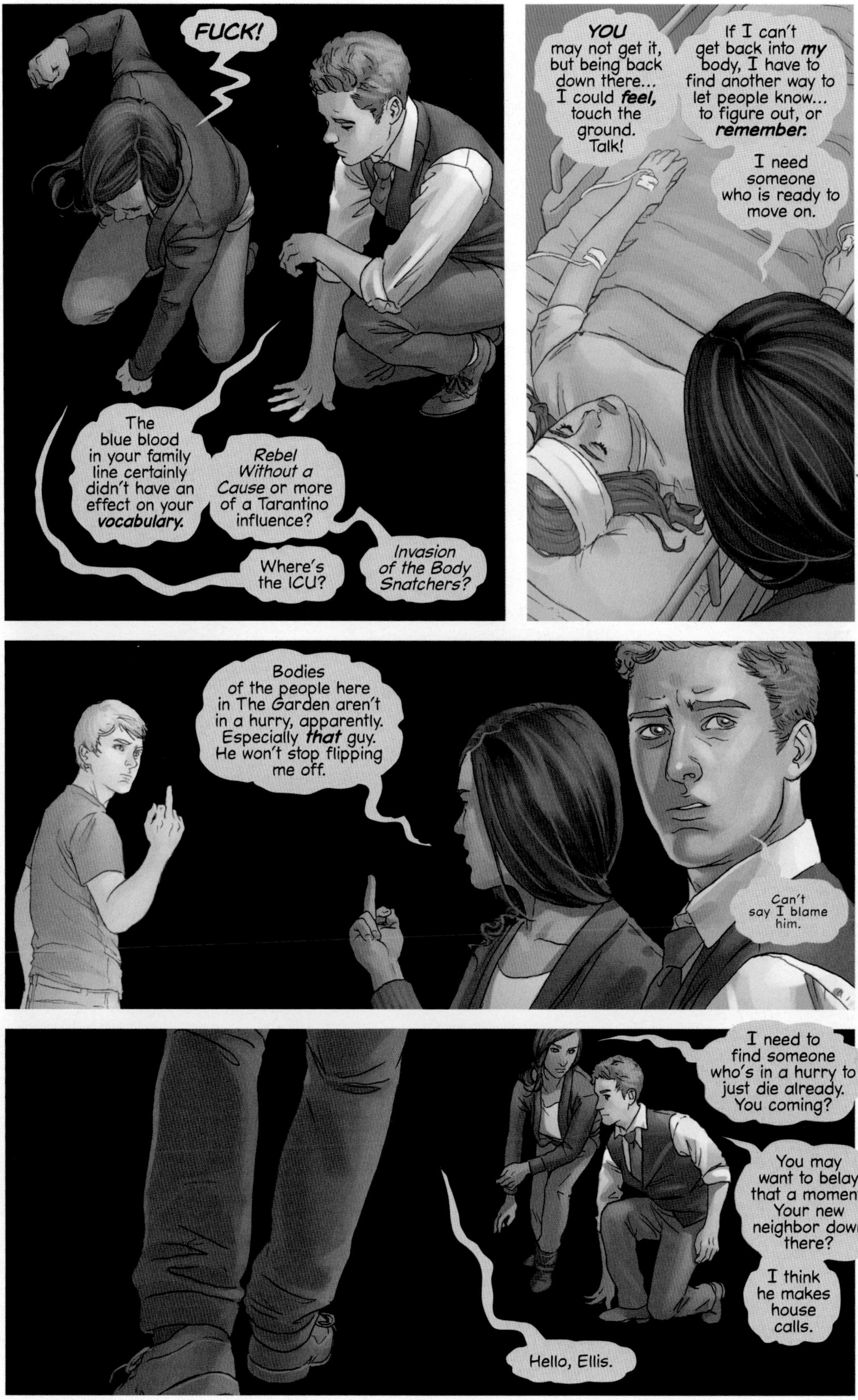
FUCK!
The blue blood in your family line certainly didn't have an effect on your *vocabulary.*
Rebel Without a Cause or more of a Tarantino influence?
Where's the ICU?
Invasion of the Body Snatchers?
YOU may not get it, but being back down there... I could ***feel,*** touch the ground. Talk!
If I can't get back into ***my*** body, I have to find another way to let people know... to figure out, or ***remember.***
I need someone who is ready to move on.
Bodies of the people here in The Garden aren't in a hurry, apparently. Especially ***that*** guy. He won't stop flipping me off.
Can't say I blame him.
I need to find someone who's in a hurry to just die already. You coming?
You may want to belay that a moment. Your new neighbor down there?
I think he makes house calls.
Hello, Ellis.

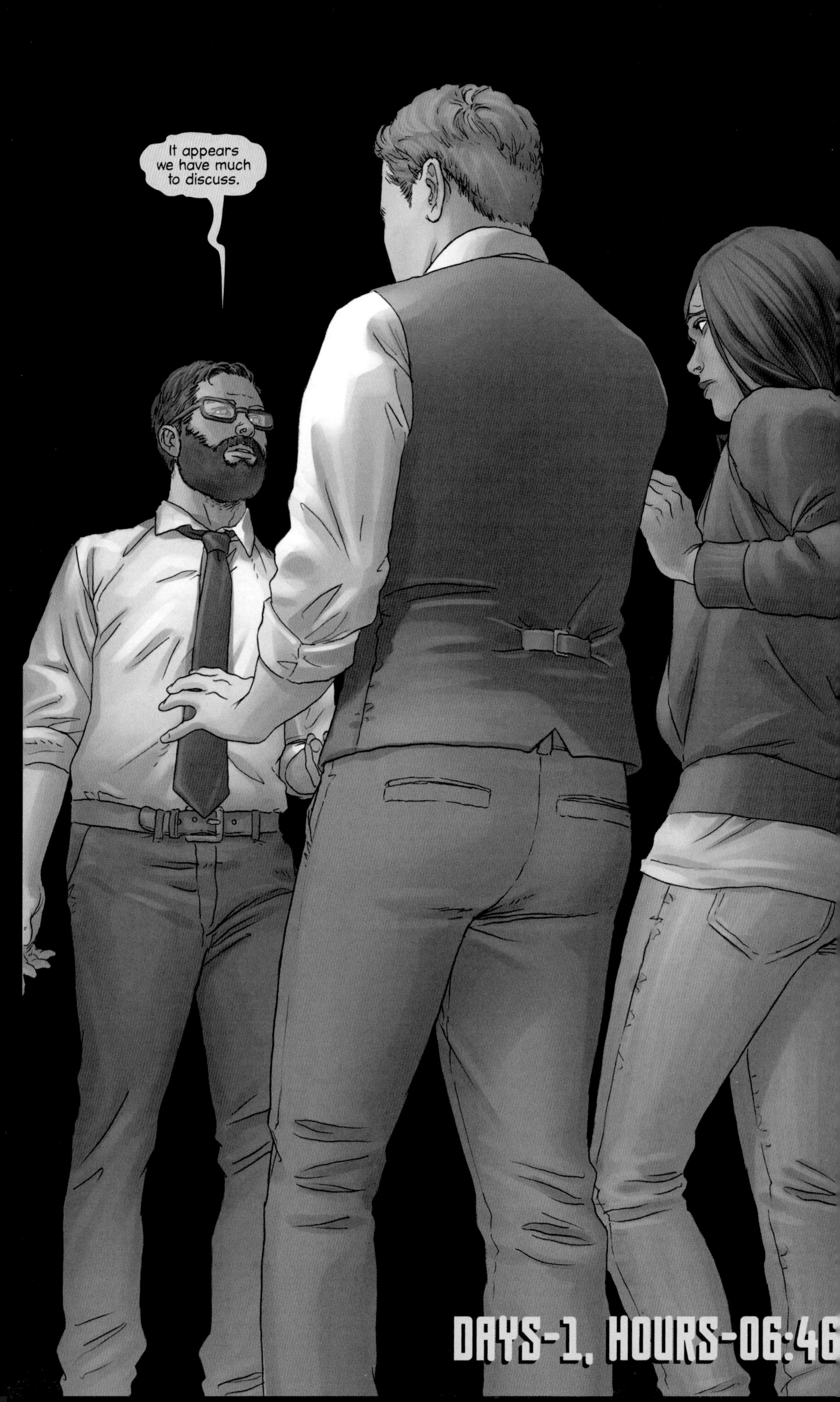
It appears we have much to discuss.
DAYS-1, HOURS-06:46

"We all live in a house on fire, no fire department to call; no way out, just the upstairs window to look out of while the fire burns the house down with us trapped, locked in it."

-Tennessee Williams

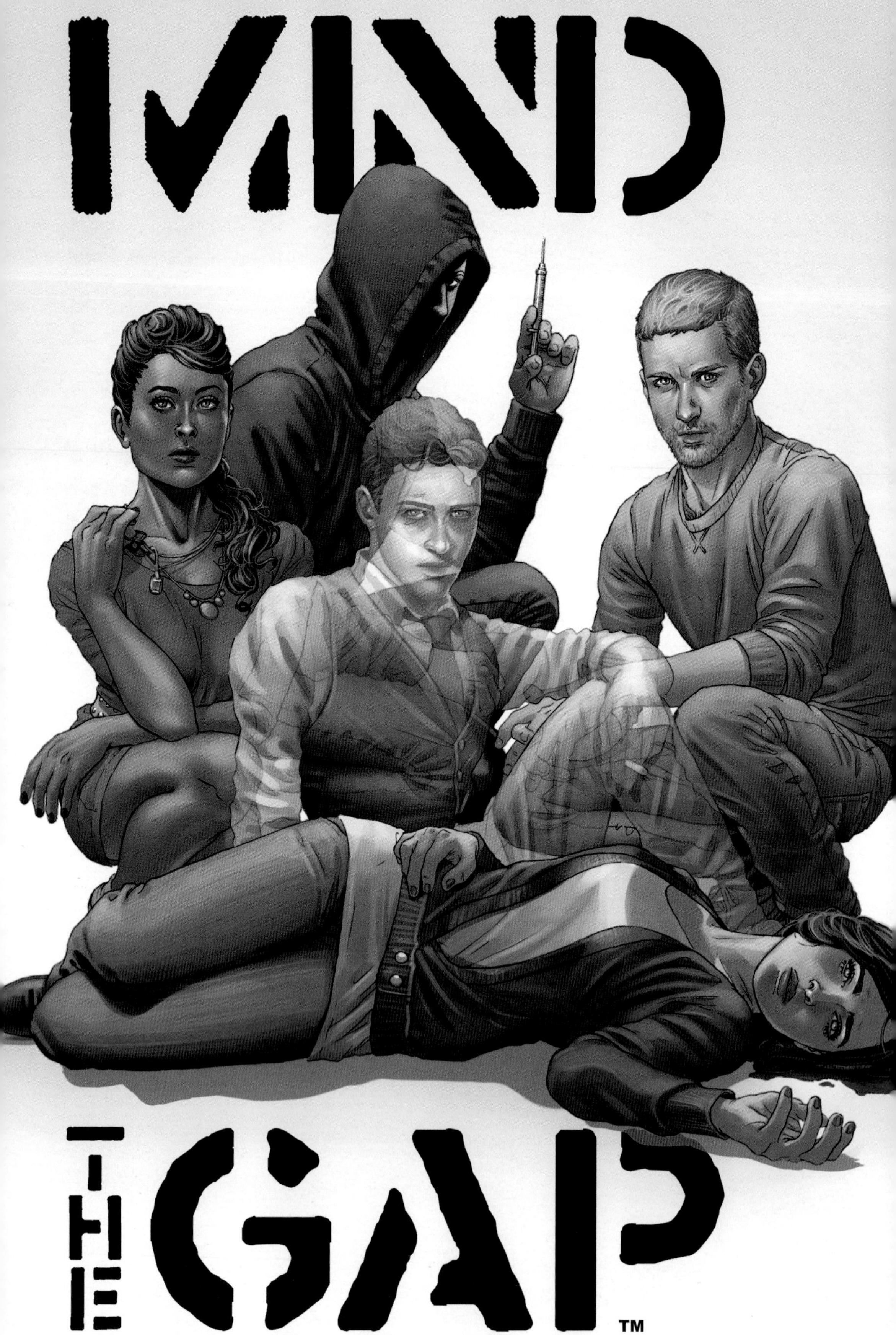
MIND
THE GAP™

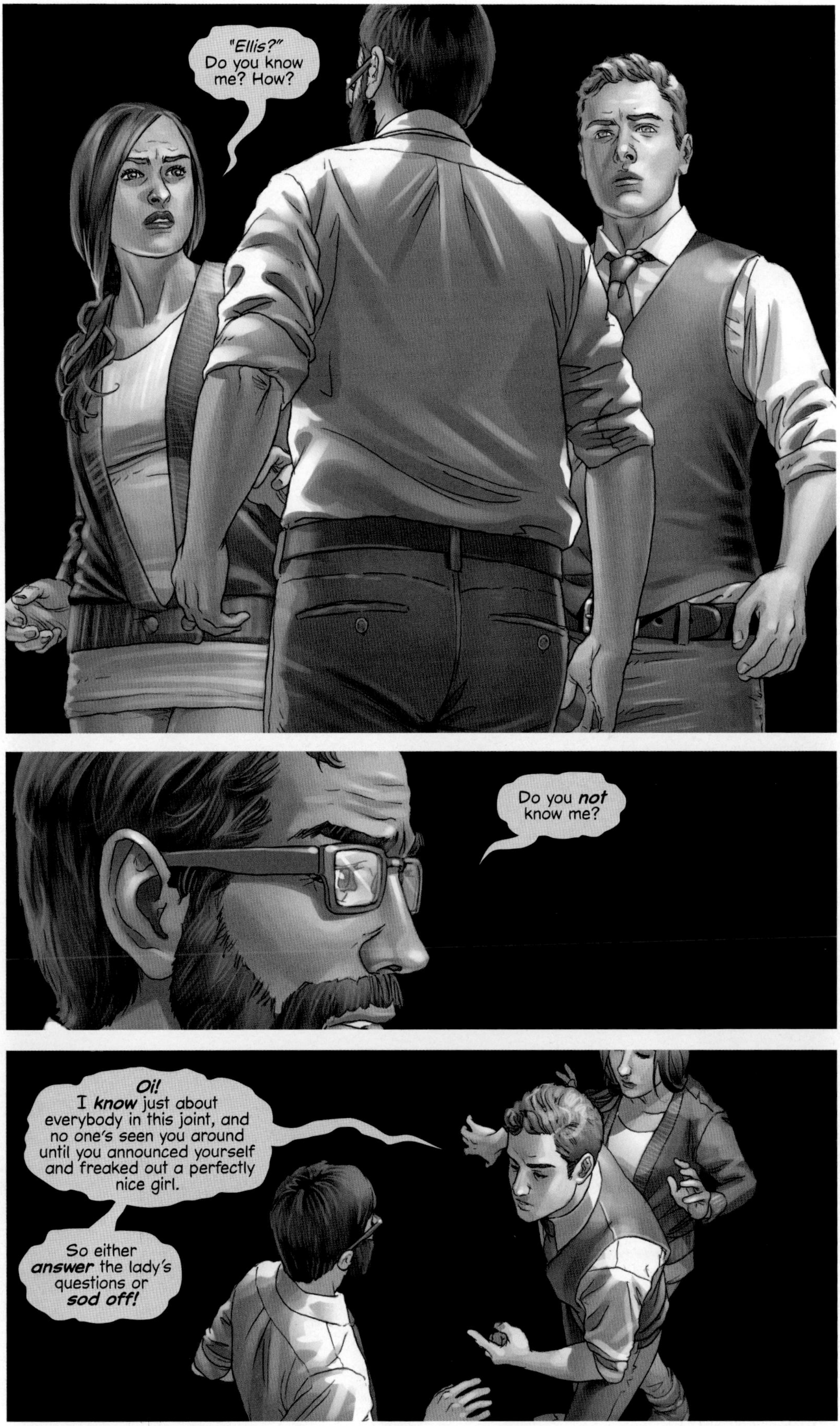
"*Ellis?*" Do you know me? How?
Do you ***not*** know me?
Oi! I ***know*** just about everybody in this joint, and no one's seen you around until you announced yourself and freaked out a perfectly nice girl.
So either ***answer*** the lady's questions or ***sod off!***

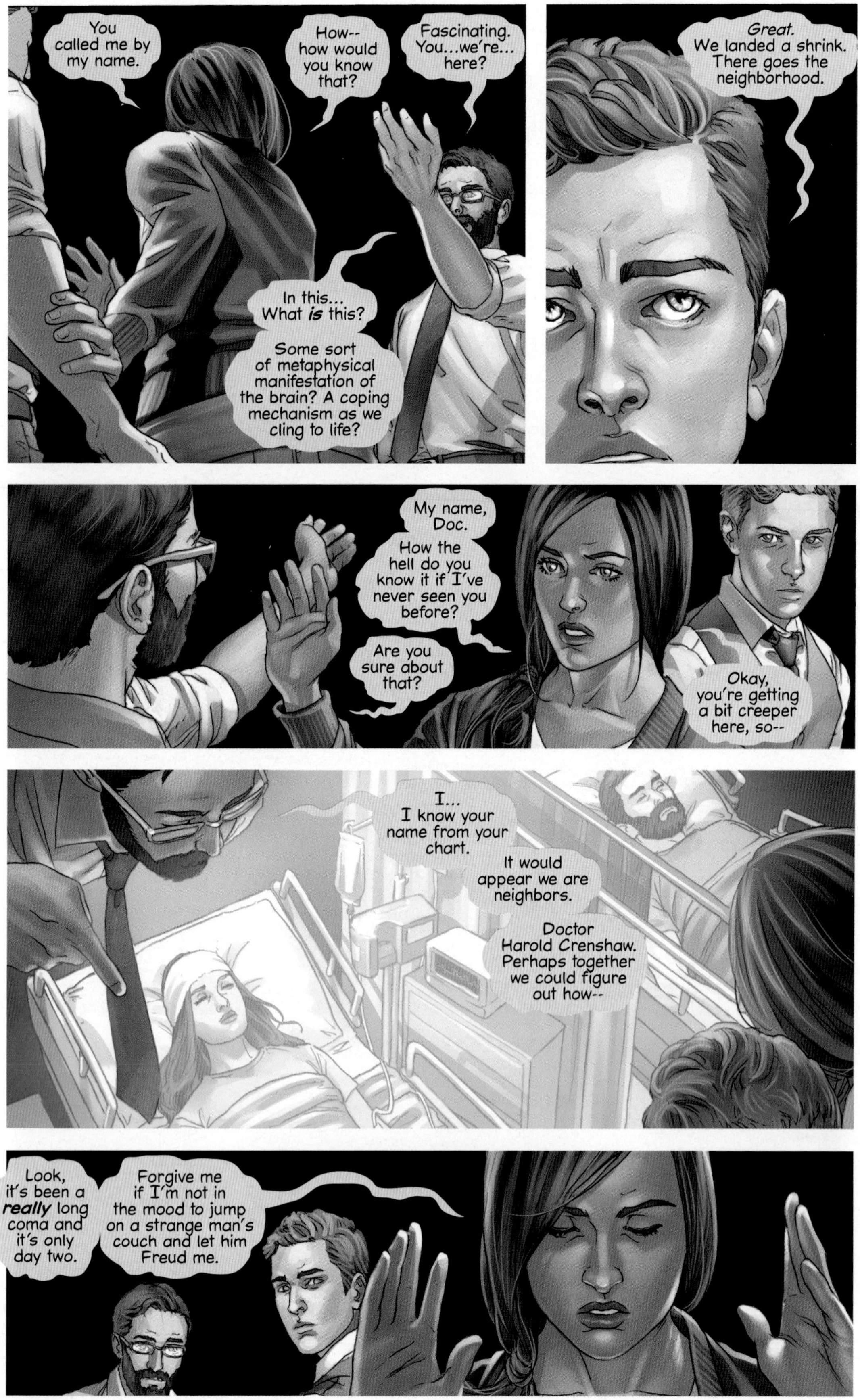

You called me by my name.
How-- how would you know that?
Fascinating. You...we're... here?
In this... What *is* this?
Some sort of metaphysical manifestation of the brain? A coping mechanism as we cling to life?
Great. We landed a shrink. There goes the neighborhood.
My name, Doc.
How the hell do you know it if I've never seen you before?
Are you sure about that?
Okay, you're getting a bit creeper here, so--
I... I know your name from your chart.
It would appear we are neighbors.
Doctor Harold Crenshaw. Perhaps together we could figure out how--
Look, it's been a ***really*** long coma and it's only day two.
Forgive me if I'm not in the mood to jump on a strange man's couch and let him Freud me.

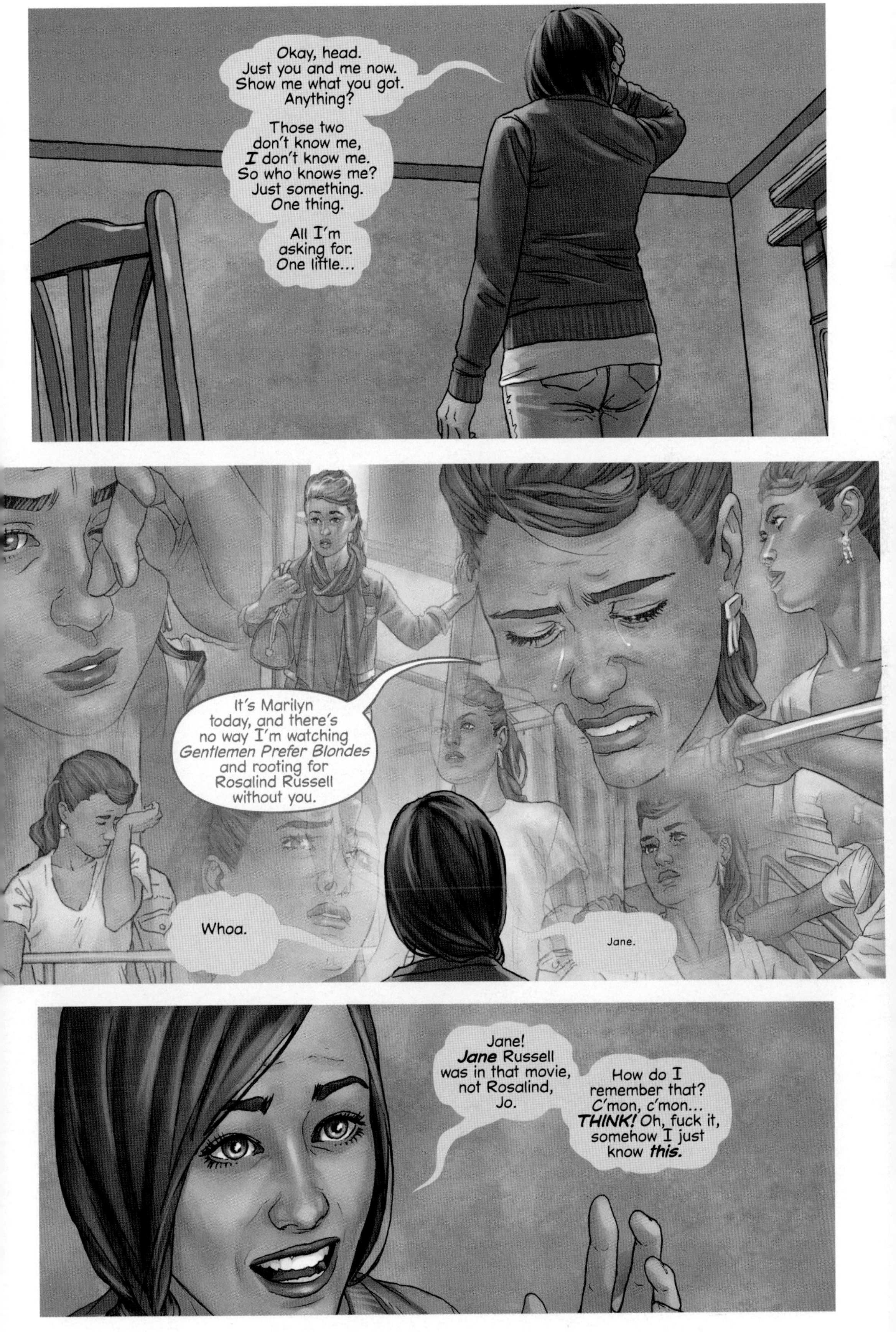
Okay, head. Just you and me now. Show me what you got. Anything?
Those two don't know me, *I* don't know me. So who knows me? Just something. One thing.
All I'm asking for. One little...
It's Marilyn today, and there's no way I'm watching *Gentlemen Prefer Blondes* and rooting for Rosalind Russell without you.
Whoa.
Jane.
Jane! ***Jane*** Russell was in that movie, not Rosalind, Jo.
How do I remember that? C'mon, c'mon... ***THINK!*** Oh, fuck it, somehow I just know ***this.***

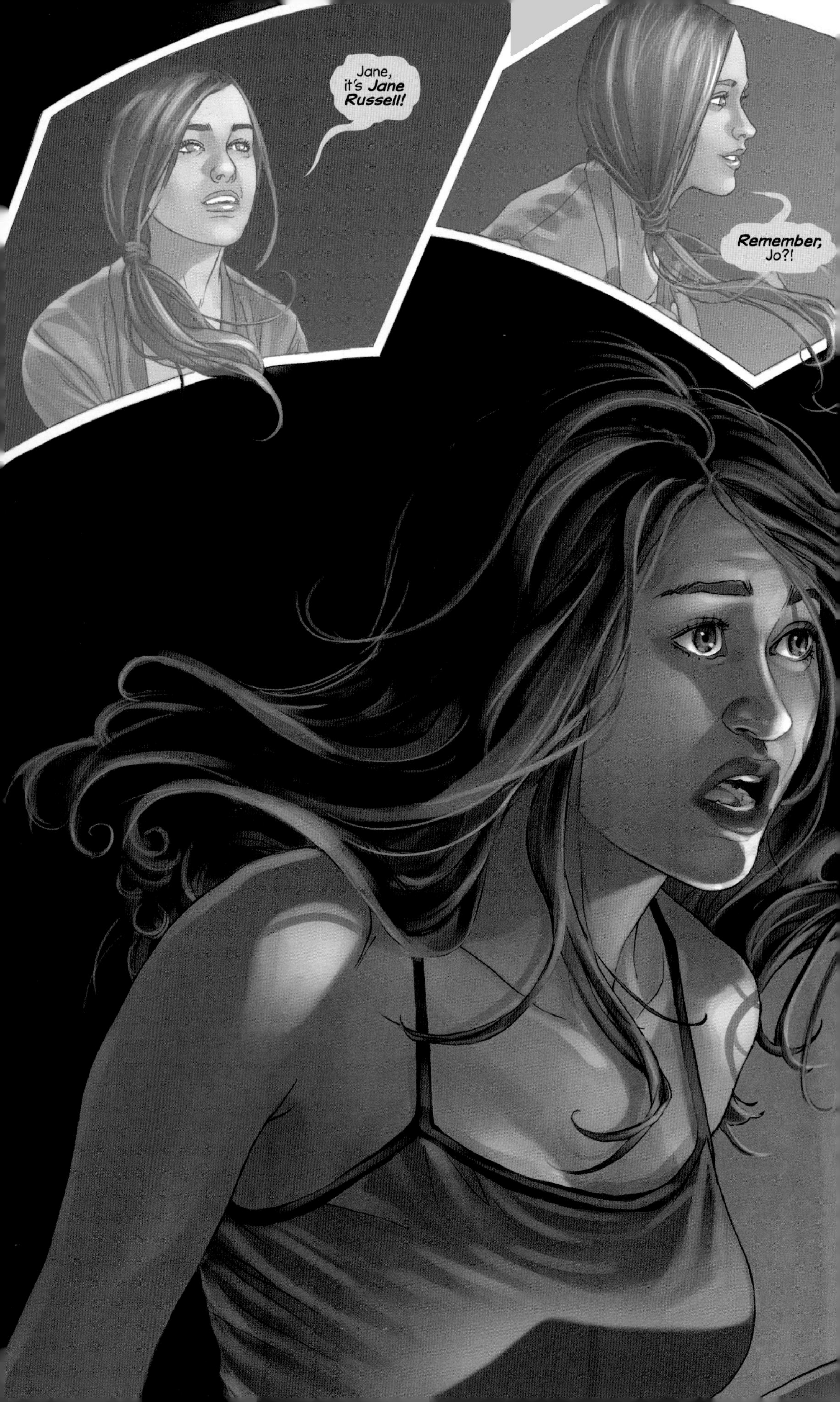
Jane,
it's *Jane Russell!*
Remember,
Jo?!

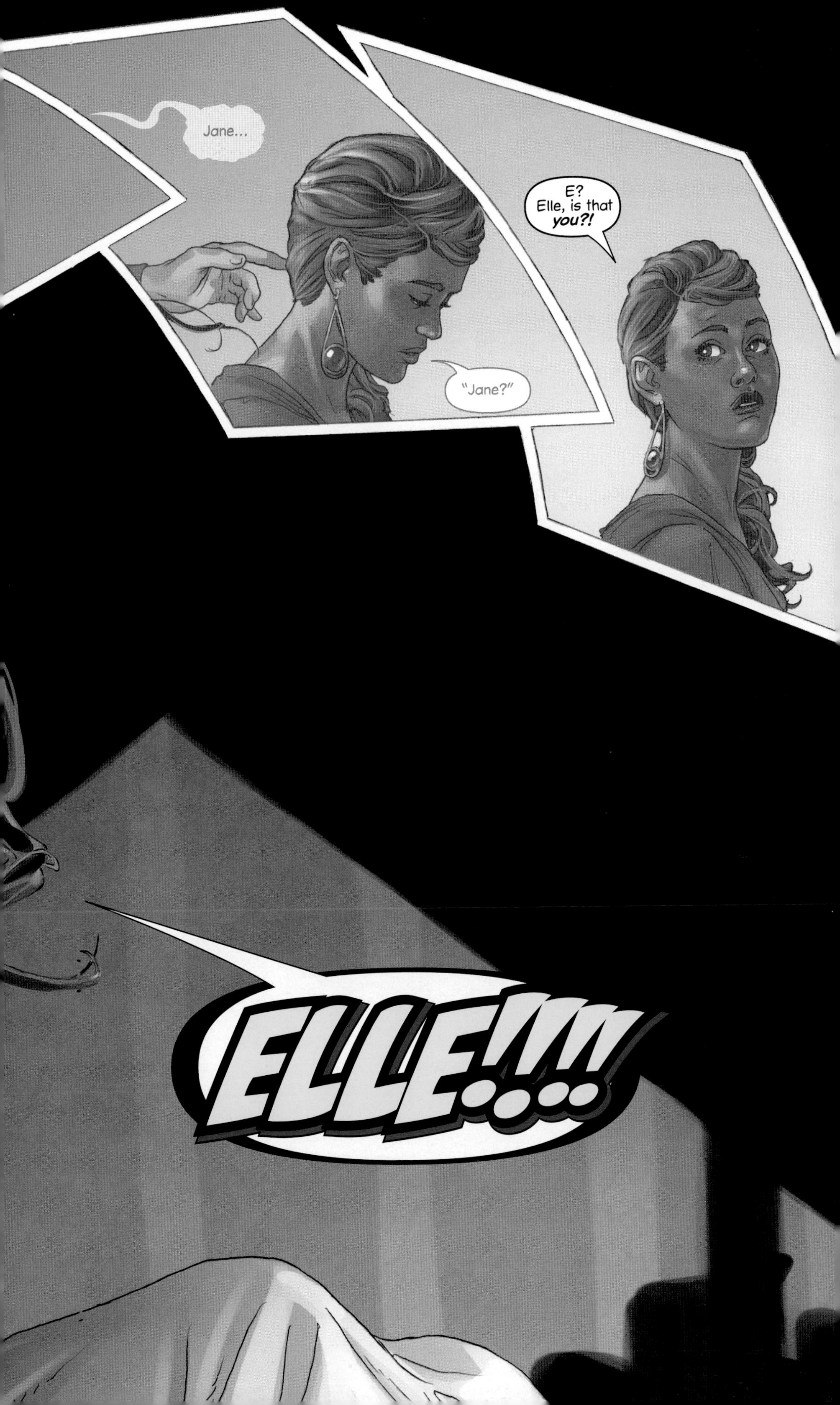
Jane...
"Jane?"
E? Elle, is that *you?!*
ELLE!!!!

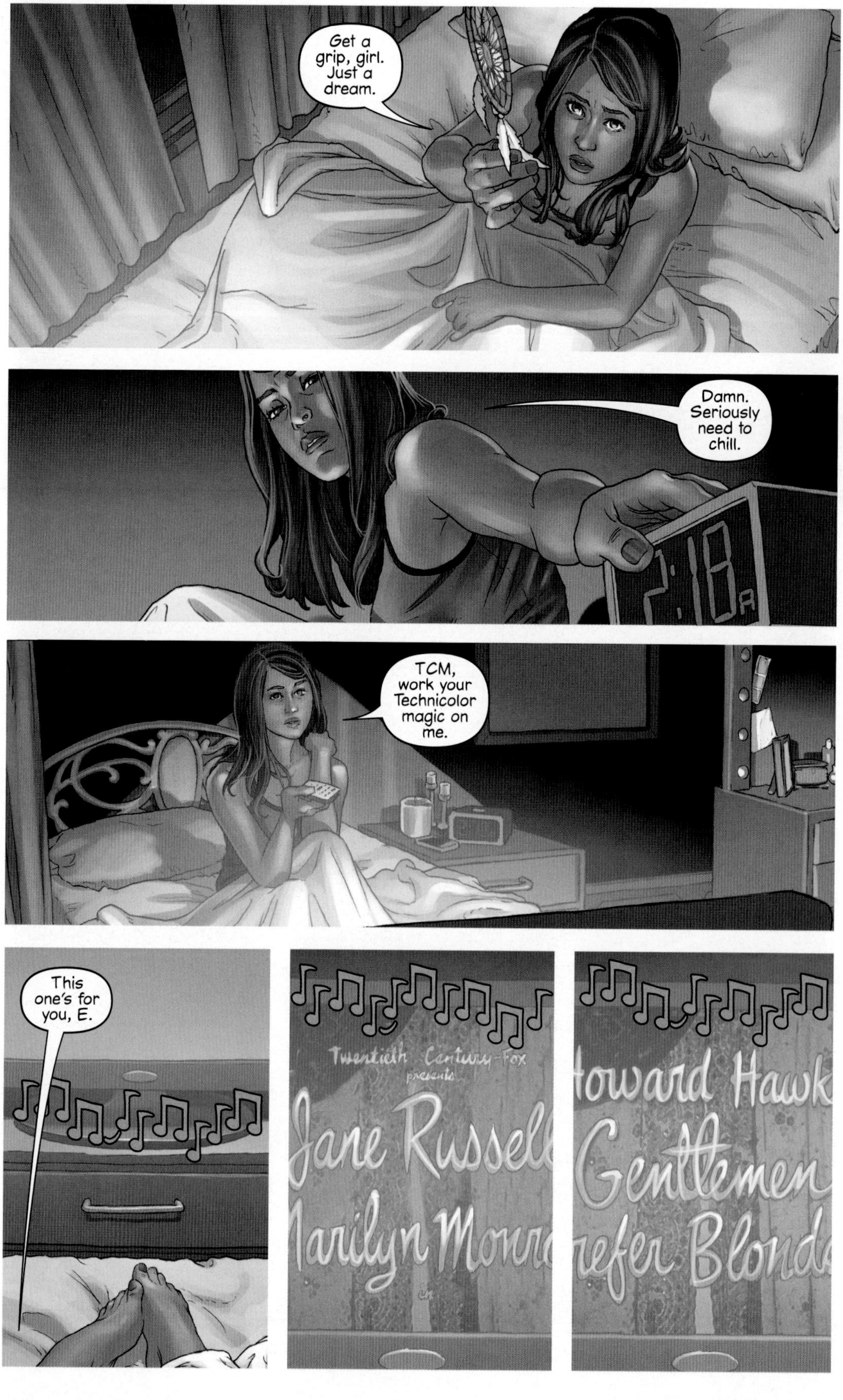
Get a grip, girl. Just a dream.
Damn. Seriously need to chill.
TCM, work your Technicolor magic on me.
This one's for you, E.
Twentieth Century-Fox presents
Jane Russell
Marilyn Monro
Howard Hawk
Gentlemen
efer Blond

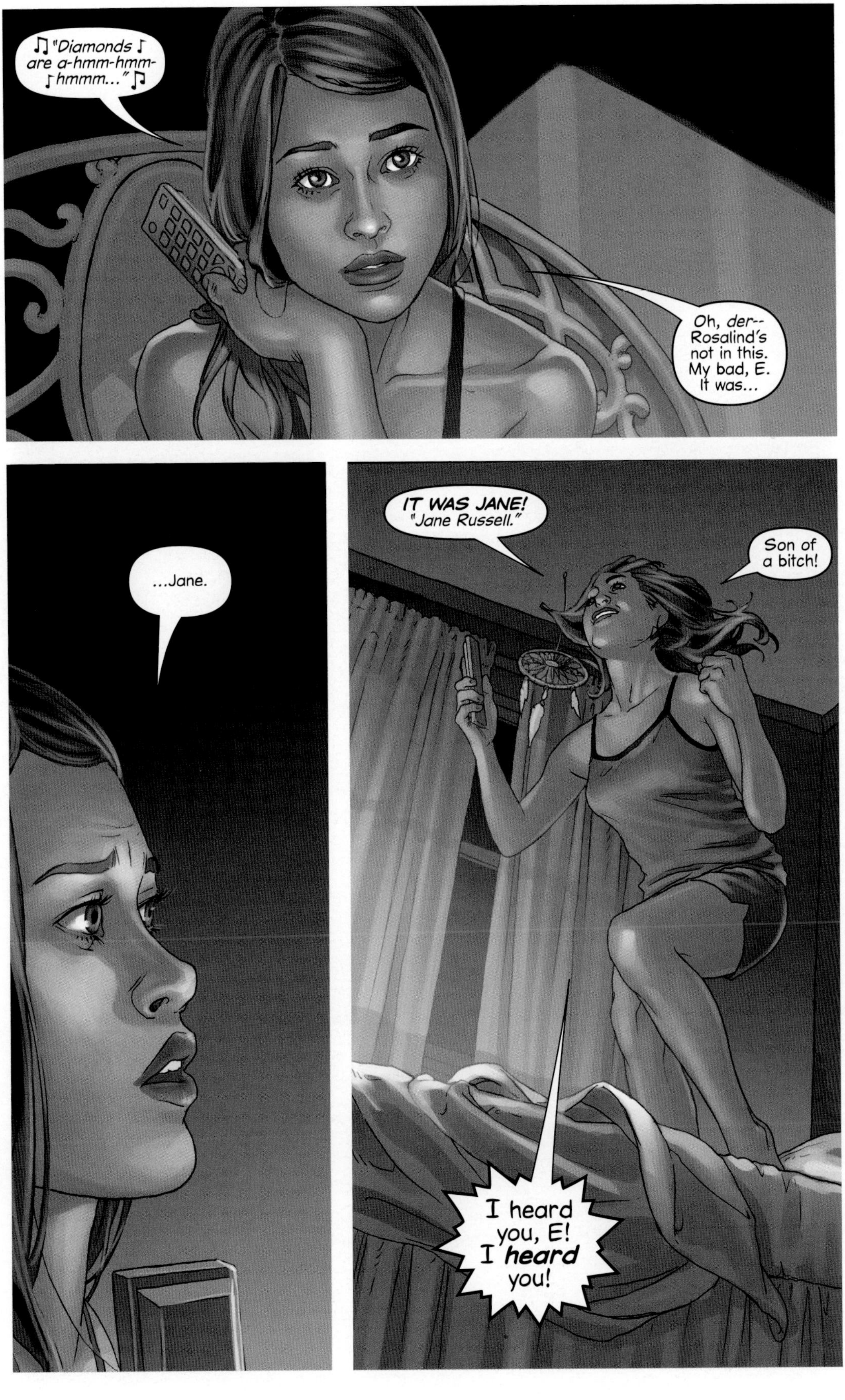
♫ "Diamonds ♩ are a-hmm-hmm- ♩ hmmm..." ♫
Oh, *der*-- Rosalind's not in this. My bad, E. It was...
...Jane.
IT WAS JANE! *"Jane Russell."*
Son of a bitch!
I heard you, E! I ***heard*** you!

INTIMATE STRANGERS
PART 3
"JANE"

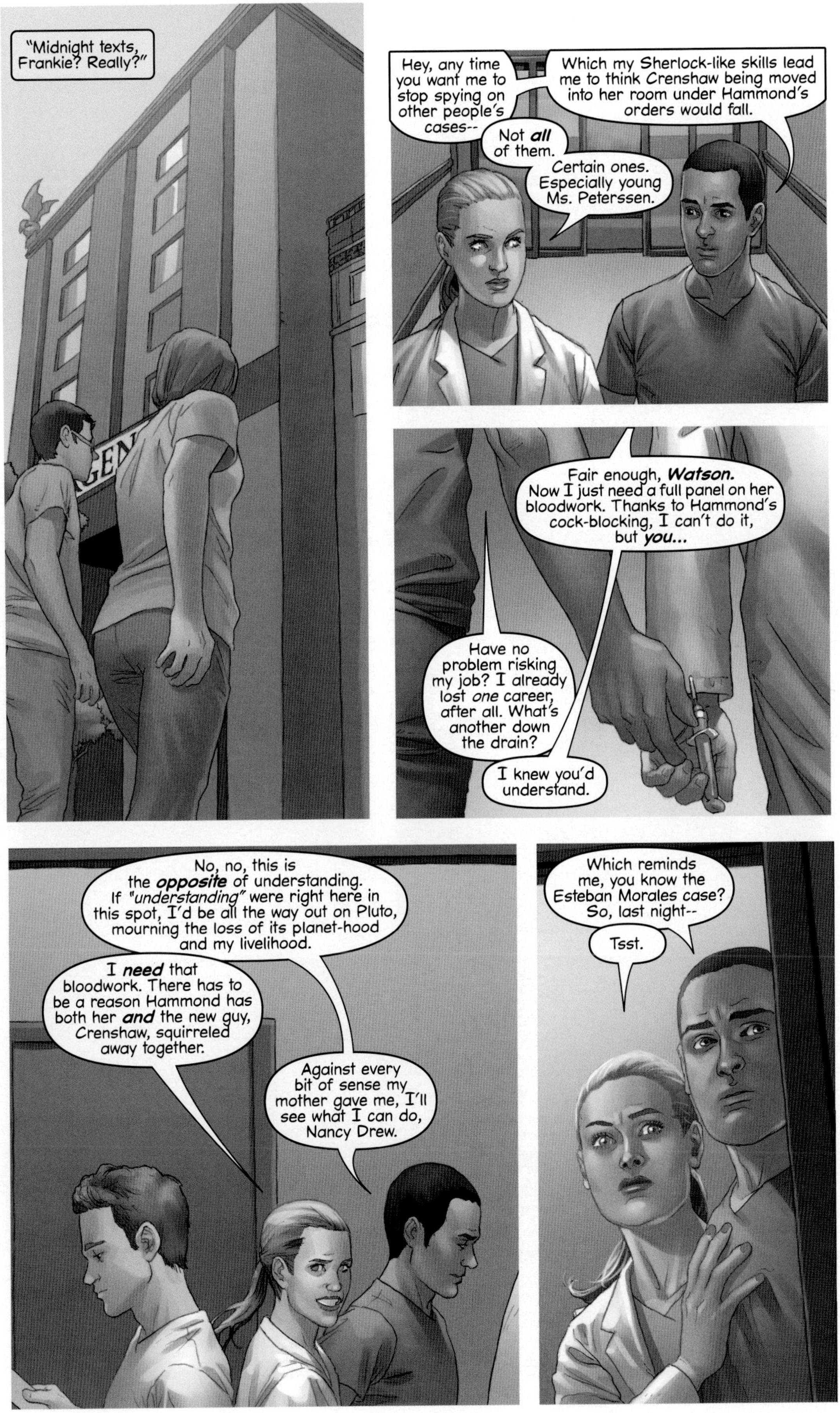
"Midnight texts, Frankie? Really?"
Hey, any time you want me to stop spying on other people's cases--
Which my Sherlock-like skills lead me to think Crenshaw being moved into her room under Hammond's orders would fall.
Not *all* of them.
Certain ones. Especially young Ms. Peterssen.
Fair enough, ***Watson.*** Now I just need a full panel on her bloodwork. Thanks to Hammond's cock-blocking, I can't do it, but ***you...***
Have no problem risking my job? I already lost *one* career, after all. What's another down the drain?
I knew you'd understand.
No, no, this is the ***opposite*** of understanding. If *"understanding"* were right here in this spot, I'd be all the way out on Pluto, mourning the loss of its planet-hood and my livelihood.
I ***need*** that bloodwork. There has to be a reason Hammond has both her ***and*** the new guy, Crenshaw, squirreled away together.
Against every bit of sense my mother gave me, I'll see what I can do, Nancy Drew.
Which reminds me, you know the Esteban Morales case? So, last night--
Tsst.

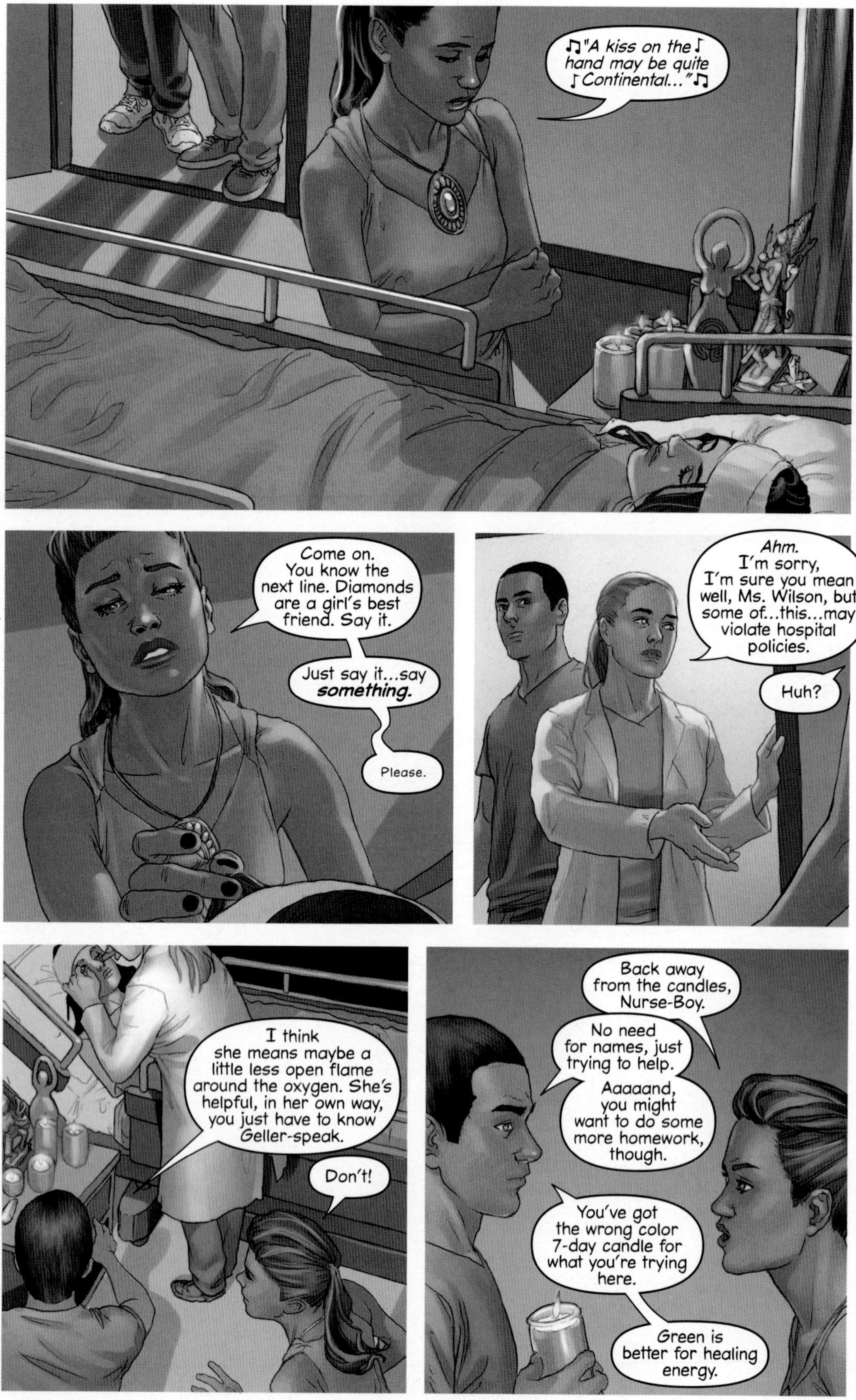

♫"A kiss on the ♪ hand may be quite ♪ Continental..."♫
Come on. You know the next line. Diamonds are a girl's best friend. Say it.
Just say it...say **something.**
Please.
Ahm. I'm sorry, I'm sure you mean well, Ms. Wilson, but some of...this...may violate hospital policies.
Huh?
I think she means maybe a little less open flame around the oxygen. She's helpful, in her own way, you just have to know Geller-speak.
Don't!
Back away from the candles, Nurse-Boy.
No need for names, just trying to help.
Aaaaand, you might want to do some more homework, though.
You've got the wrong color 7-day candle for what you're trying here.
Green is better for healing energy.

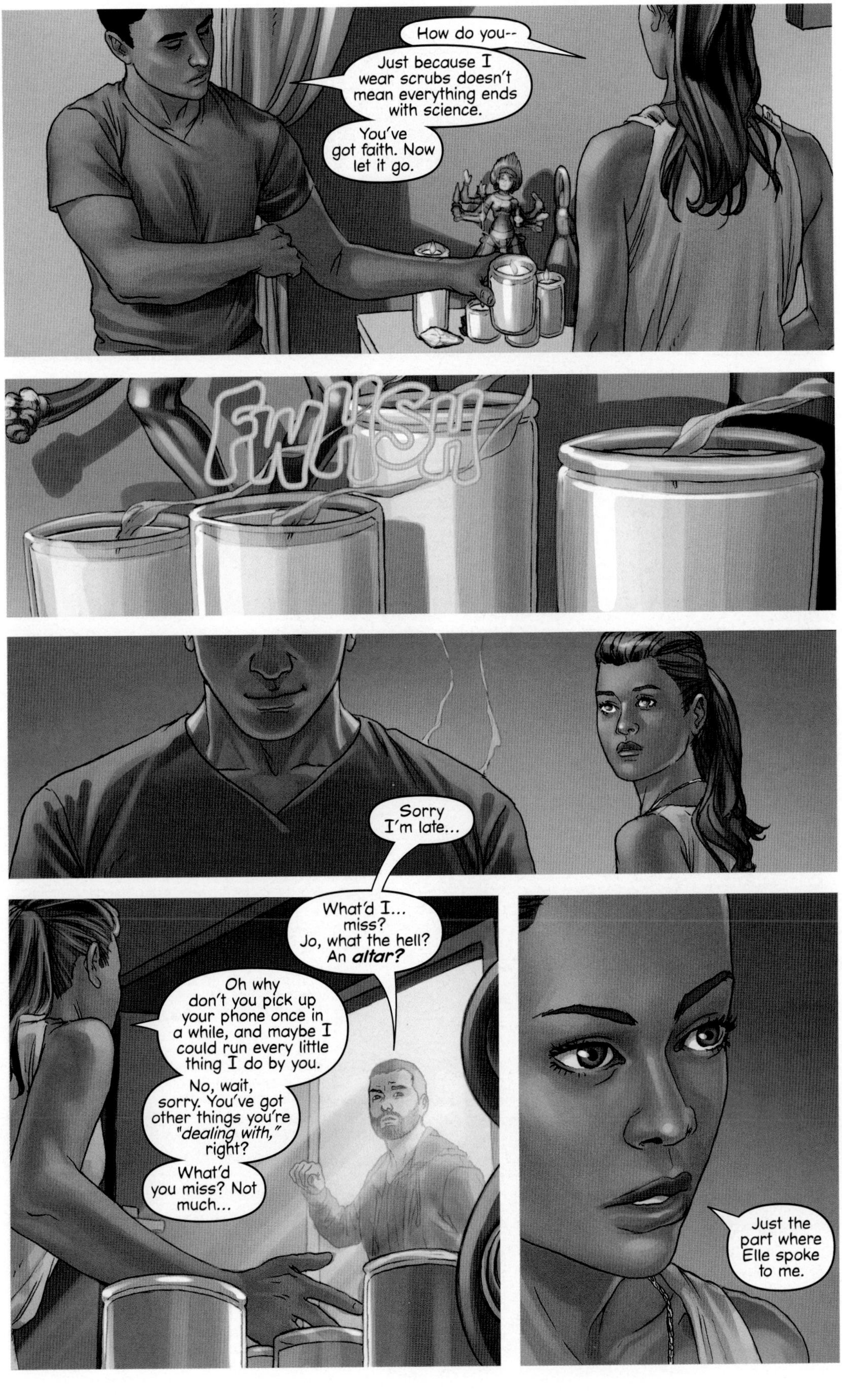
How do you--
Just because I wear scrubs doesn't mean everything ends with science.
You've got faith. Now let it go.
FWUSH
Sorry I'm late...
What'd I... miss? Jo, what the hell? An *altar?*
Oh why don't you pick up your phone once in a while, and maybe I could run every little thing I do by you.
No, wait, sorry. You've got other things you're *"dealing with,"* right?
What'd you miss? Not much...
Just the part where Elle spoke to me.

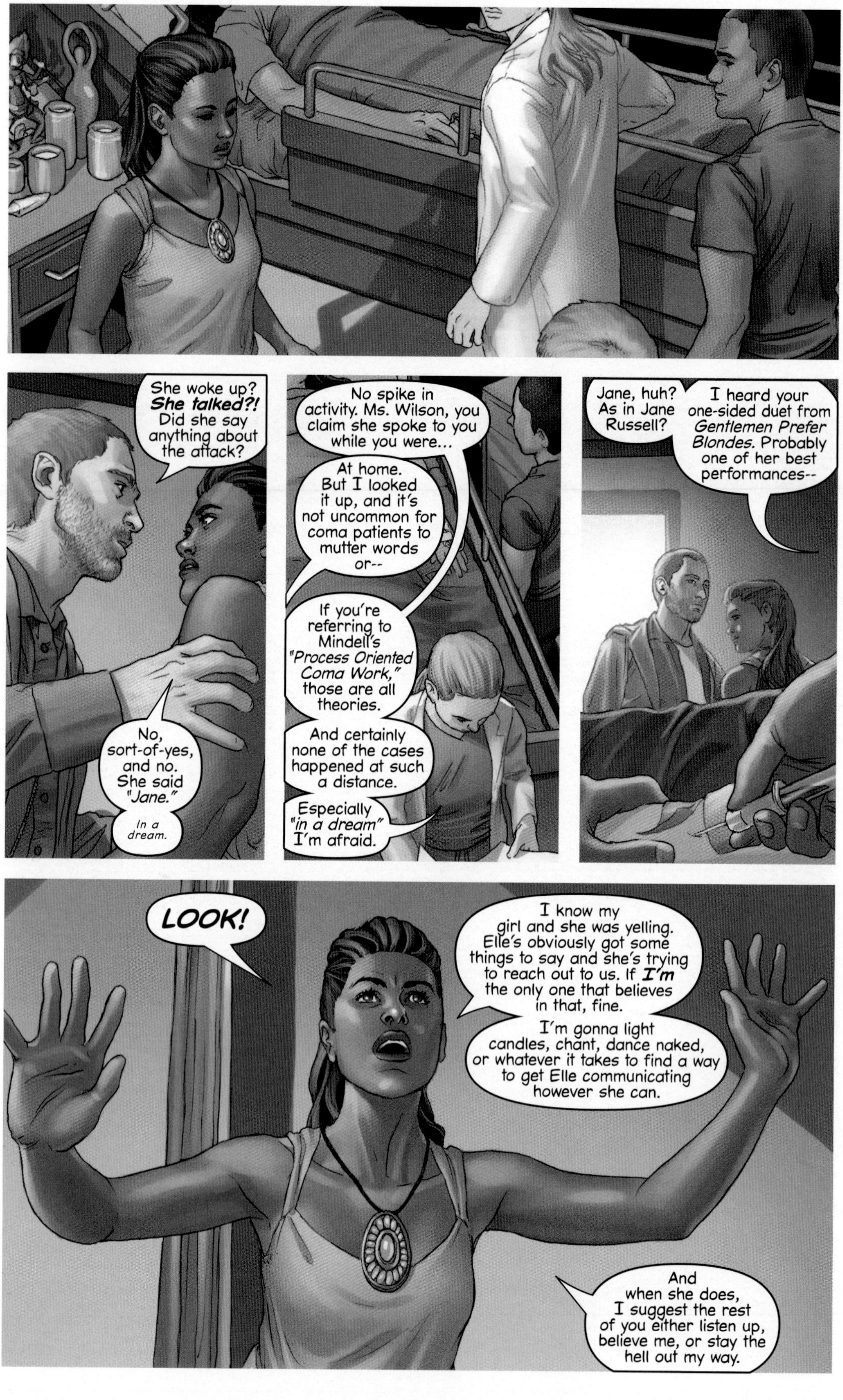

She woke up? She talked?! Did she say anything about the attack?
No, sort-of-yes, and no. She said "Jane."
In a dream.
No spike in activity. Ms. Wilson, you claim she spoke to you while you were...
At home. But I looked it up, and it's not uncommon for coma patients to mutter words or--
If you're referring to Mindell's "Process Oriented Coma Work," those are all theories.
And certainly none of the cases happened at such a distance.
Especially "in a dream" I'm afraid.
Jane, huh? As in Jane Russell?
I heard your one-sided duet from Gentlemen Prefer Blondes. Probably one of her best performances--
LOOK!
I know my girl and she was yelling. Elle's obviously got some things to say and she's trying to reach out to us. If I'm the only one that believes in that, fine.
I'm gonna light candles, chant, dance naked, or whatever it takes to find a way to get Elle communicating however she can.
And when she does, I suggest the rest of you either listen up, believe me, or stay the hell out my way.

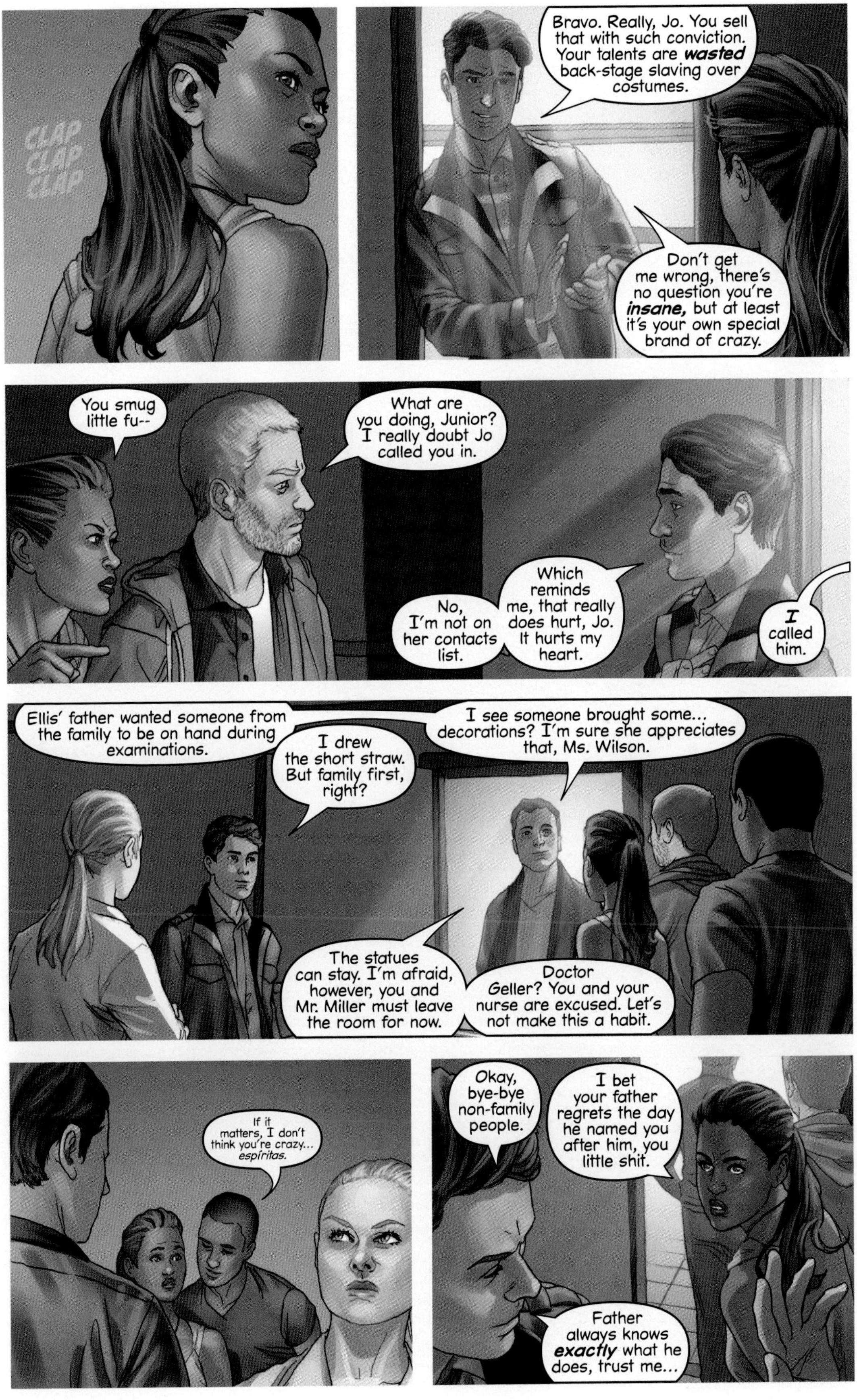
CLAP
CLAP
CLAP
Bravo. Really, Jo. You sell that with such conviction. Your talents are ***wasted*** back-stage slaving over costumes.
Don't get me wrong, there's no question you're ***insane,*** but at least it's your own special brand of crazy.
You smug little fu--
What are you doing, Junior? I really doubt Jo called you in.
No, I'm not on her contacts list.
Which reminds me, that really does hurt, Jo. It hurts my heart.
I called him.
Ellis' father wanted someone from the family to be on hand during examinations.
I drew the short straw. But family first, right?
I see someone brought some... decorations? I'm sure she appreciates that, Ms. Wilson.
The statues can stay. I'm afraid, however, you and Mr. Miller must leave the room for now.
Doctor Geller? You and your nurse are excused. Let's not make this a habit.
If it matters, I don't think you're crazy... *espíritas.*
Okay, bye-bye non-family people.
I bet your father regrets the day he named you after him, you little shit.
Father always knows ***exactly*** what he does, trust me...

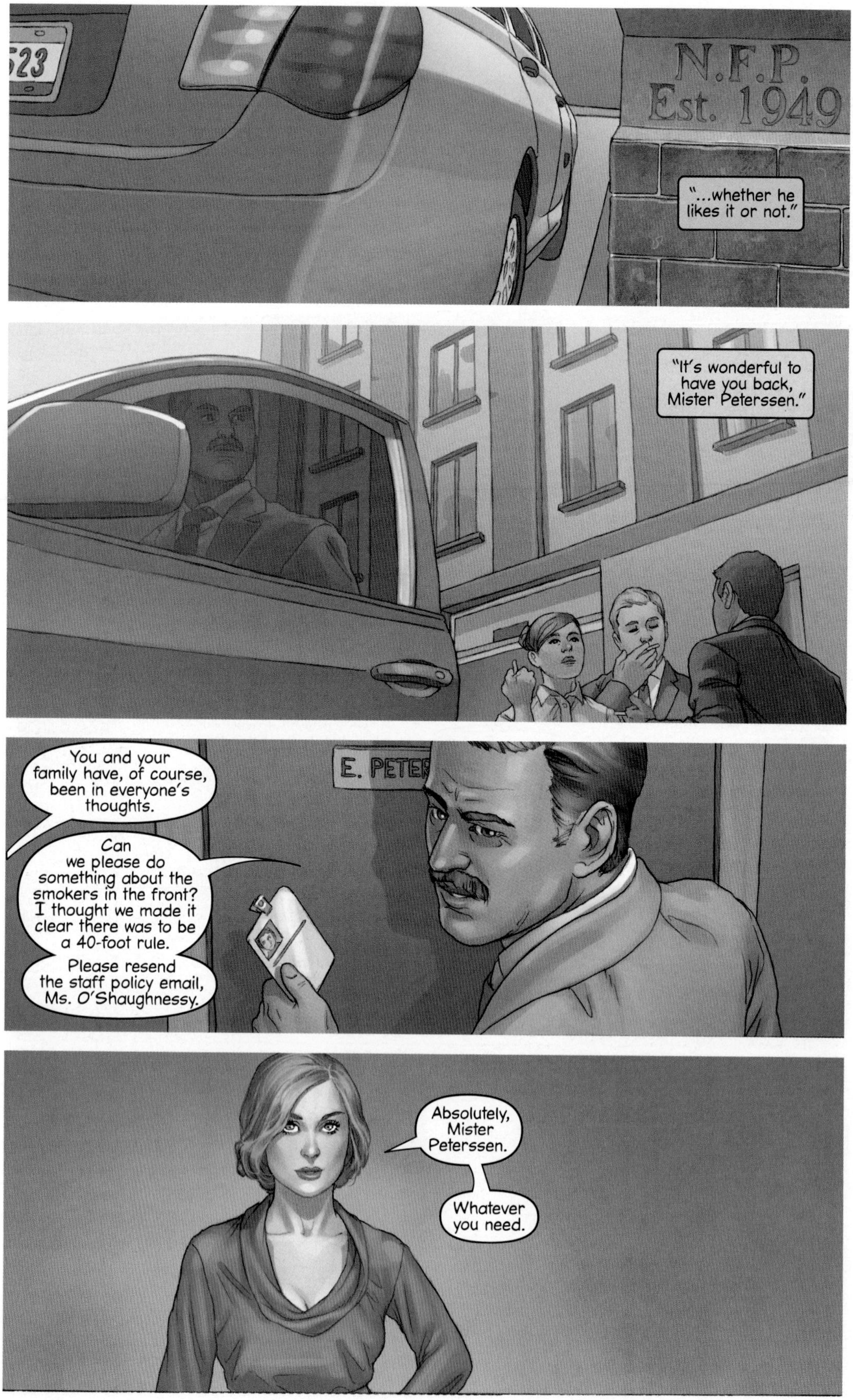
523
N.F.P. Est. 1949
"...whether he likes it or not."
"It's wonderful to have you back, Mister Peterssen."
E. PETER
You and your family have, of course, been in everyone's thoughts.
Can we please do something about the smokers in the front? I thought we made it clear there was to be a 40-foot rule.
Please resend the staff policy email, Ms. O'Shaughnessy.
Absolutely, Mister Peterssen.
Whatever you need.

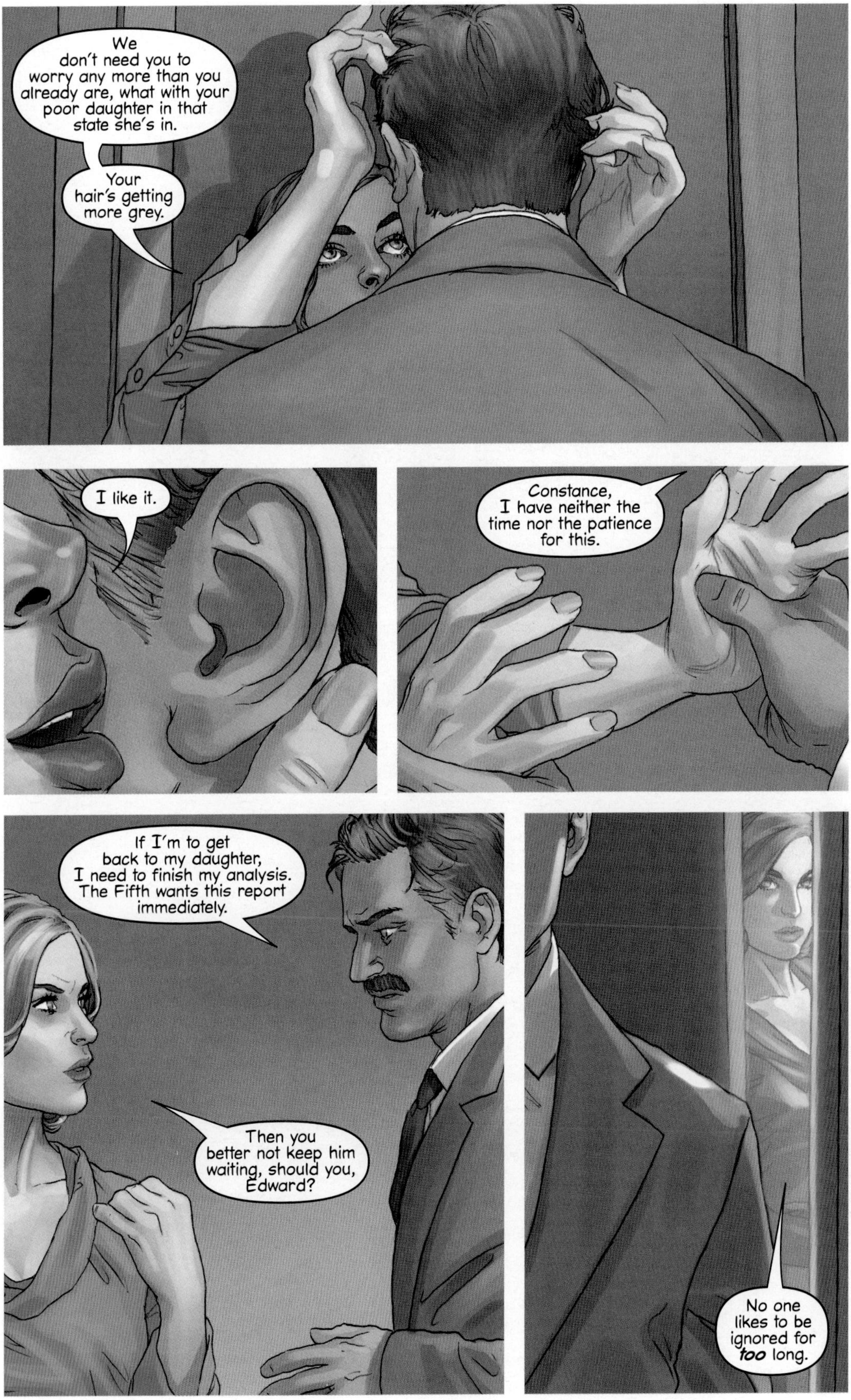
We don't need you to worry any more than you already are, what with your poor daughter in that state she's in.
Your hair's getting more grey.
I like it.
Constance, I have neither the time nor the patience for this.
If I'm to get back to my daughter, I need to finish my analysis. The Fifth wants this report immediately.
Then you better not keep him waiting, should you, Edward?
No one likes to be ignored for *too* long.

Jane! Jane, Jane, Jane!

No! Don't leave! What other word do you want me to say?!

ARGH!

She heard me. Somehow, in a dream, we "touched" and...

And she's the *only* one. She's different. Safe and always there for me. Like a bollard. I just don't know what rope to throw her.

Bollard, huh? You sail?

I guess? How the hell should I know? Most things are blank in my head and the rest are just jumbled up and I can't seem to get them out in any order.

Like I'm putting together a puzzle without the picture on the box. And half the pieces are overturned.

God help me that I'm even saying this, but maybe you should bring in Doctor Shrink out there to help you sort the mess.

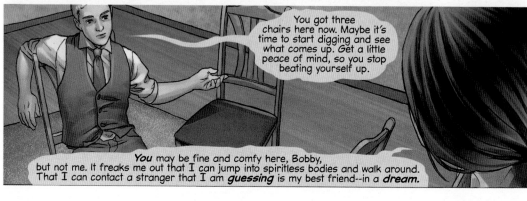

You got three chairs here now. Maybe it's time to start digging and see what comes up. Get a little peace of mind, so you stop beating yourself up.

You may be fine and comfy here, Bobby, but not me. It freaks me out that I can jump into spiritless bodies and walk around. That I can contact a stranger that I am *guessing* is my best friend--in a *dream*.

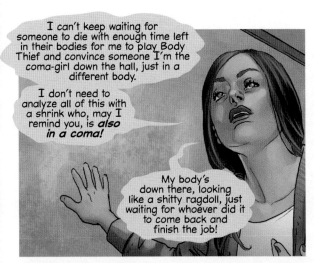

I can't keep waiting for someone to die with enough time left in their bodies for me to play Body Thief and convince someone I'm the coma-girl down the hall, just in a different body.

I don't need to analyze all of this with a shrink who, may I remind you, is *also in a coma!*

My body's down there, looking like a shitty ragdoll, just waiting for whoever did it to come back and finish the job!

Someone put me here and I can't wait on my own mind's fucked-up timetable to figure out how or why.

What I need right now...

...is a memory... ANY memory...

...to give me a clue to answer...

WHAT THE HELL AM I?!?!

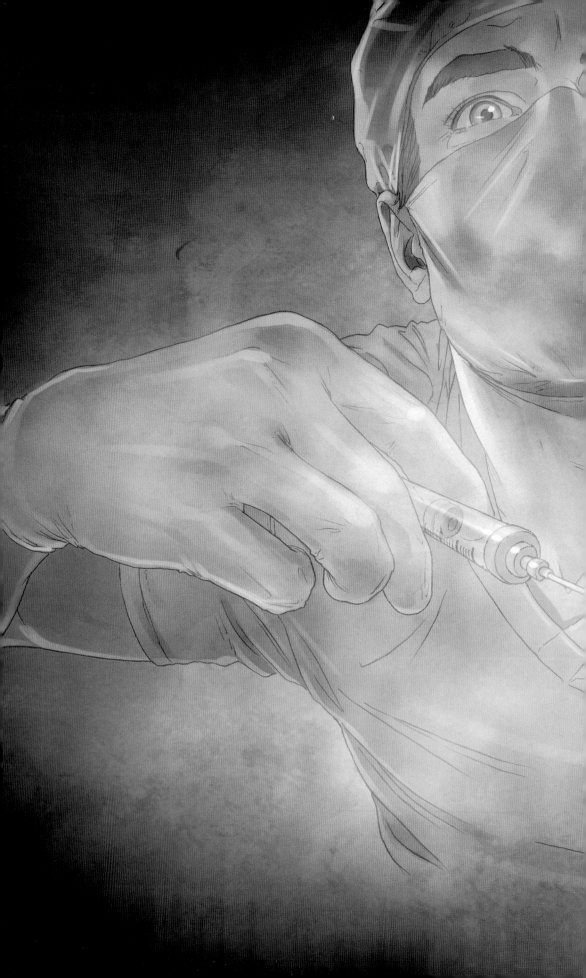

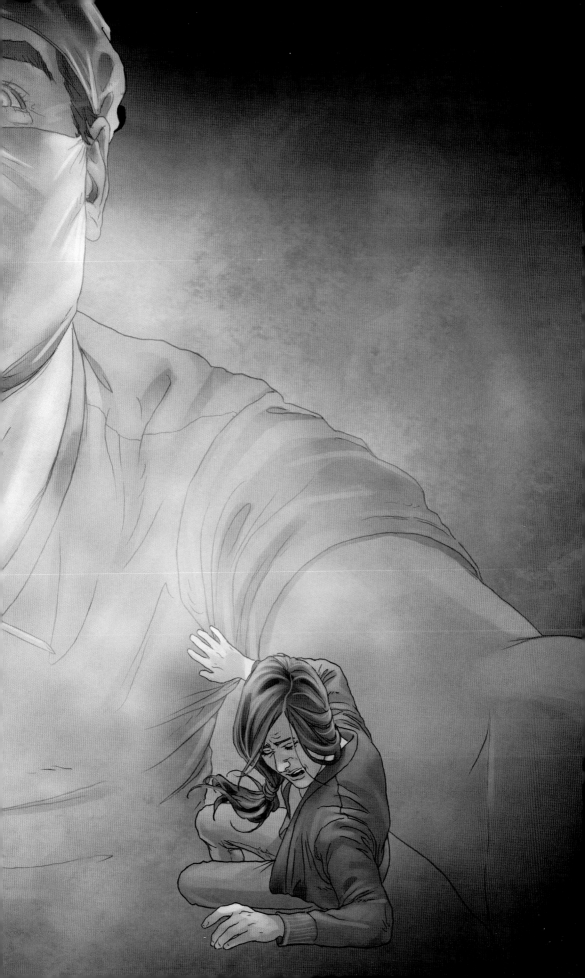

Elle?
You there, luv?

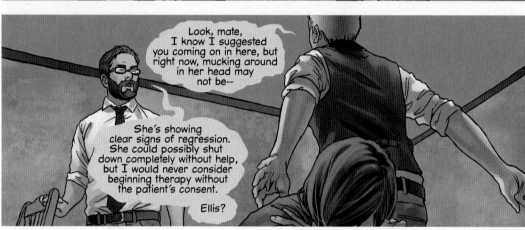

Look, mate, I know I suggested you coming on in here, but right now, mucking around in her head may not be--

She's showing clear signs of regression. She could possibly shut down completely without help, but I would never consider beginning therapy without the patient's consent.

Ellis?

Okay. Now remember, Ellis, whenever you feel scared, this is a safe place. No one here wants to hurt you. Can you show me that you understand what it is I'm saying?

Very good. Now, let's begin.

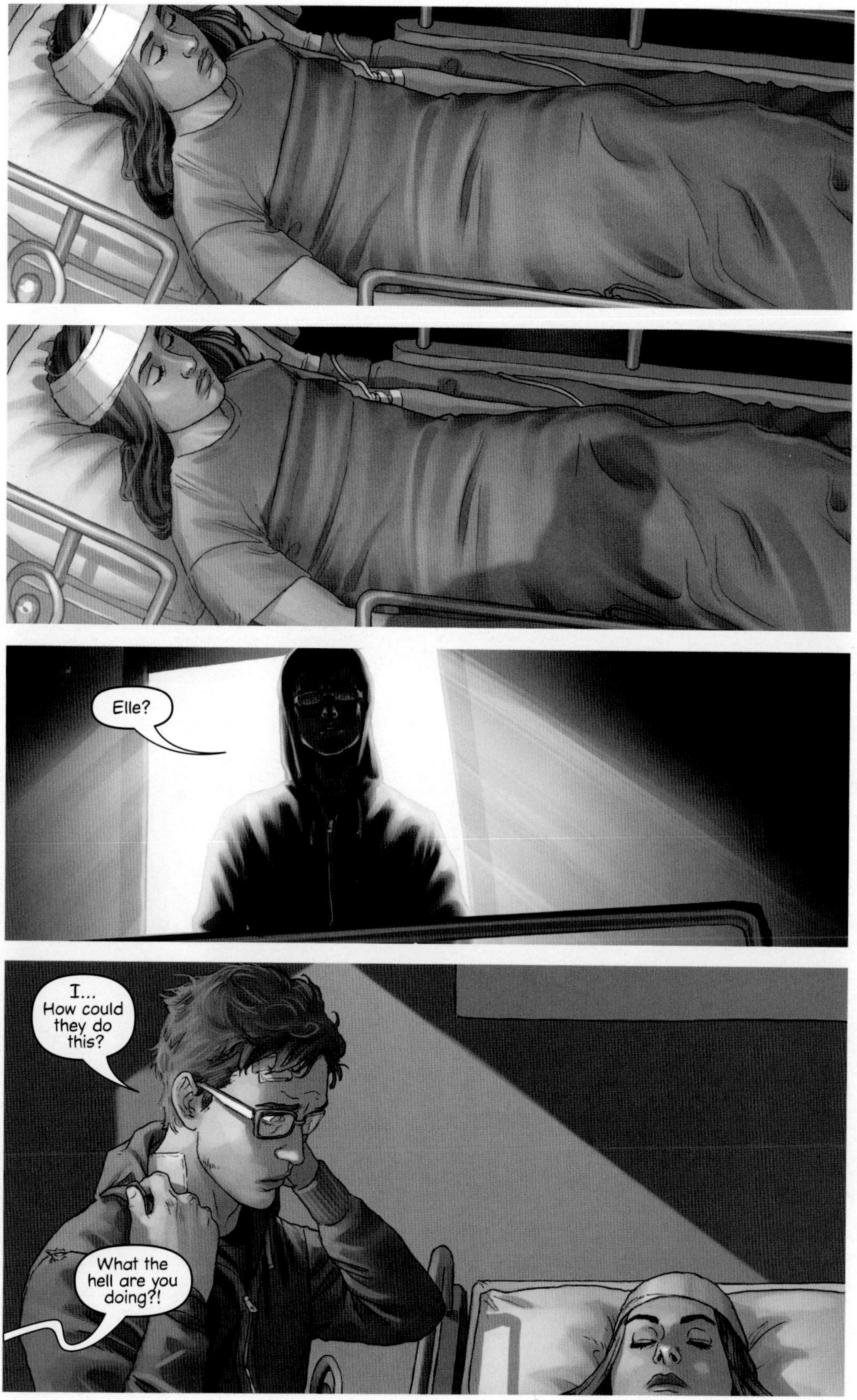
Elle?
I... How could they do this?
What the hell are you doing?!

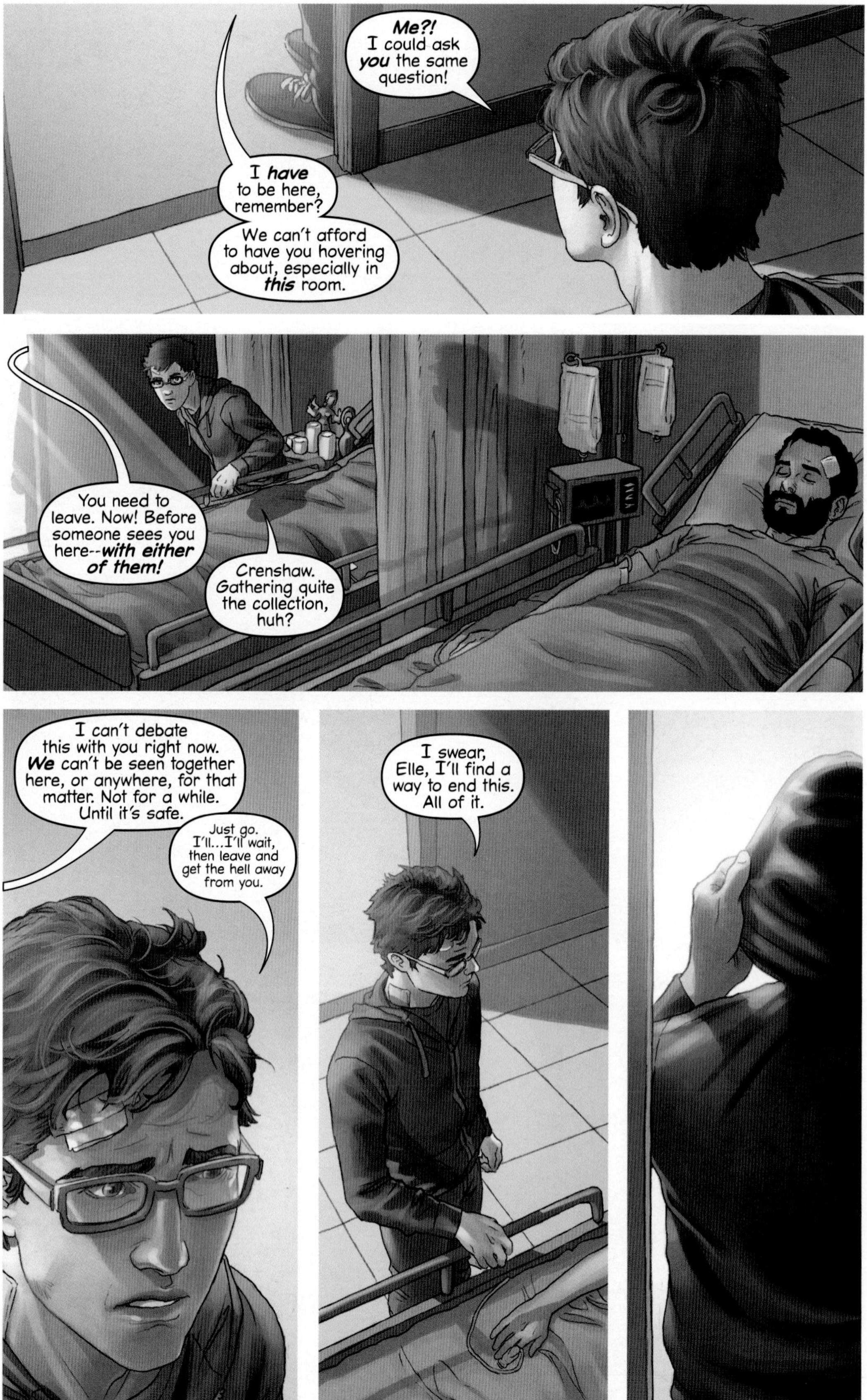
Me?! I could ask *you* the same question!
I *have* to be here, remember?
We can't afford to have you hovering about, especially in *this* room.
You need to leave. Now! Before someone sees you here--*with either of them!*
Crenshaw. Gathering quite the collection, huh?
I can't debate this with you right now. *We* can't be seen together here, or anywhere, for that matter. Not for a while. Until it's safe.
Just go. I'll...I'll wait, then leave and get the hell away from you.
I swear, Elle, I'll find a way to end this. All of it.

Sorry.

BRRZT

Hey, Annie.

Hon, are you ready for a bit of "there are no coincidences?"

As long as it doesn't involve candles or crystals.

I won't even ask.

So you know how the Peterssen case was shut down before it could even really begin?

Turns out our big-time shrink had some interesting people on his client list. Including, get this, one *Ellis Peterssen.*

Shit. That's it, then, right? A workaround to reopen the case?

Not yet. Far as we can tell, all case notes were destroyed; forensics is working what they can. But Crenshaw's secretary, Louise, has been a doll in providing us with his client list.

If there's a connection, we'll find it.

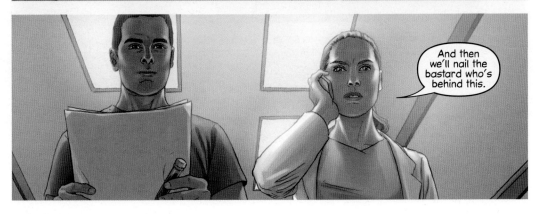

And then we'll nail the bastard who's behind this.

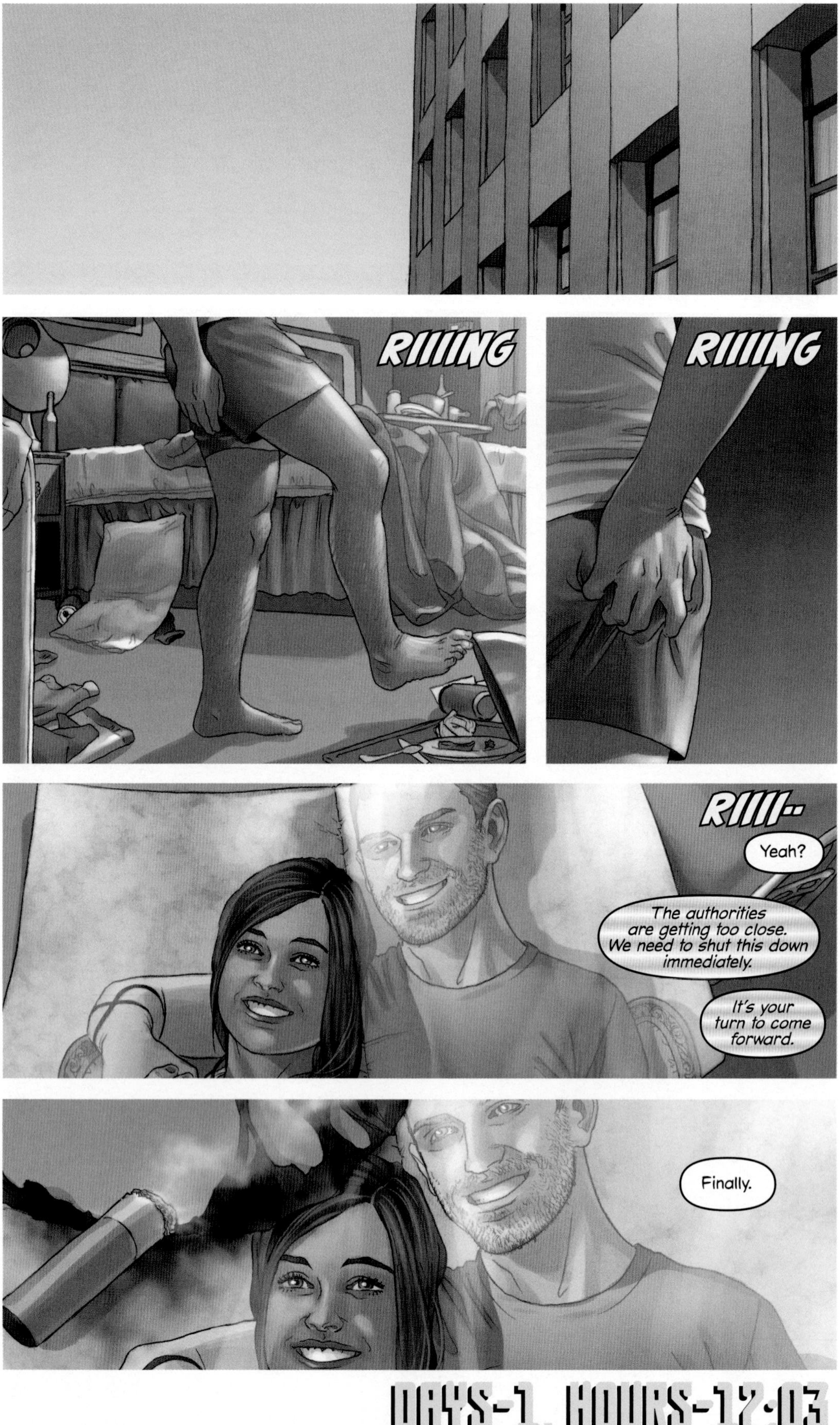
RIIIING
RIIIING
RIIII--
Yeah?
The authorities are getting too close. We need to shut this down immediately.
It's your turn to come forward.
Finally.

DAYS-1, HOURS-17:03

"The past is not simply the past, but a prism through which the subject filters their own changing self-image."

-Doris Kearns Goodwin

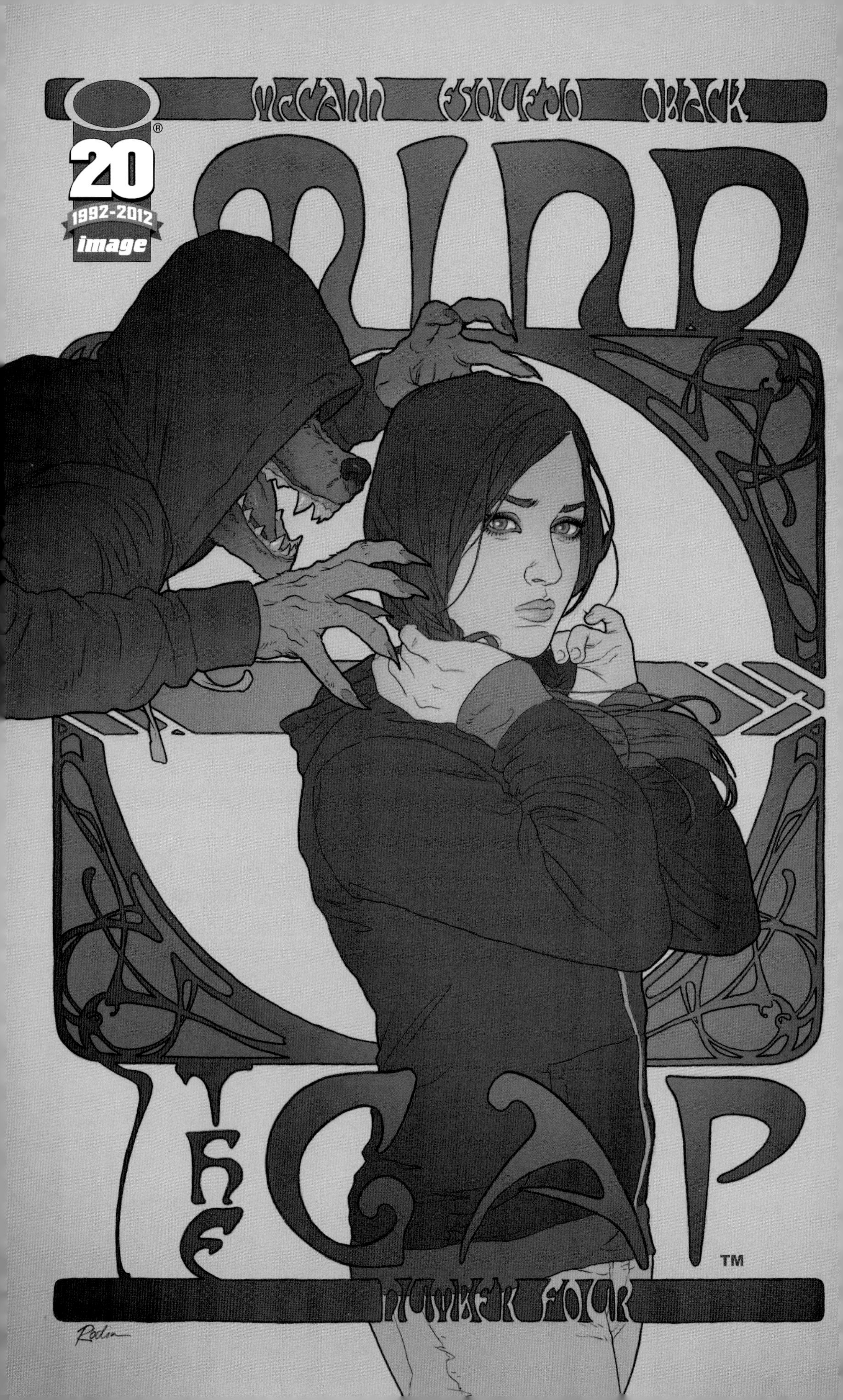

20
1992-2012
image
MIND THE GAP
NUMBER FOUR

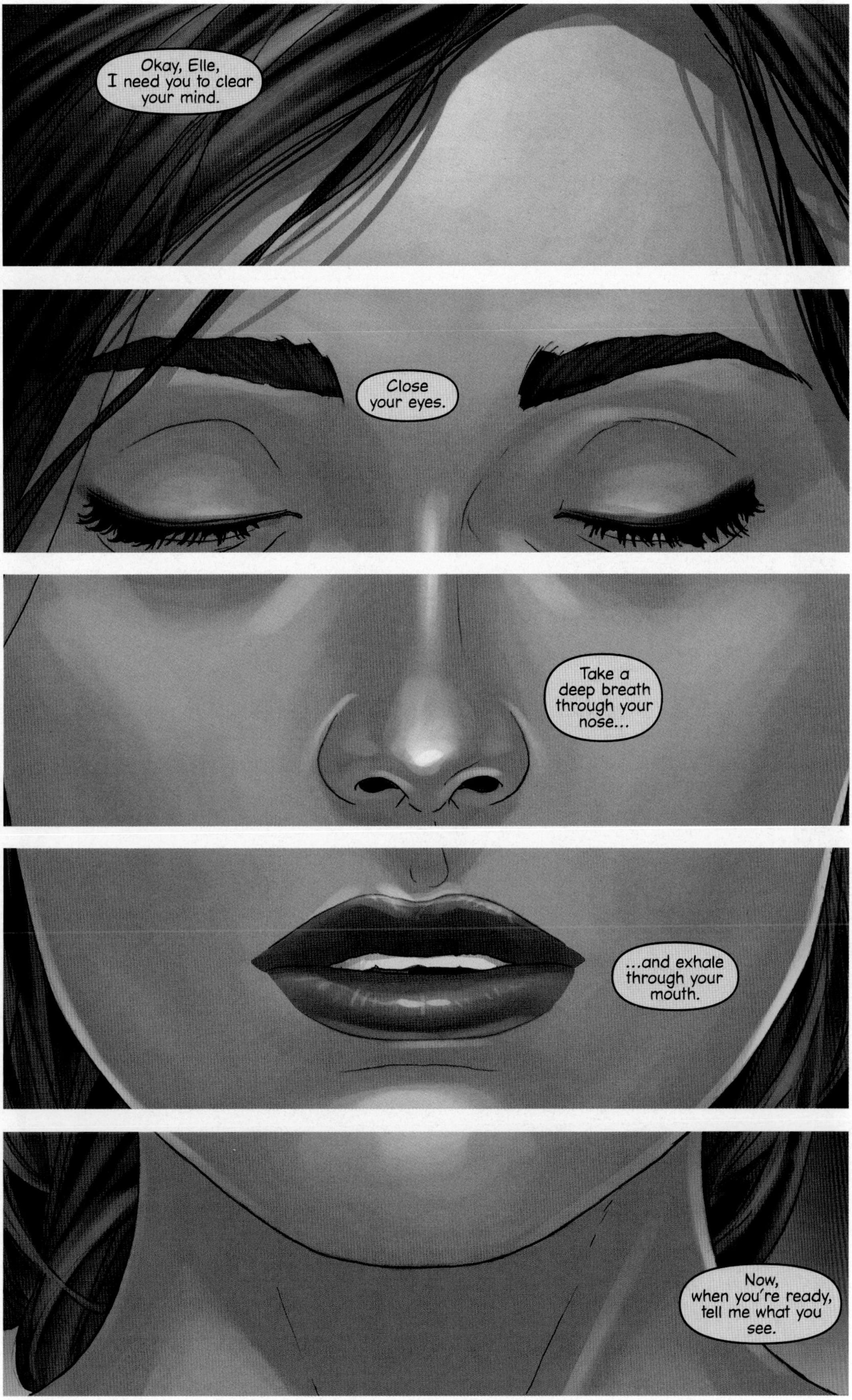
Okay, Elle, I need you to clear your mind.
Close your eyes.
Take a deep breath through your nose...
...and exhale through your mouth.
Now, when you're ready, tell me what you see.

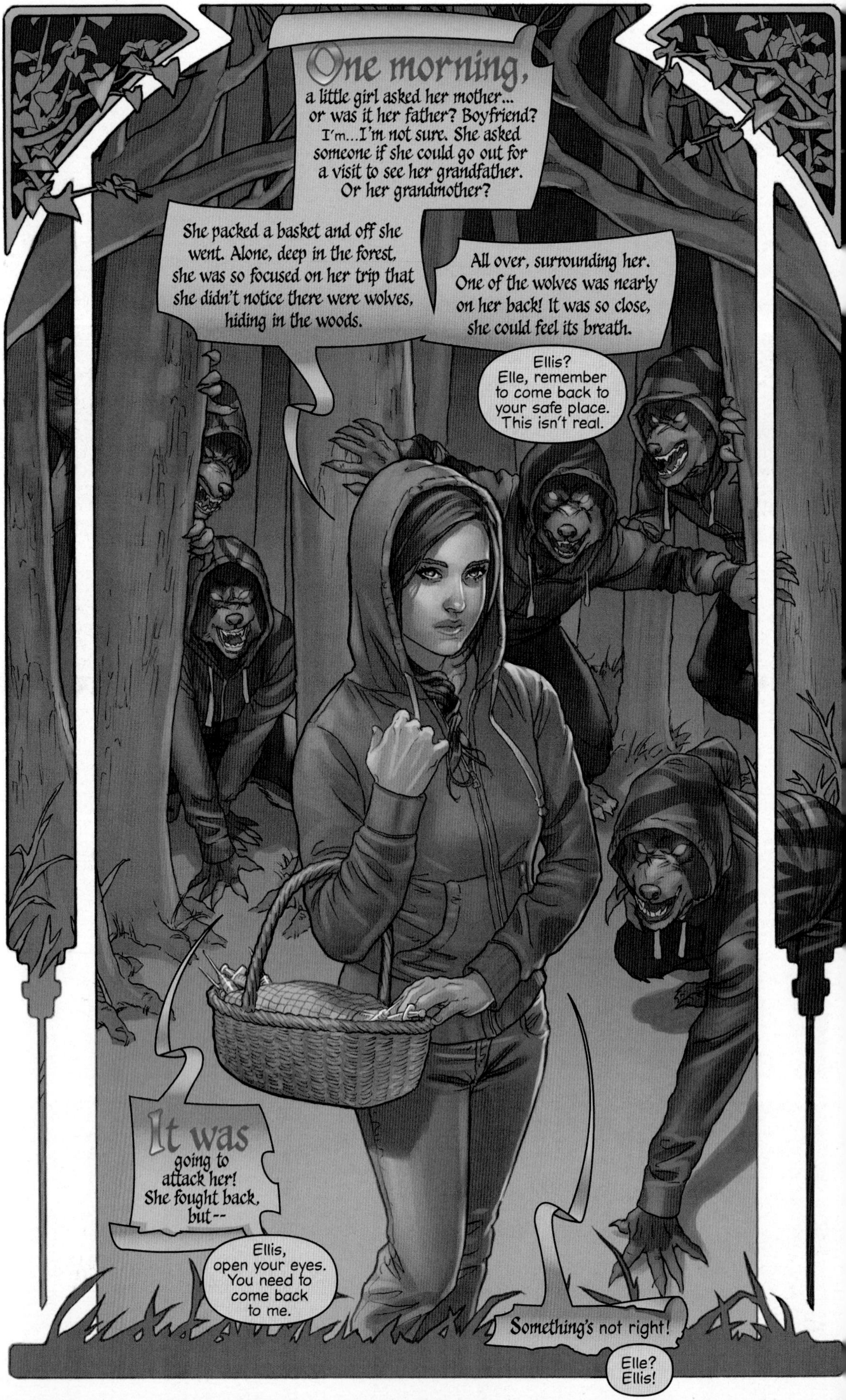

One morning, a little girl asked her mother... or was it her father? Boyfriend? I'm...I'm not sure. She asked someone if she could go out for a visit to see her grandfather. Or her grandmother?
She packed a basket and off she went. Alone, deep in the forest, she was so focused on her trip that she didn't notice there were wolves, hiding in the woods.
All over, surrounding her. One of the wolves was nearly on her back! It was so close, she could feel its breath.
Ellis? Elle, remember to come back to your safe place. This isn't real.
It was going to attack her! She fought back, but--
Ellis, open your eyes. You need to come back to me.
Something's not right!
Elle? Ellis!

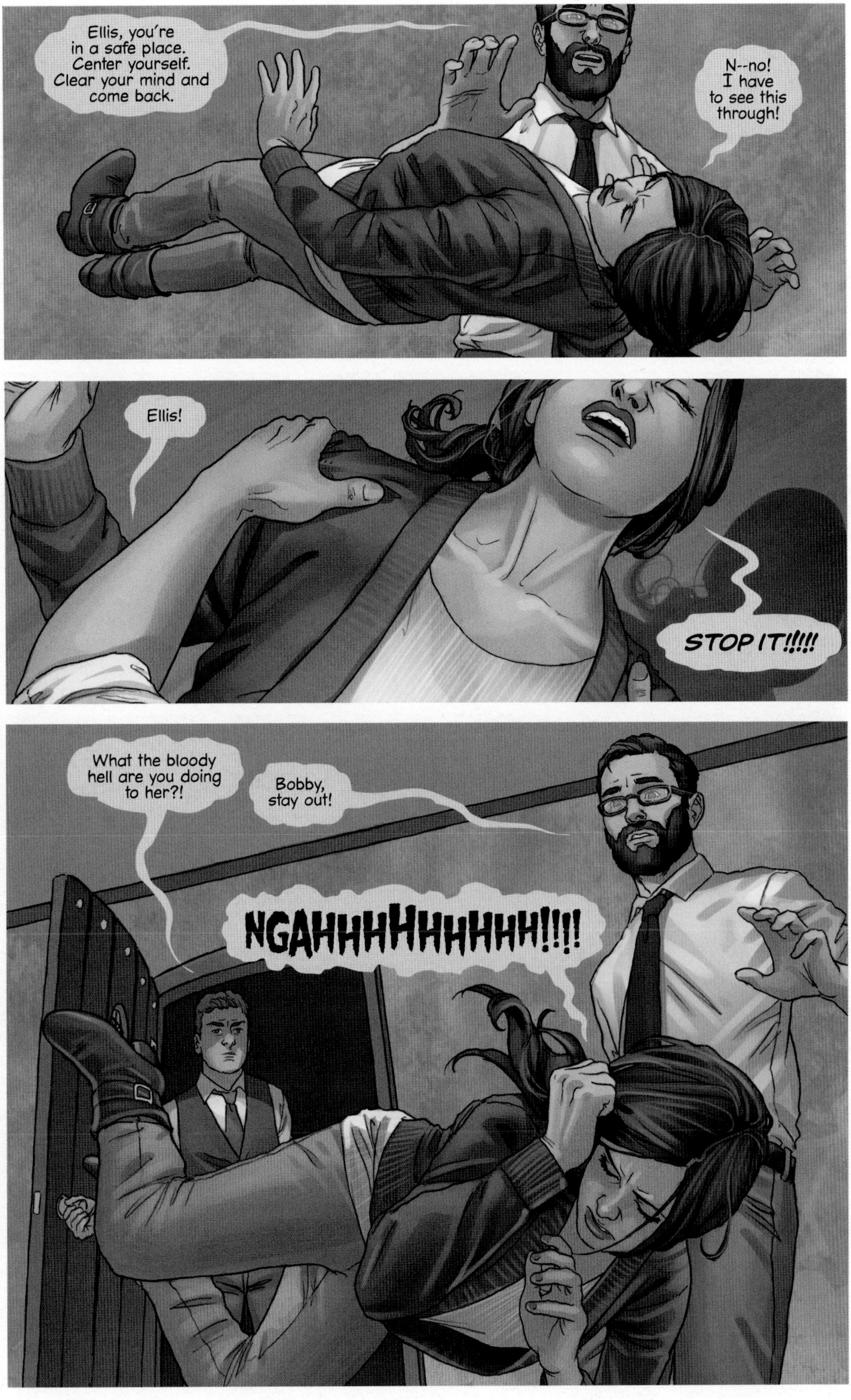

Ellis, you're in a safe place. Center yourself. Clear your mind and come back.
N--no! I have to see this through!
Ellis!
STOP IT!!!!!
What the bloody hell are you doing to her?!
Bobby, stay out!
NGAHHHHHHHHH!!!!

I *knew* letting you near her was a right proper mistake!

This is hardly the time for debate.

Elle's trapped in a state of great mental distress. I need you to stay back so I can guide her back before her mind is further damaged.

No... no, no, no, no...

Ellis, listen only to my voice. The woods are not real. Nothing is attacking you.

safe?

Yes, yes, that's right, Elle! You are back in your safe place. Out of the woods.

Open your eyes...

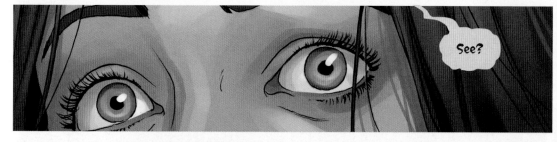

See?

There are no wolves.

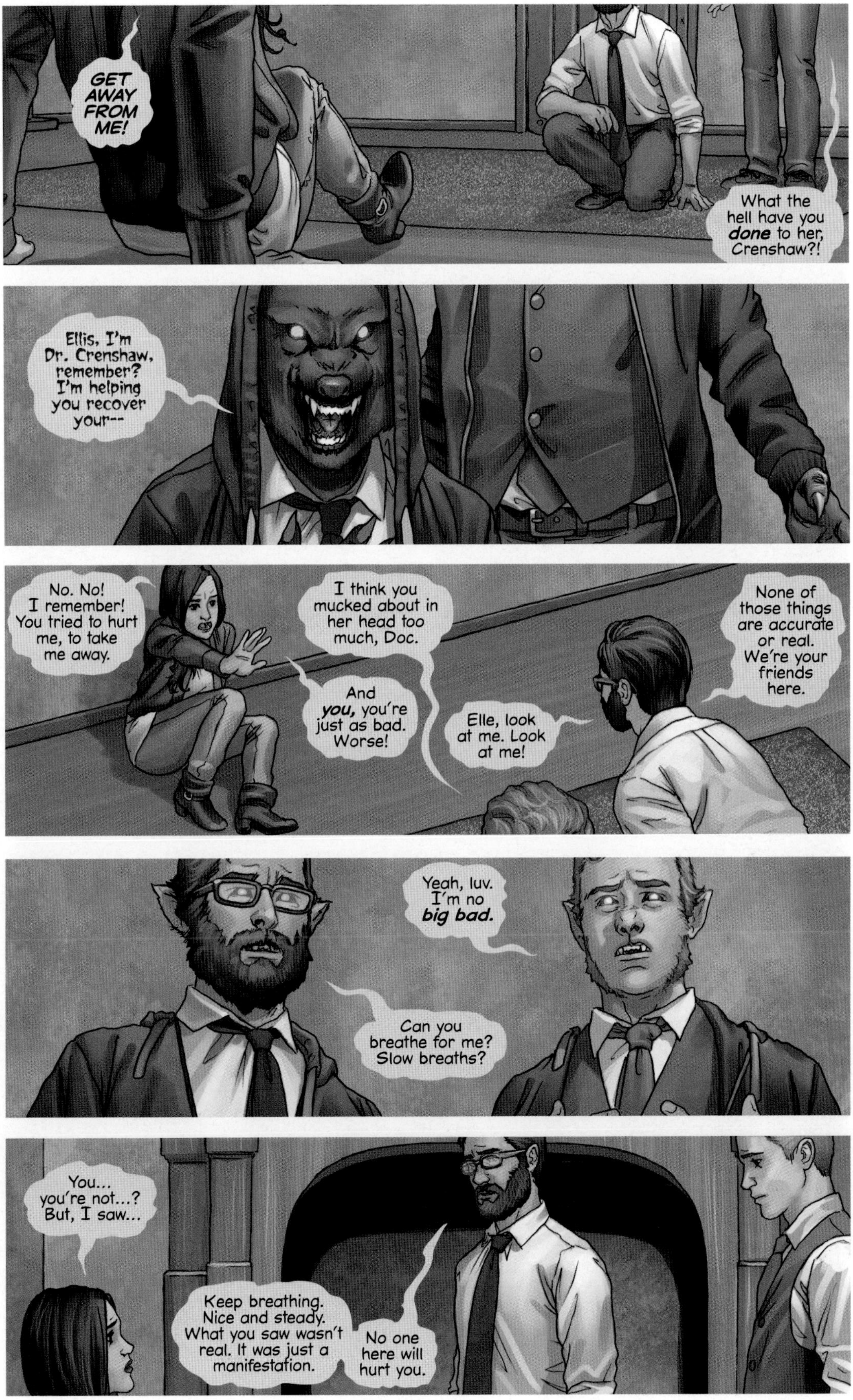
GET AWAY FROM ME!
What the hell have you **done** to her, Crenshaw?!
Ellis, I'm Dr. Crenshaw, remember? I'm helping you recover your--
No. No! I remember! You tried to hurt me, to take me away.
I think you mucked about in her head too much, Doc.
And **you,** you're just as bad. Worse!
Elle, look at me. Look at me!
None of those things are accurate or real. We're your friends here.
Yeah, luv. I'm no **big bad.**
Can you breathe for me? Slow breaths?
You... you're not...? But, I saw...
Keep breathing. Nice and steady. What you saw wasn't real. It was just a manifestation.
No one here will hurt you.

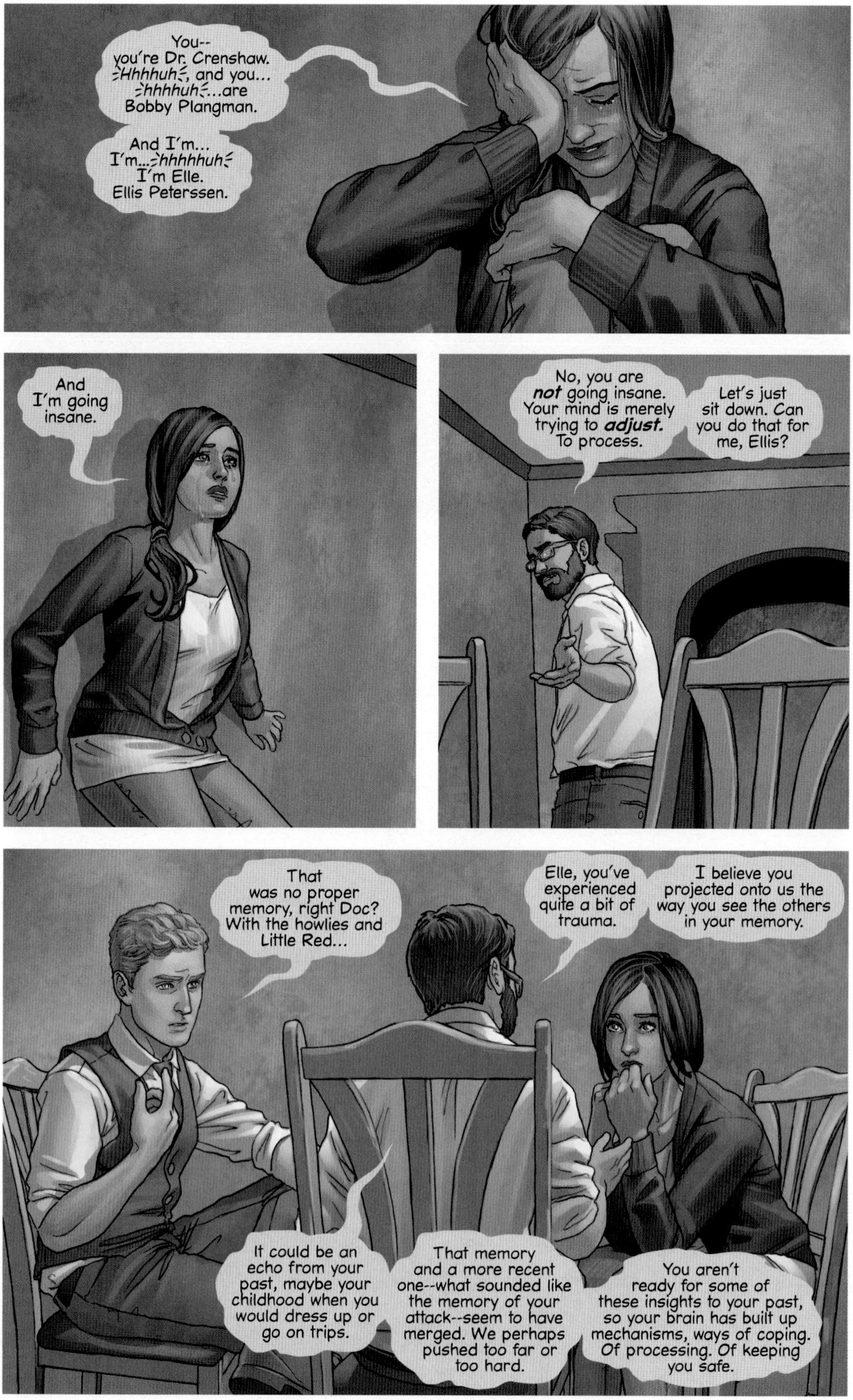
You-- you're Dr. Crenshaw. ≈Hhhhuh≈, and you... ≈hhhhuh≈...are Bobby Plangman.
And I'm... I'm...≈hhhhuh≈ I'm Elle. Ellis Peterssen.
And I'm going insane.
No, you are **not** going insane. Your mind is merely trying to ***adjust.*** To process.
Let's just sit down. Can you do that for me, Ellis?
That was no proper memory, right Doc? With the howlies and Little Red...
Elle, you've experienced quite a bit of trauma.
I believe you projected onto us the way you see the others in your memory.
It could be an echo from your past, maybe your childhood when you would dress up or go on trips.
That memory and a more recent one--what sounded like the memory of your attack--seem to have merged. We perhaps pushed too far or too hard.
You aren't ready for some of these insights to your past, so your brain has built up mechanisms, ways of coping. Of processing. Of keeping you safe.

Just how the hell is my brain forgetting everything about my life--except that maybe I dressed up as fucking Little Red *Riding* Hood as a kid--a way of keeping me safe?

I-- I'm not entirely sure, to be frank.

This, this place, these surroundings, they are all foreign to me.

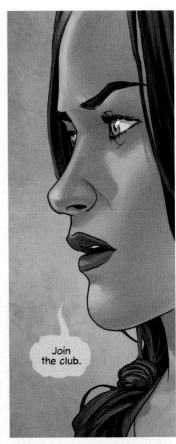

Join the club.

But you've been-- Ah, no. You're right. There's no reason to assume *any* of this would be familiar to you. Or to any of us.

In fact, there's no reason to assume that we are all having the same experience. Or possibly not here at all. We could merely be manifestations of what you are perceiving in your current state.

What, you, Bobby...this house? All this is in my *head*?!

It is an option.

Now wait just a minute there, Doc. I've been here a long time, longer than you, mate, and definitely longer than Elle.

My *real* body's over in--Right, look, no bloody way am I some figment of her imagination. No offense, luv.

I'm not suggesting we don't exist. I mean that we each may see and cope with things differently.

For example, this house. It can change based on Ellis' mental wishes. It's already become more than just shelter. It is appearing now to be a home.

So, I'm "living" this all in my *mind?*

Exactly! These are all reflections of your thoughts, which is why the walls are blank slates.

Not completely blank. There's some pretty terrifying images there, see? The needle-loving doctor... Little Red Me-Hood...

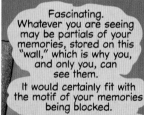

Fascinating. Whatever you are seeing may be partials of your memories, stored on this "wall," which is why you, and only you, can see them.

It would certainly fit with the motif of your memories being blocked.

If there is something you don't want to be seen on this plane by others, you can simply make it so.

There have never been such vividly documented memories in cases of what I can only ascribe to being altered states, or more commonly known as "Near Death Experiences."

This goes far beyond a simple tunnel of light, or seeing a loved one. This...This is a plane of reality between ours that we've known and whatever-if anything-lies beyond!

Ellis, you-- this is something to behold, something you *must* remember when you awaken from--

Hold up, Doc.

This psycho-babble about walls and dream worlds...Too much. Right now, I just need "me" time.

You said there's some things only I can see here? Let's try the opposite, then. If I *don't* want to see something, then...

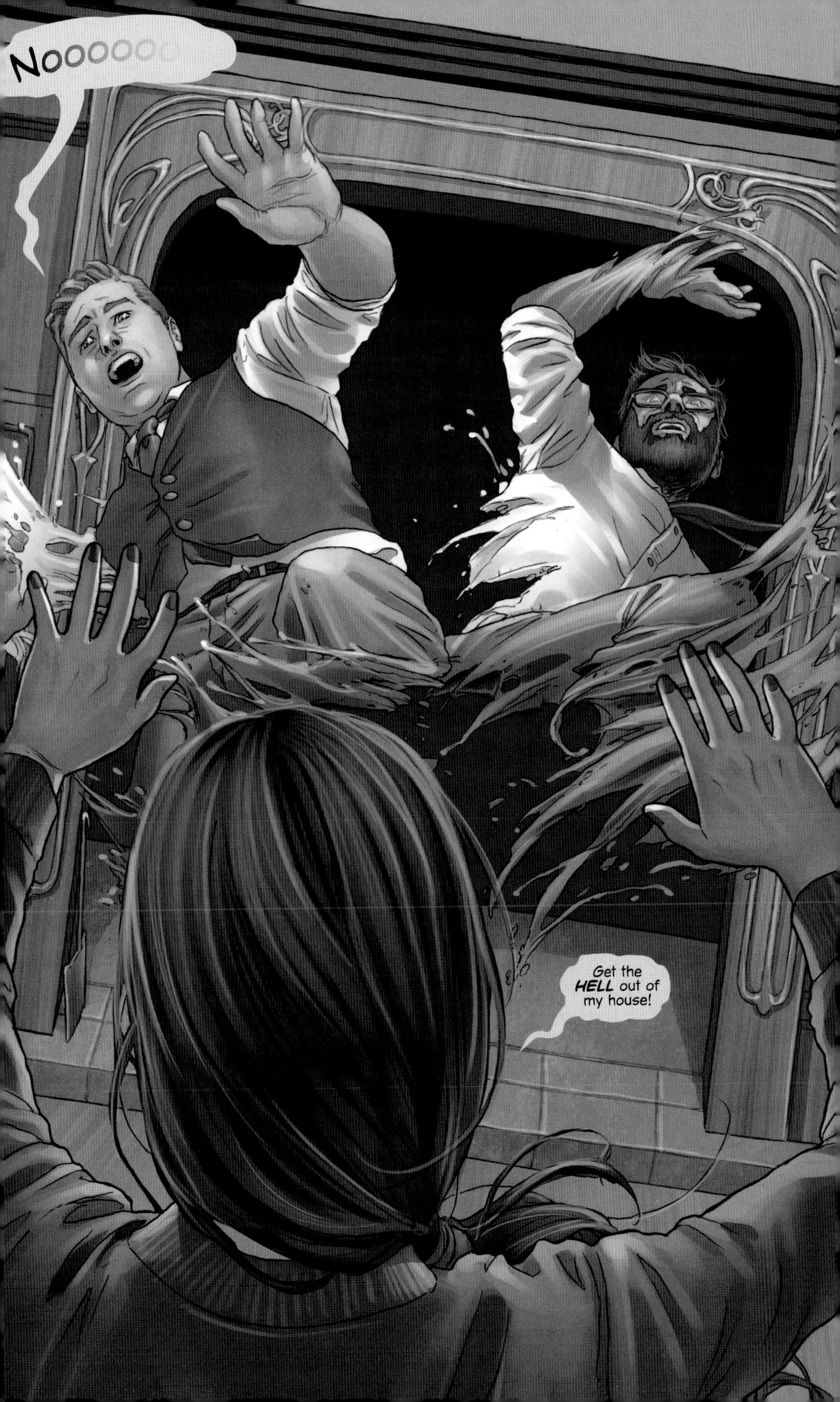
Nooooooo
Get the HELL out of my house!

INTIMATE STRANGERS
PART 4
"BIG. BAD."

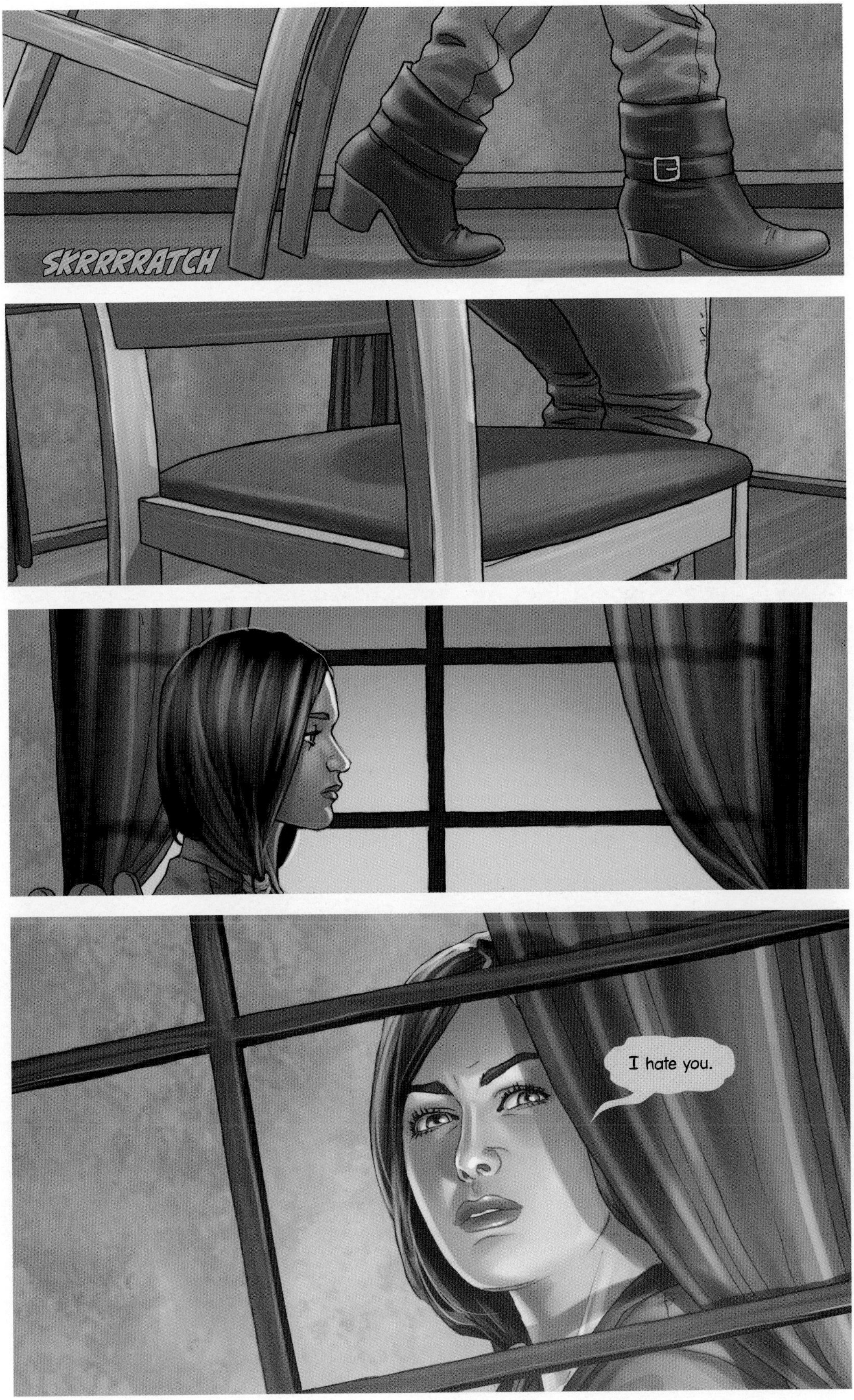
SKRRRRATCH
I hate you.

I mean it. I truly hate you.

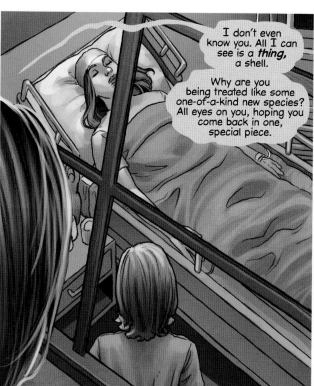

I don't even know you. All I can see is a *thing,* a shell.

Why are you being treated like some one-of-a-kind new species? All eyes on you, hoping you come back in one, special piece.

Flip side, why's someone out there wanting you dead?

And me...

A ghosty-whatever that builds mental houses, or can possess people's dying bodies?

Why do I have to be the one who fucking puts us back together? The one who has to live through this. To fight.

To remember.

We'd better be worth it.

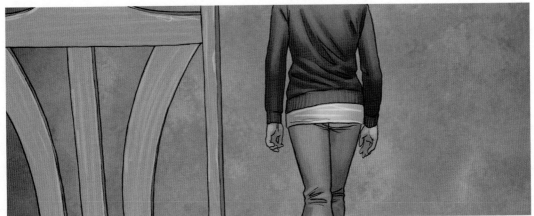

"Coping mechanisms."

If I'm the fighter then I better start fighting to remember. Screw processing and screw playing safe.

RRRRRRMMM

MMBB

HRRROWNNNK

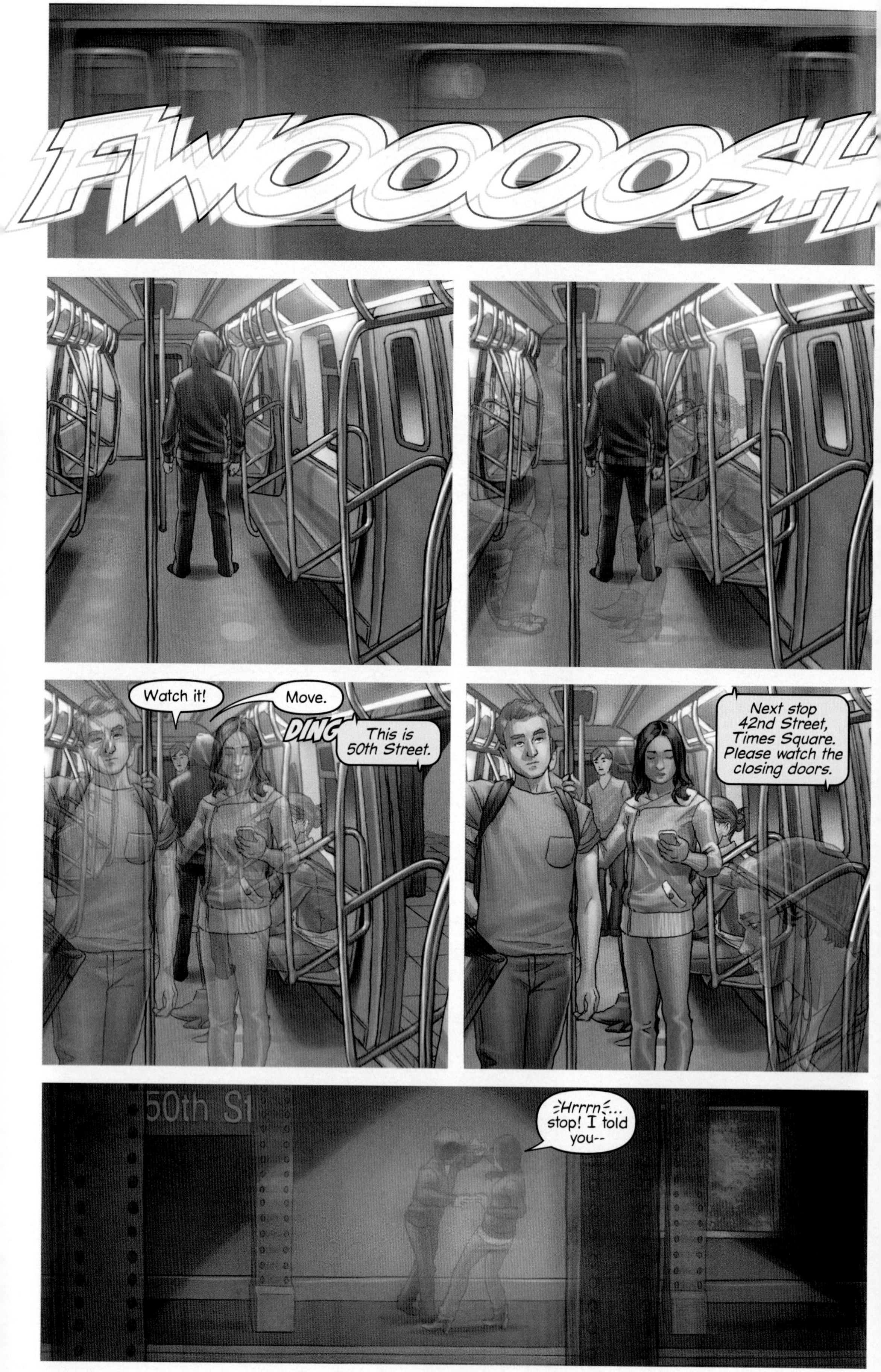
FWOOOOSH
Watch it!
Move.
DING
This is 50th Street.
Next stop 42nd Street, Times Square. Please watch the closing doors.
50th St
Hrrrn... stop! I told you--

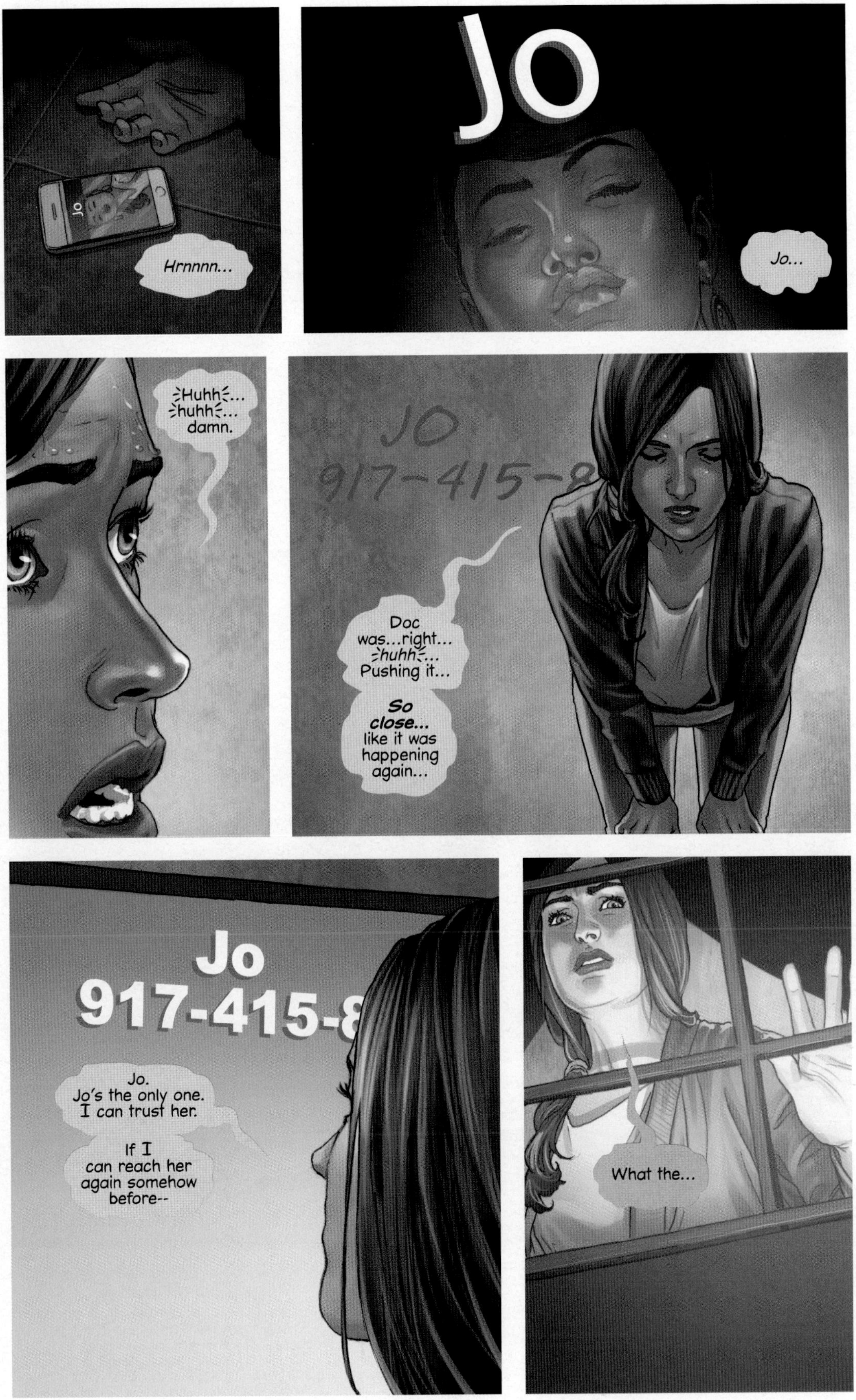

Jo
Hrnnnn...
JO
Jo...
Huhh... huhh... damn.
JO
917-415-8
Doc was...right... huhh... Pushing it...
So close... like it was happening again...
Jo
917-415-8
Jo. Jo's the only one. I can trust her.
If I can reach her again somehow before--
What the...

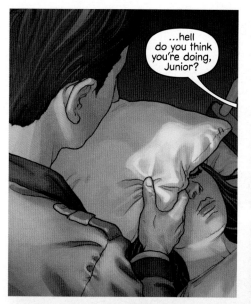

...hell do you think you're doing, Junior?

I'm trying to make my sister more comfortable. I assume that's okay by you, Jo?

With all the money my family donates to this place, you'd think they'd buy high-end bedding rather than what I can only assume came from a fire sale at a prison.

Since when have you **ever** cared about making Elle comfortable?

You have never, nor will you ever, understand the complexities of the relationships my sister forms.

You should know that better than any, Miller.

You wanna know my fist in your face, you spoiled little--

A violent outburst. How original for you.

Jo, please remove Dane. I don't care where. Non-family visiting hours don't start for another hour.

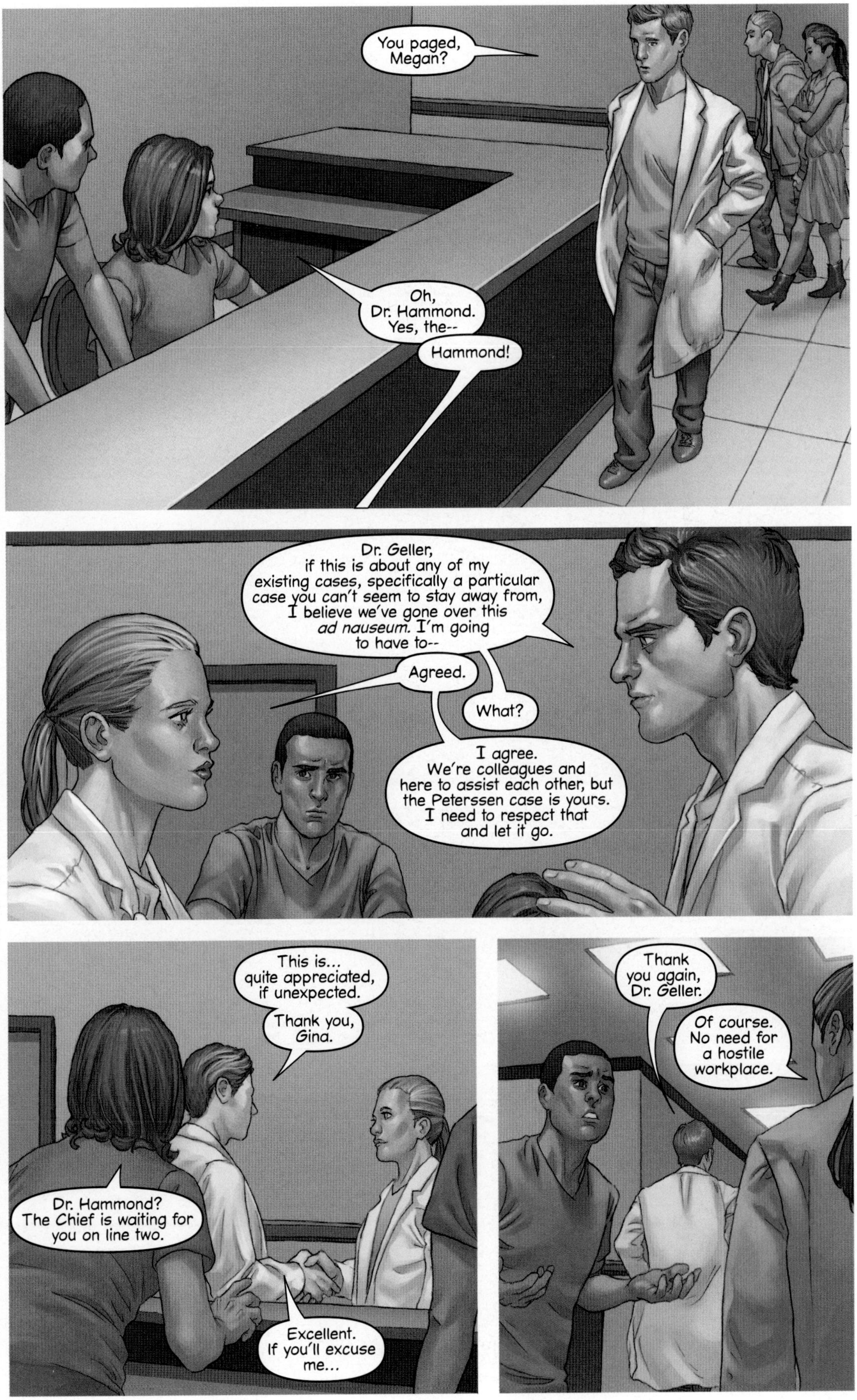

You paged, Megan?
Oh, Dr. Hammond. Yes, the--
Hammond!
Dr. Geller, if this is about any of my existing cases, specifically a particular case you can't seem to stay away from, I believe we've gone over this *ad nauseum*. I'm going to have to--
Agreed.
What?
I agree. We're colleagues and here to assist each other, but the Peterssen case is yours. I need to respect that and let it go.
This is... quite appreciated, if unexpected.
Thank you, Gina.
Dr. Hammond? The Chief is waiting for you on line two.
Excellent. If you'll excuse me...
Thank you again, Dr. Geller.
Of course. No need for a hostile workplace.

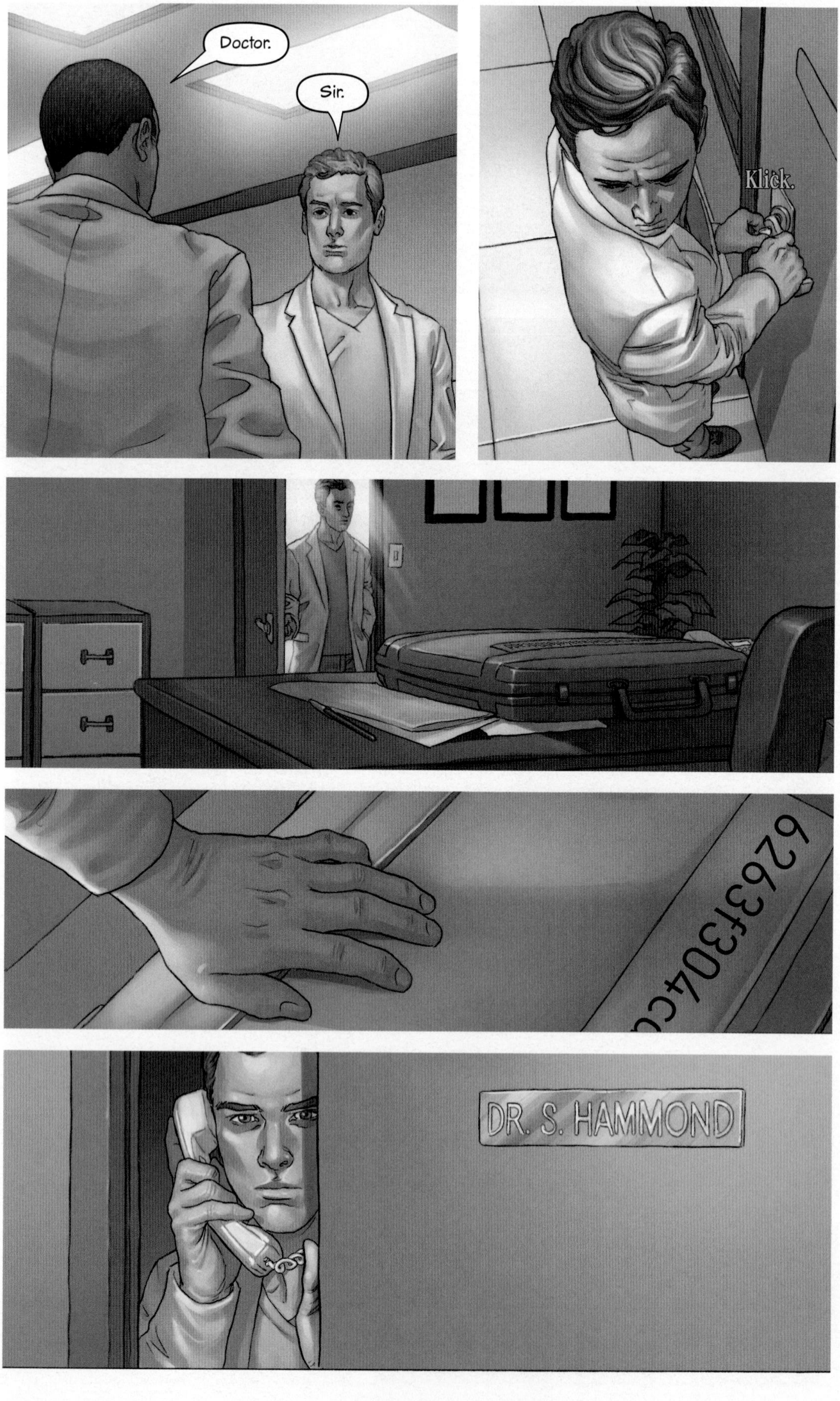
Doctor.
Sir.
Klick.
6263f304c
DR. S. HAMMOND

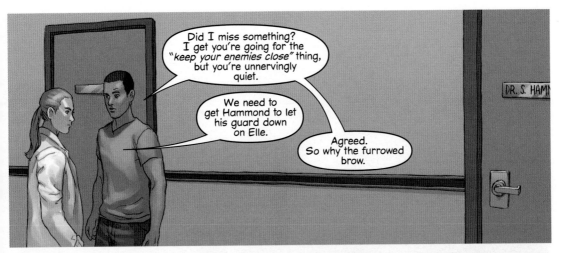

Did I miss something? I get you're going for the "*keep your enemies close*" thing, but you're unnervingly quiet.

We need to get Hammond to let his guard down on Elle.

Agreed. So why the furrowed brow.

DR. S. HAMM

There's something... off. Normally he would've relished in my "apologetic" state.

Maybe he went to faint? Or laugh maniacally. I can see either option.

The chief! She said "*the chief.*"

Nurse Kyle. Megan!

You told Hammond the Chief wanted to speak with him. But that's highly improbable, seeing as the hospital Chief-of-Staff is on vacation.

As in "*do not disturb me unless you want 36-hour shifts for the next month*" vacation. Nor does Hammond report directly to the Chief.

I-- I'm sorry, that's all I know.

If there is an emergency or a reorganization, I should be alerted. Now, who was that on the phone, Nurse?

The "*Chief*" wanted Dr. Hammond. Privately. That, Doctor, is all I can relay.

You do an amazing Jack Bauer. Did you know that? I mean, scary good. And your *wife's* supposed to be the cop?!

She's lying. See what you can find out, overhear, or whatever.

Sure. I'll just go get my audio surveillance equipment that I don't own and--

Gossip. Go out for drinks. Be...social. I don't know, just hang around other nurses.

She says, without meaning to stereotype an entire field of medicine.

BRRRZZZT

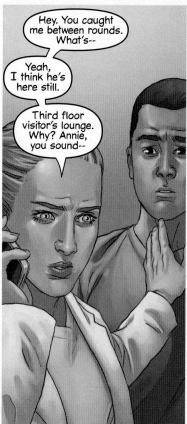

Hey. You caught me between rounds. What's--

Yeah, I think he's here still.

Third floor visitor's lounge. Why? Annie, you sound--

He's *what?!*

Yeah, yeah... I'll make sure. See you when you get here.

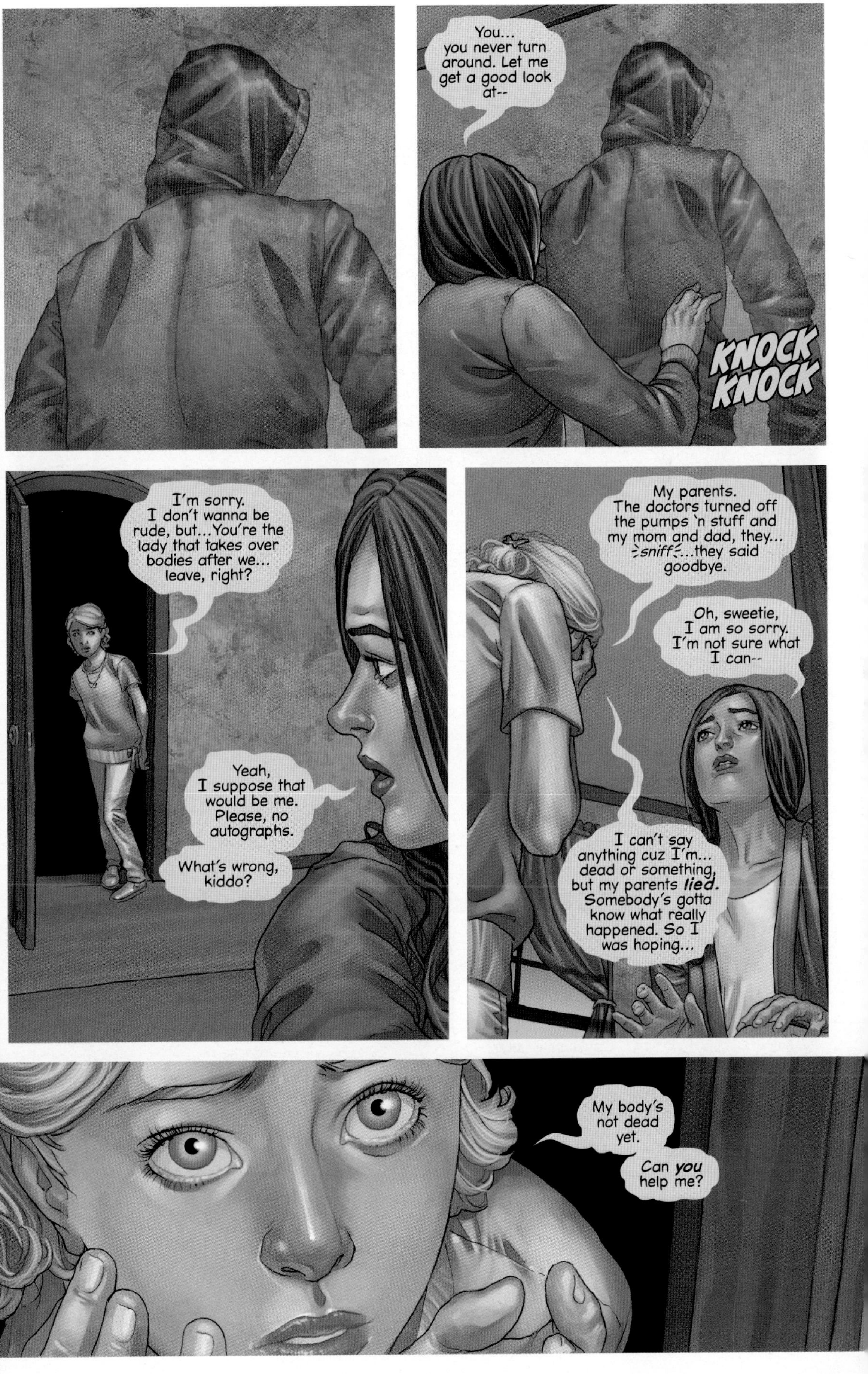
You... you never turn around. Let me get a good look at--
KNOCK KNOCK
I'm sorry. I don't wanna be rude, but... You're the lady that takes over bodies after we... leave, right?
Yeah, I suppose that would be me. Please, no autographs.
What's wrong, kiddo?
My parents. The doctors turned off the pumps 'n stuff and my mom and dad, they... *sniff*... they said goodbye.
Oh, sweetie, I am so sorry. I'm not sure what I can--
I can't say anything cuz I'm... dead or something, but my parents ***lied.*** Somebody's gotta know what really happened. So I was hoping...
My body's not dead yet.
Can ***you*** help me?

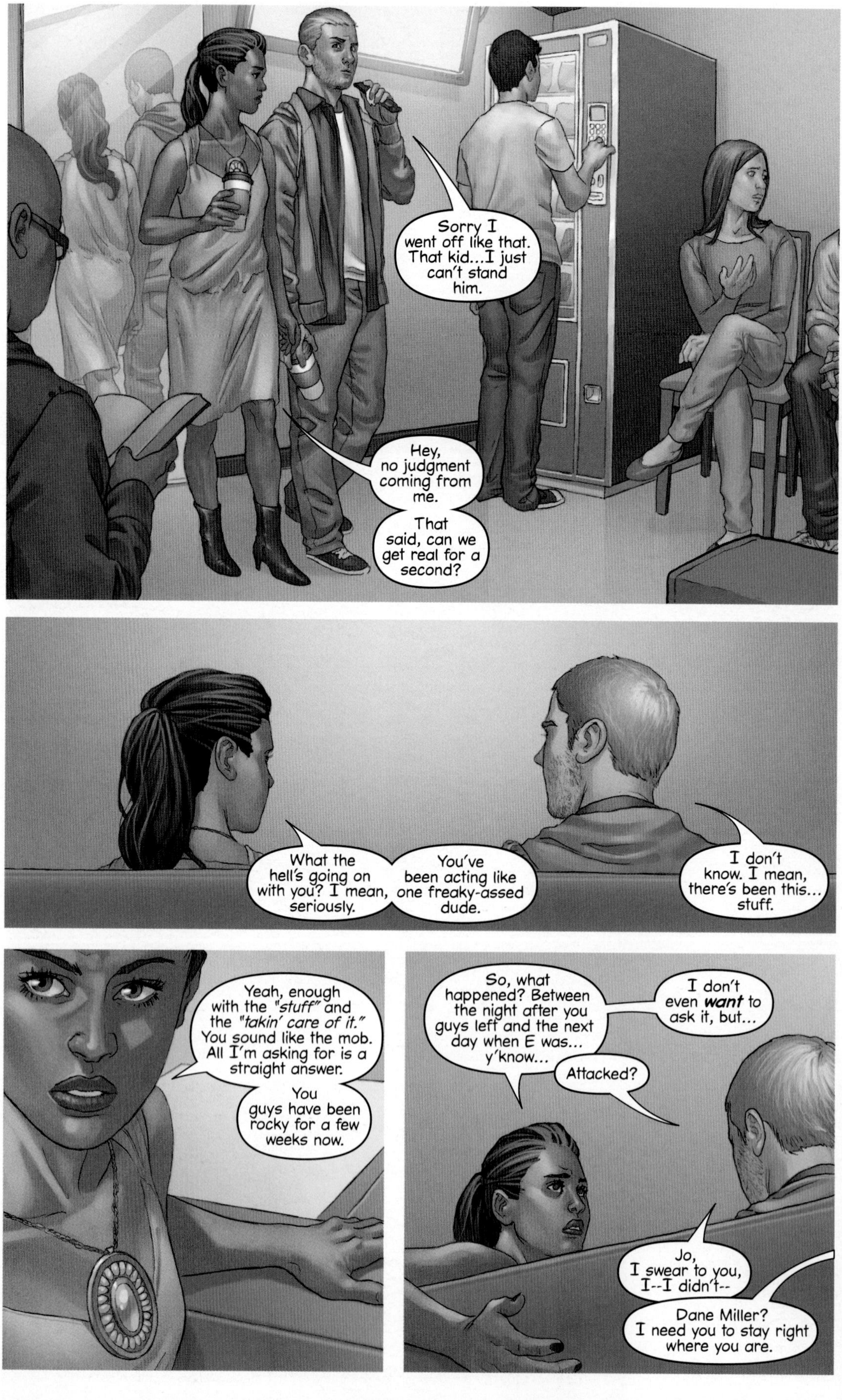
Sorry I went off like that. That kid...I just can't stand him.
Hey, no judgment coming from me.
That said, can we get real for a second?
What the hell's going on with you? I mean, seriously.
You've been acting like one freaky-assed dude.
I don't know. I mean, there's been this... stuff.
Yeah, enough with the *"stuff"* and the *"takin' care of it."* You sound like the mob. All I'm asking for is a straight answer.
You guys have been rocky for a few weeks now.
So, what happened? Between the night after you guys left and the next day when E was... y'know...
I don't even ***want*** to ask it, but...
Attacked?
Jo, I swear to you, I--I didn't--
Dane Miller? I need you to stay right where you are.

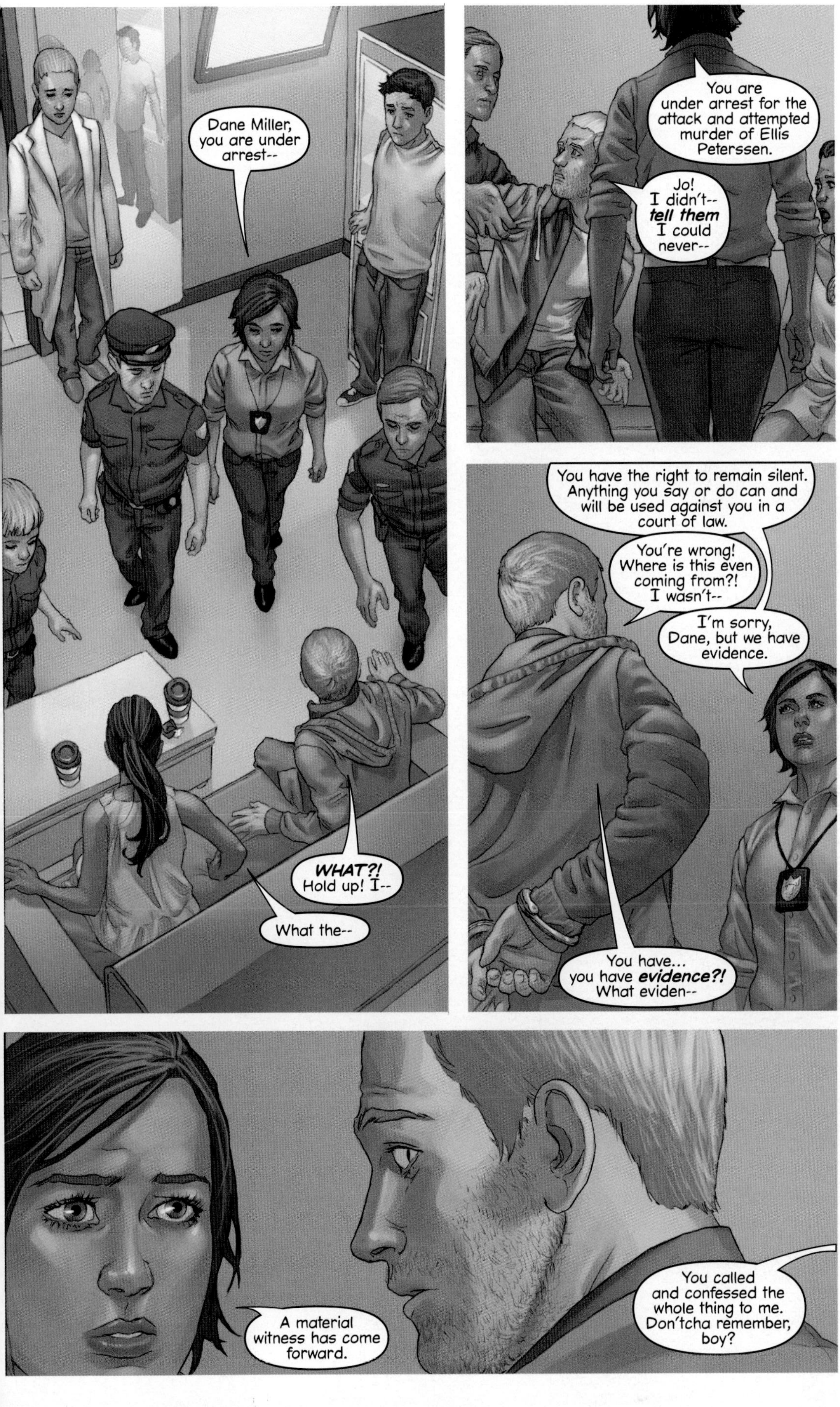

Dane Miller, you are under arrest--
WHAT?! Hold up! I--
What the--
You are under arrest for the attack and attempted murder of Ellis Peterssen.
Jo! I didn't-- tell them I could never--
You have the right to remain silent. Anything you say or do can and will be used against you in a court of law.
You're wrong! Where is this even coming from?! I wasn't--
I'm sorry, Dane, but we have evidence.
You have... you have evidence?! What eviden--
A material witness has come forward.
You called and confessed the whole thing to me. Don'tcha remember, boy?

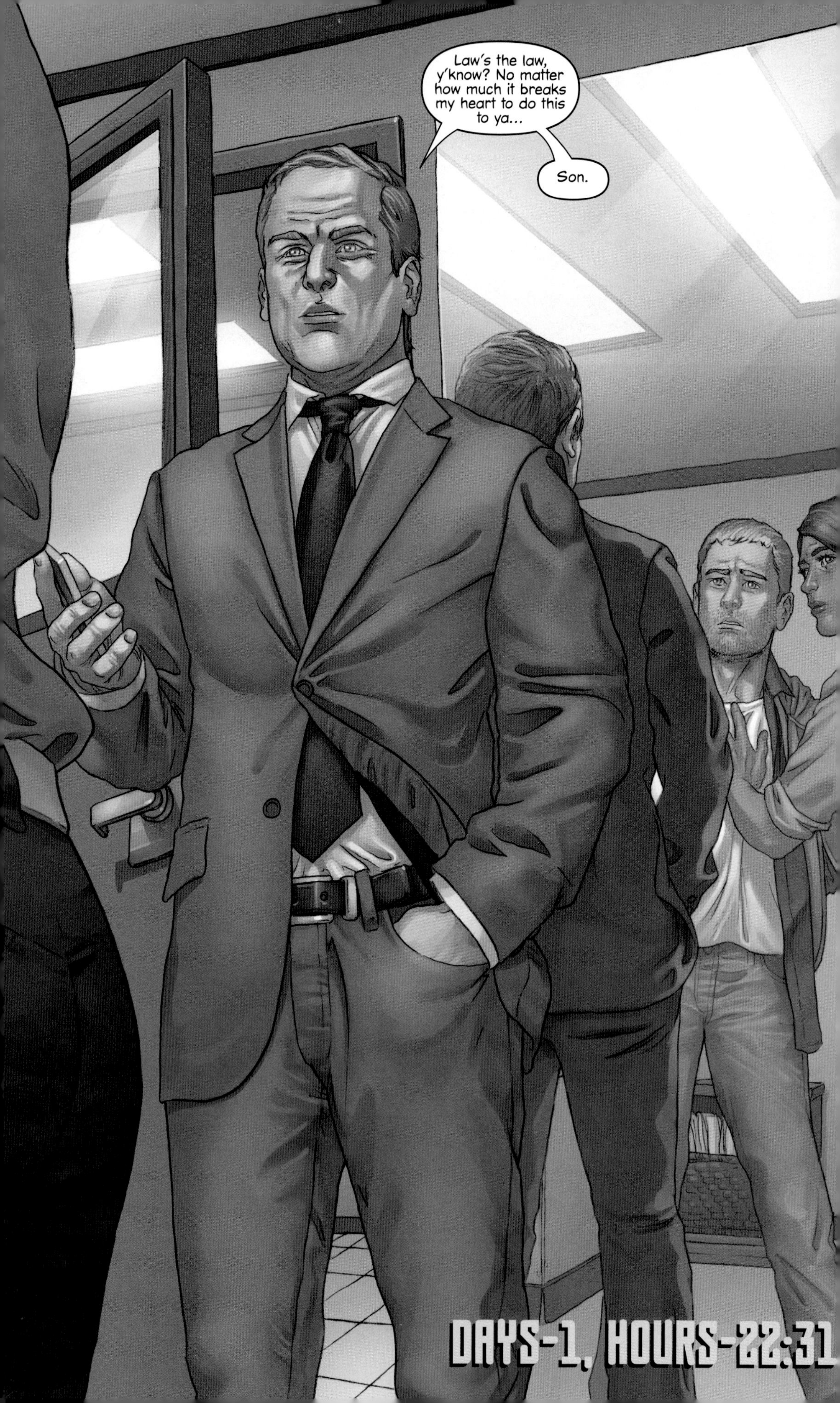
Law's the law, y'know? No matter how much it breaks my heart to do this to ya...
Son.
DAYS-1, HOURS-22:31

"All happy families resemble each other, each unhappy family is unhappy in its own way."

-LEO TOLSTOY, *Anna Karenina*

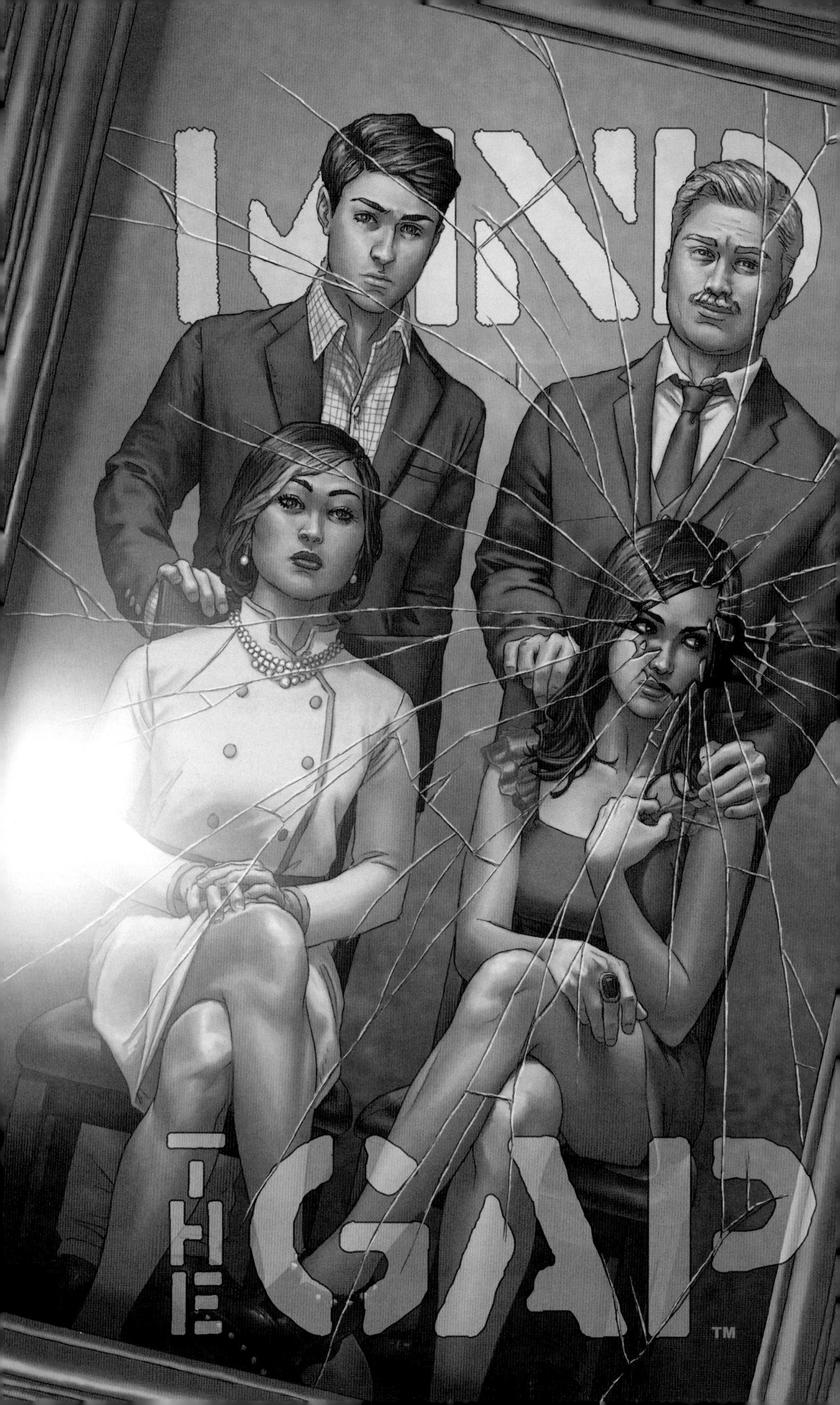
THE
TM

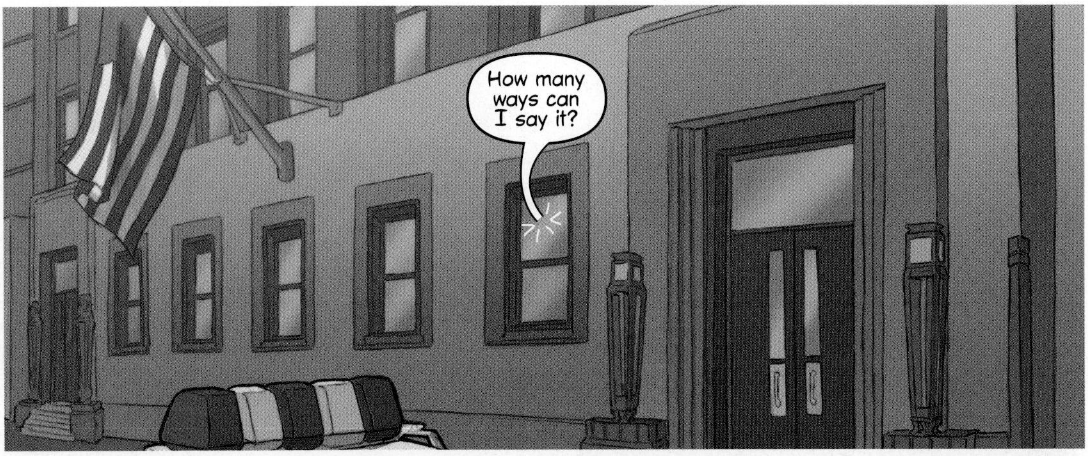
How many ways can I say it?

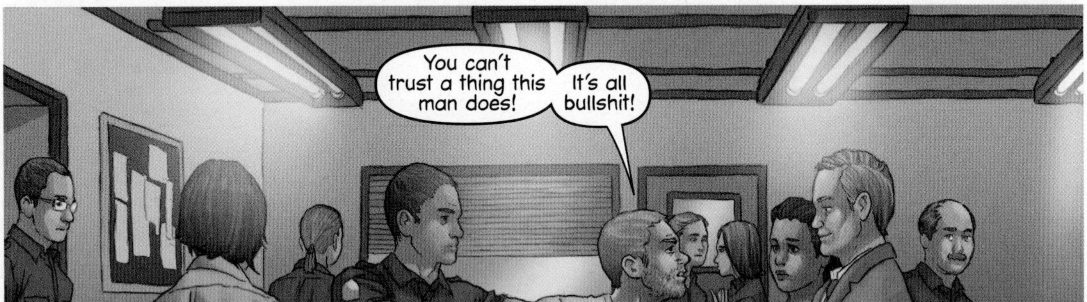
You can't trust a thing this man does!
It's all bullshit!
I'm sorry, but his evidence isn't the only thing we've based this case on.
In your statement, you claim you never saw the victim, Ellis Peterssen, after you left Ms. Wilson's house the day before.

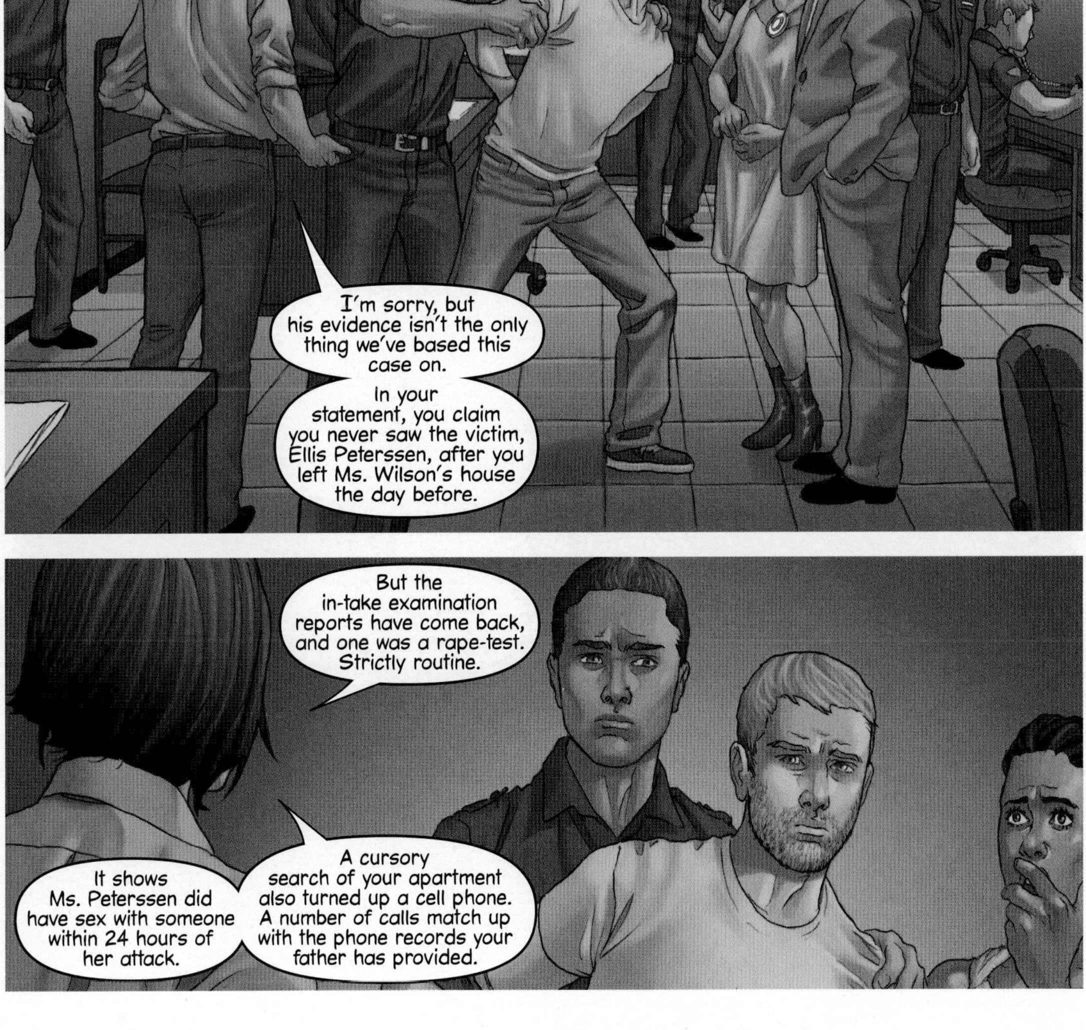
But the in-take examination reports have come back, and one was a rape-test. Strictly routine.
It shows Ms. Peterssen did have sex with someone within 24 hours of her attack.
A cursory search of your apartment also turned up a cell phone. A number of calls match up with the phone records your father has provided.

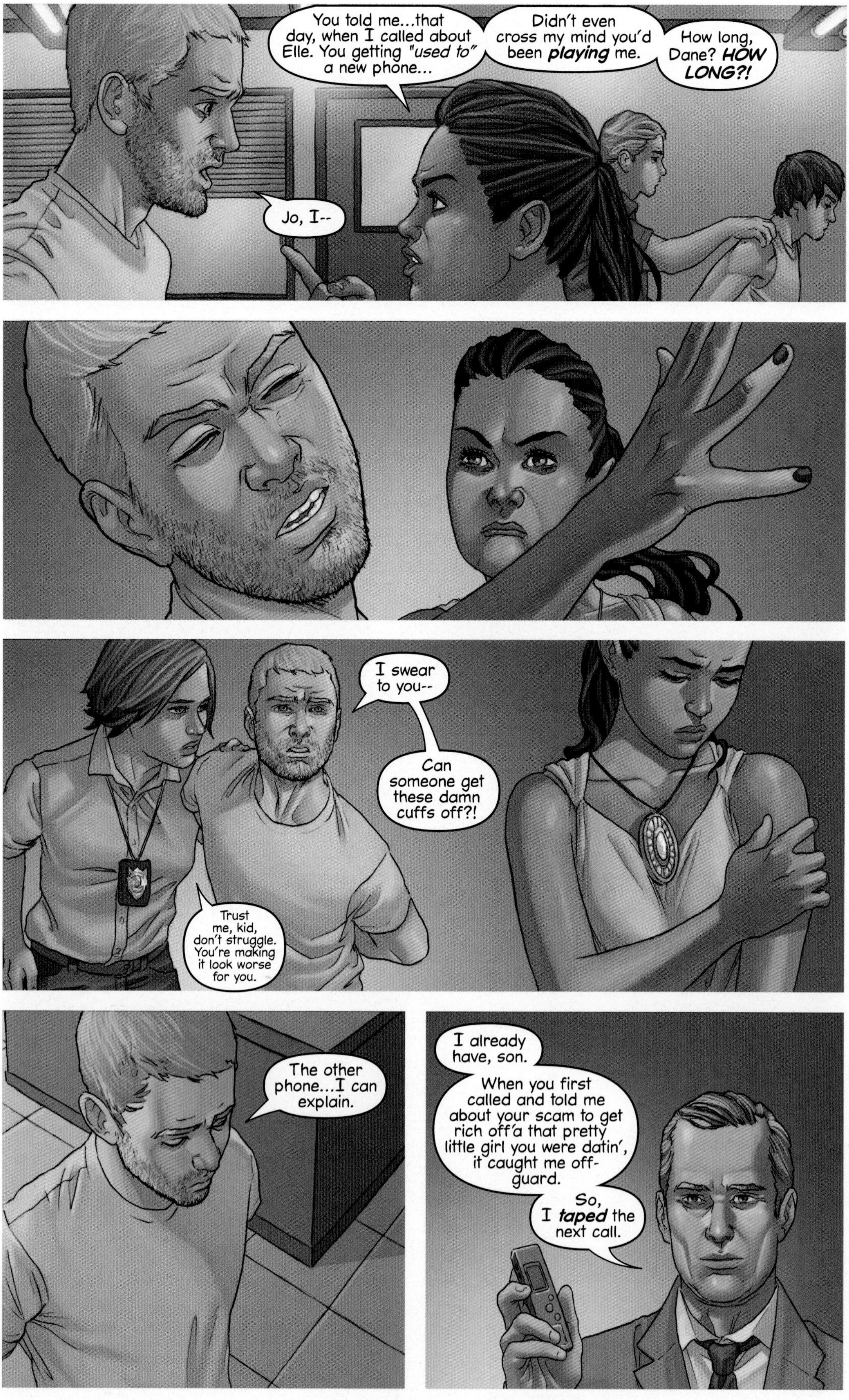
You told me...that day, when I called about Elle. You getting *"used to"* a new phone...
Didn't even cross my mind you'd been ***playing*** me.
How long, Dane? ***HOW LONG?!***
Jo, I--
I swear to you--
Can someone get these damn cuffs off?!
Trust me, kid, don't struggle. You're making it look worse for you.
The other phone...I can explain.
I already have, son.
When you first called and told me about your scam to get rich off'a that pretty little girl you were datin', it caught me off-guard.
So, I ***taped*** the next call.

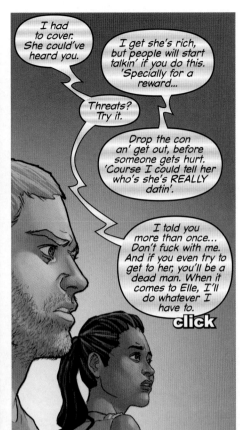

click

Breaks a father's heart to do this, but...

Hello?

I wanted to call and try and talk you outta doing this. You owe me enough to hear me out.

How'd you even get this number? I told you to use--Never mind. I don't owe you shit.

You're startin' to lose it. Let me help.

You'd fuck everything up, like you always do.

What the... This is all--

Is that why you hung up on me, Dane?

I had to cover. She could've heard you.

I get she's rich, but people will start talkin' if you do this. 'Specially for a reward...

Threats? Try it.

Drop the con an' get out, before someone gets hurt. 'Course I could tell her who's she's REALLY datin'.

I told you more than once... Don't fuck with me. And if you even try to get to her, you'll be a dead man. When it comes to Elle, I'll do whatever I have to.

click

That's *a fake!* That's *not* how it happened!! Jo, that other phone, it was never mine! This is a fucking *set up!*

We got a fighter!

SPIT

THUMP

What'd I tell ya 'bout the next time I saw you.

≶nNngh≶

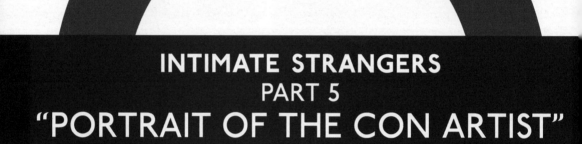

INTIMATE STRANGERS
PART 5
"PORTRAIT OF THE CON ARTIST"

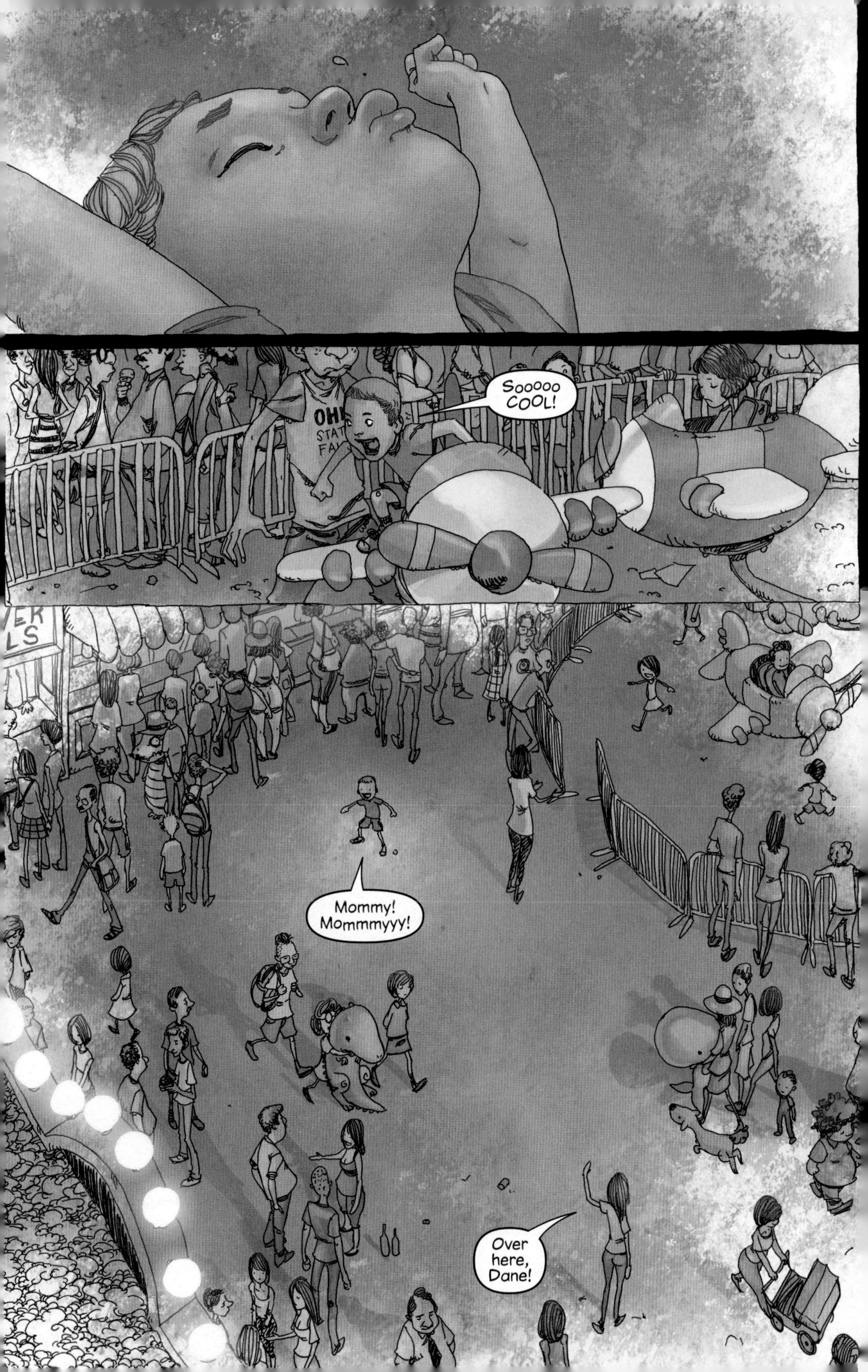
Sooooo COOL!
Mommy! Mommmyyy!
Over here, Dane!

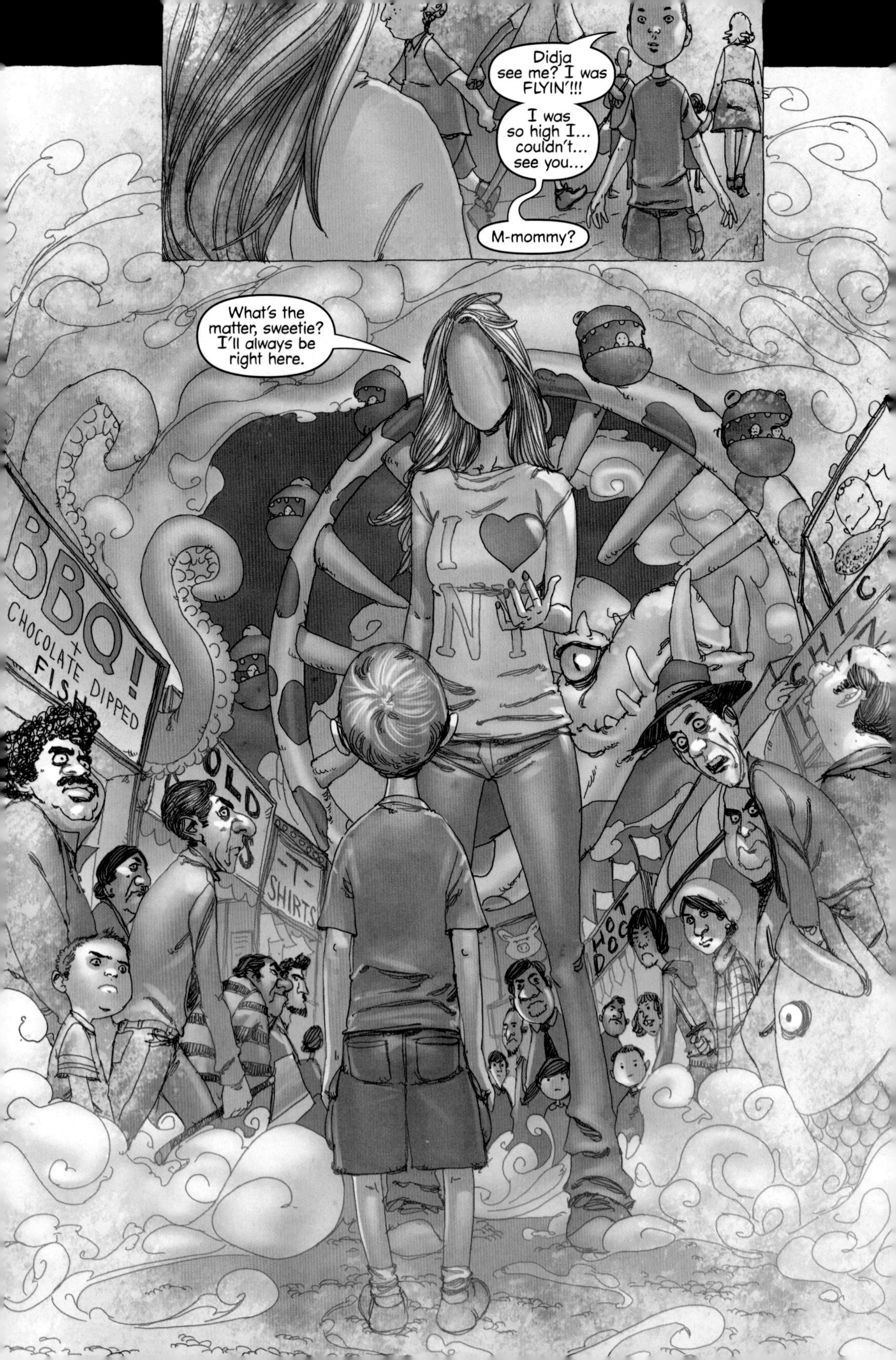
Didja see me? I was FLYIN'!!!
I was so high I... couldn't... see you...
M-mommy?
What's the matter, sweetie? I'll always be right here.
BBQ! + CHOCOLATE DIPPED FISH
OLD
T SHIRTS
HOT DOG
I ♥ NY

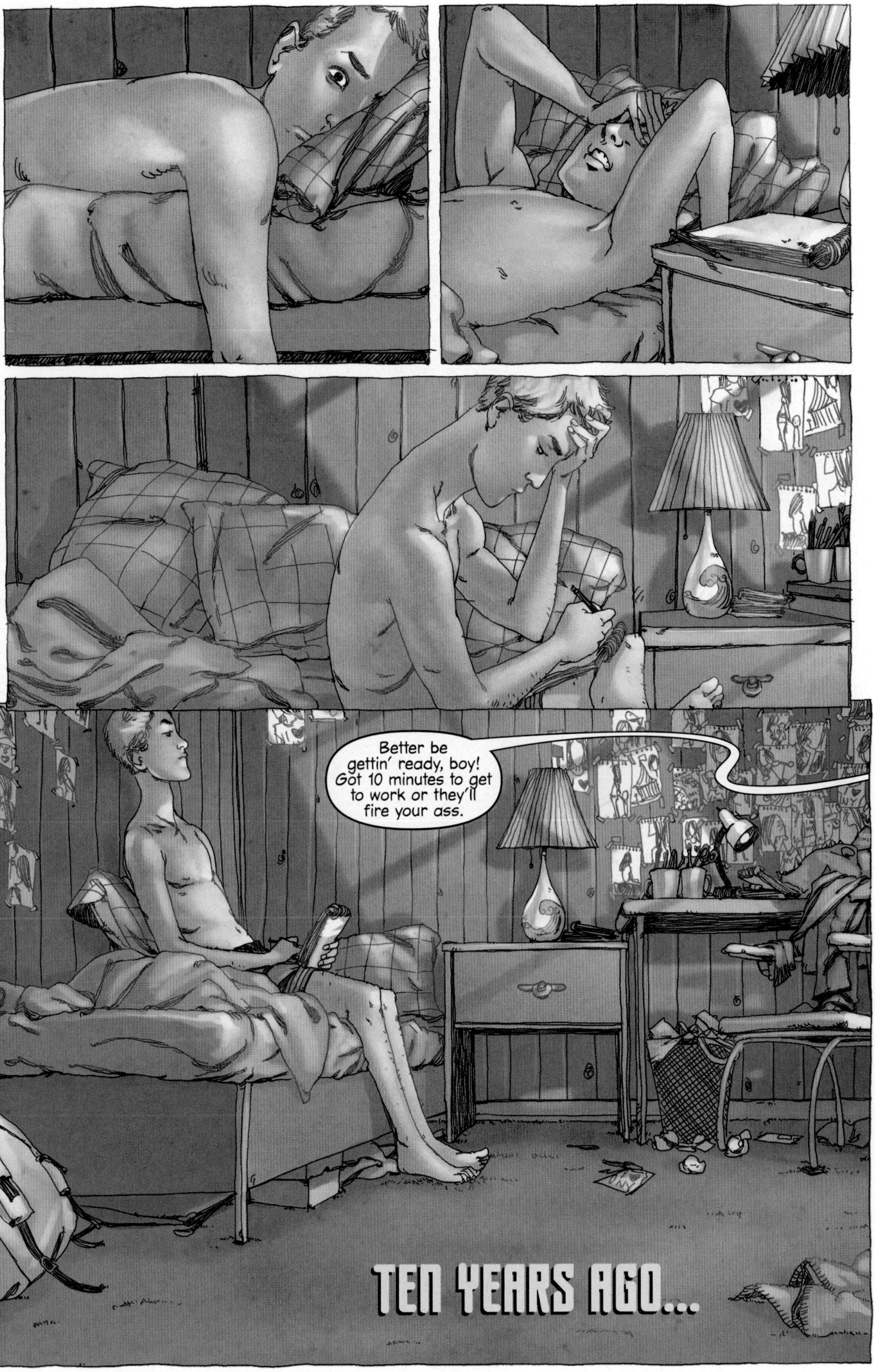
Better be gettin' ready, boy! Got 10 minutes to get to work or they'll fire your ass.
TEN YEARS AGO...

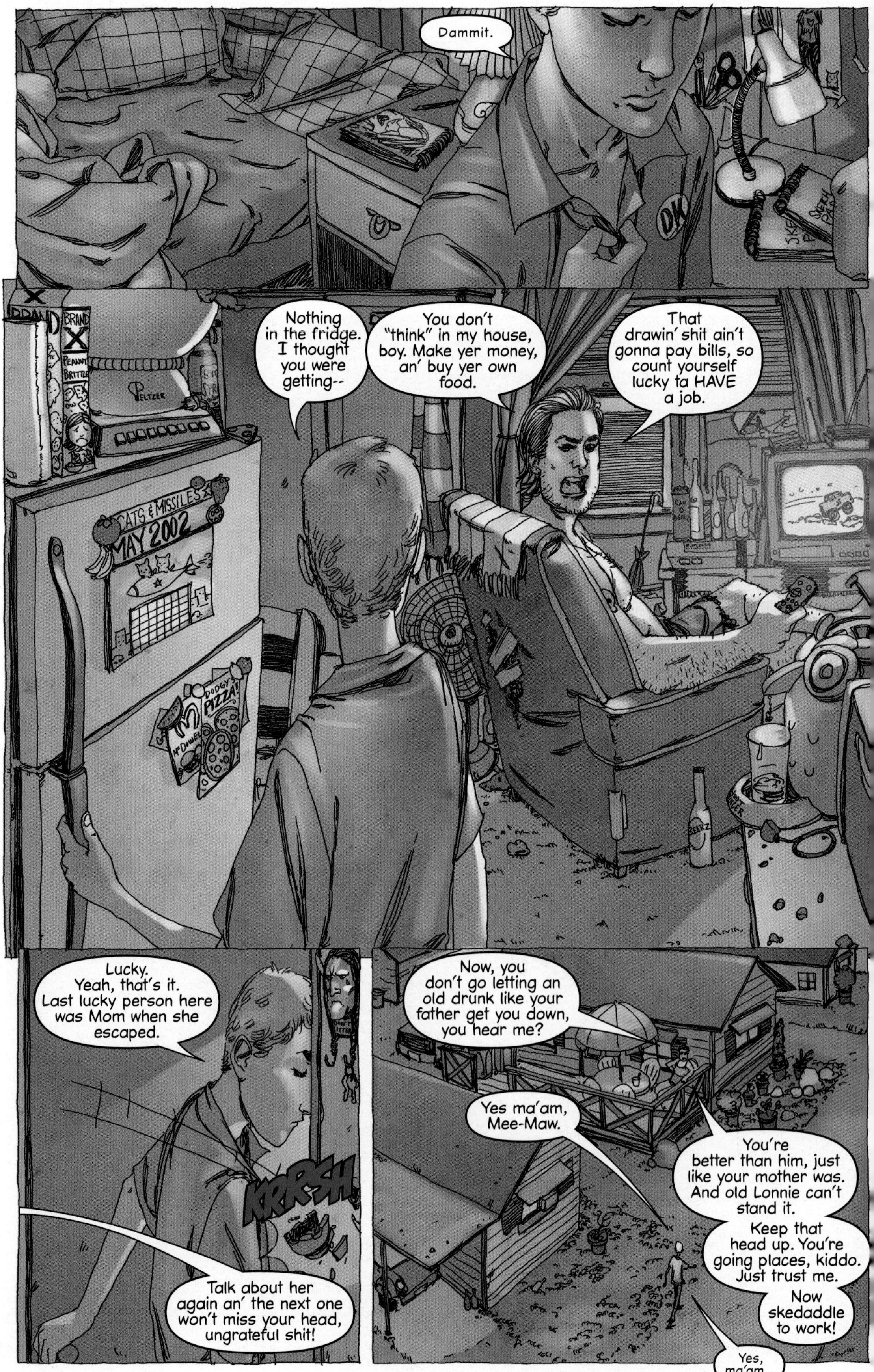
Dammit.
Nothing in the fridge. I thought you were getting--
You don't "think" in my house, boy. Make yer money, an' buy yer own food.
That drawin' shit ain't gonna pay bills, so count yourself lucky ta HAVE a job.
CATS & MISSILES MAY 2002
DODGY'S PIZZA!
BEERZ
Lucky. Yeah, that's it. Last lucky person here was Mom when she escaped.
KRRSH!
Talk about her again an' the next one won't miss your head, ungrateful shit!
Now, you don't go letting an old drunk like your father get you down, you hear me?
Yes ma'am, Mee-Maw.
You're better than him, just like your mother was. And old Lonnie can't stand it.
Keep that head up. You're going places, kiddo. Just trust me.
Now skedaddle to work!
Yes, ma'am...

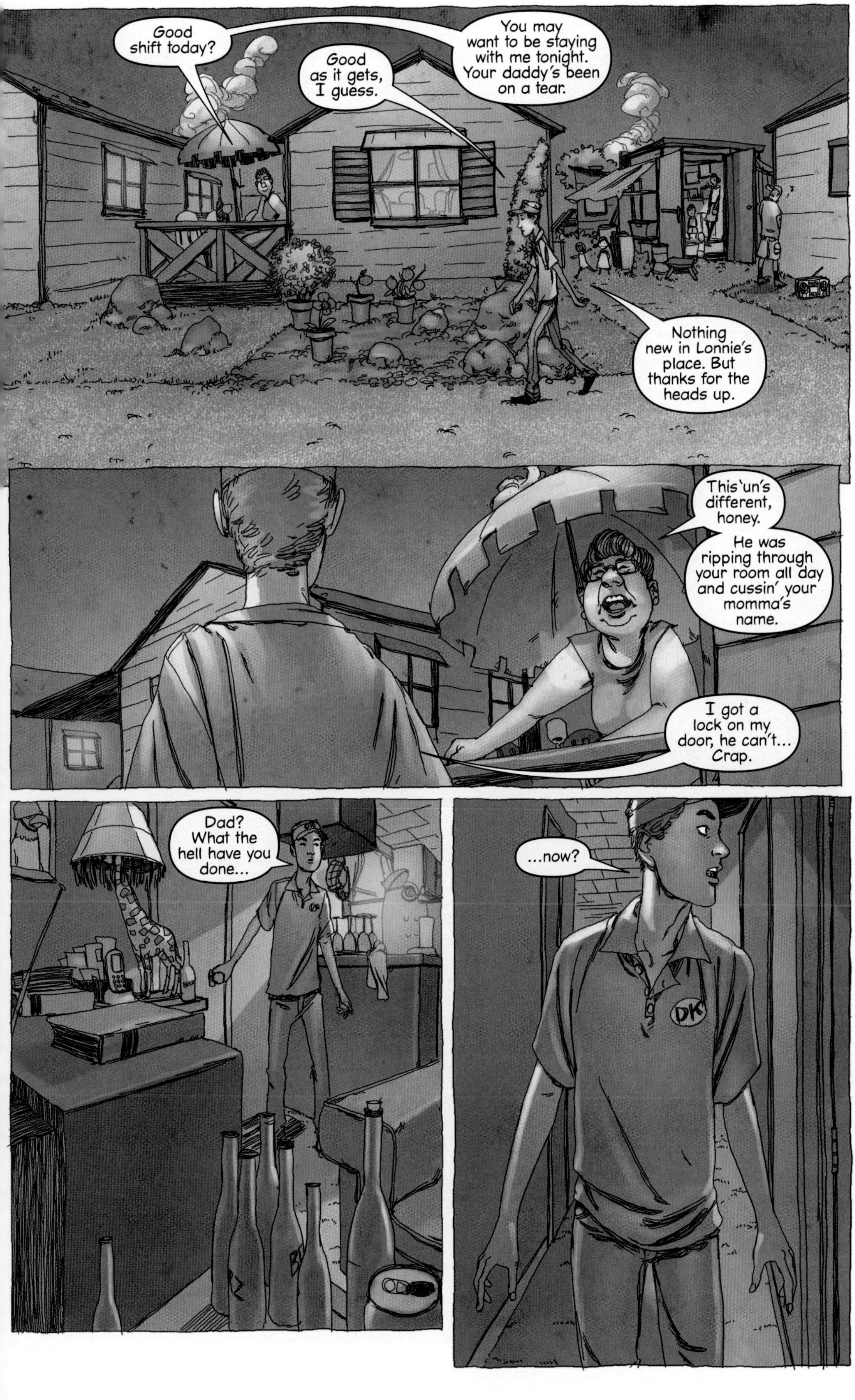
Good shift today?
Good as it gets, I guess.
You may want to be staying with me tonight. Your daddy's been on a tear.
Nothing new in Lonnie's place. But thanks for the heads up.
This 'un's different, honey.
He was ripping through your room all day and cussin' your momma's name.
I got a lock on my door, he can't... Crap.
Dad? What the hell have you done...
...now?

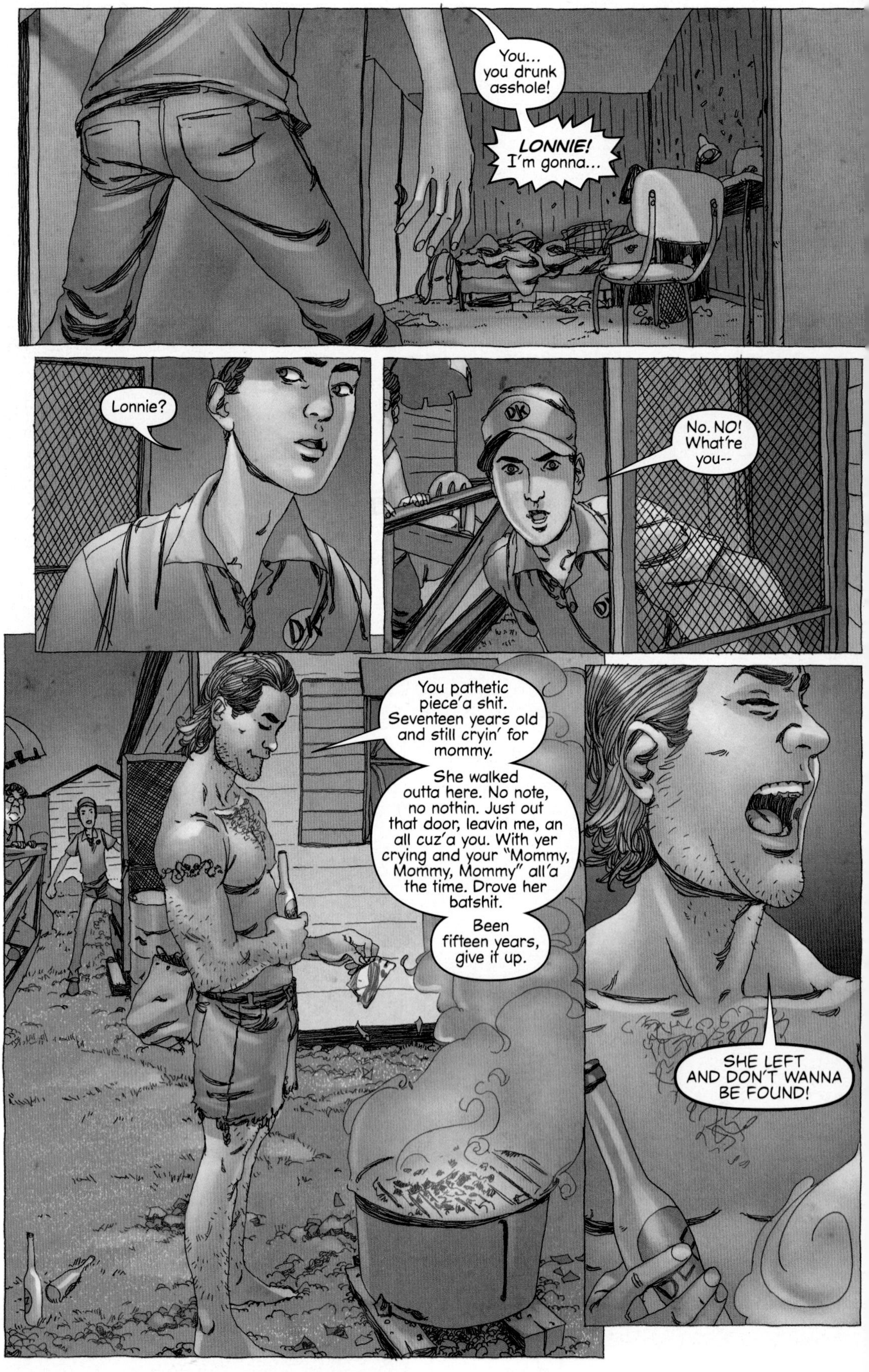
You... you drunk asshole!
LONNIE! I'm gonna...
Lonnie?
No. NO! What're you--
You pathetic piece'a shit. Seventeen years old and still cryin' for mommy.
She walked outta here. No note, no nothin. Just out that door, leavin me, an all cuz'a you. With yer crying and your "Mommy, Mommy, Mommy" all'a the time. Drove her batshit.
Been fifteen years, give it up.
SHE LEFT AND DON'T WANNA BE FOUND!

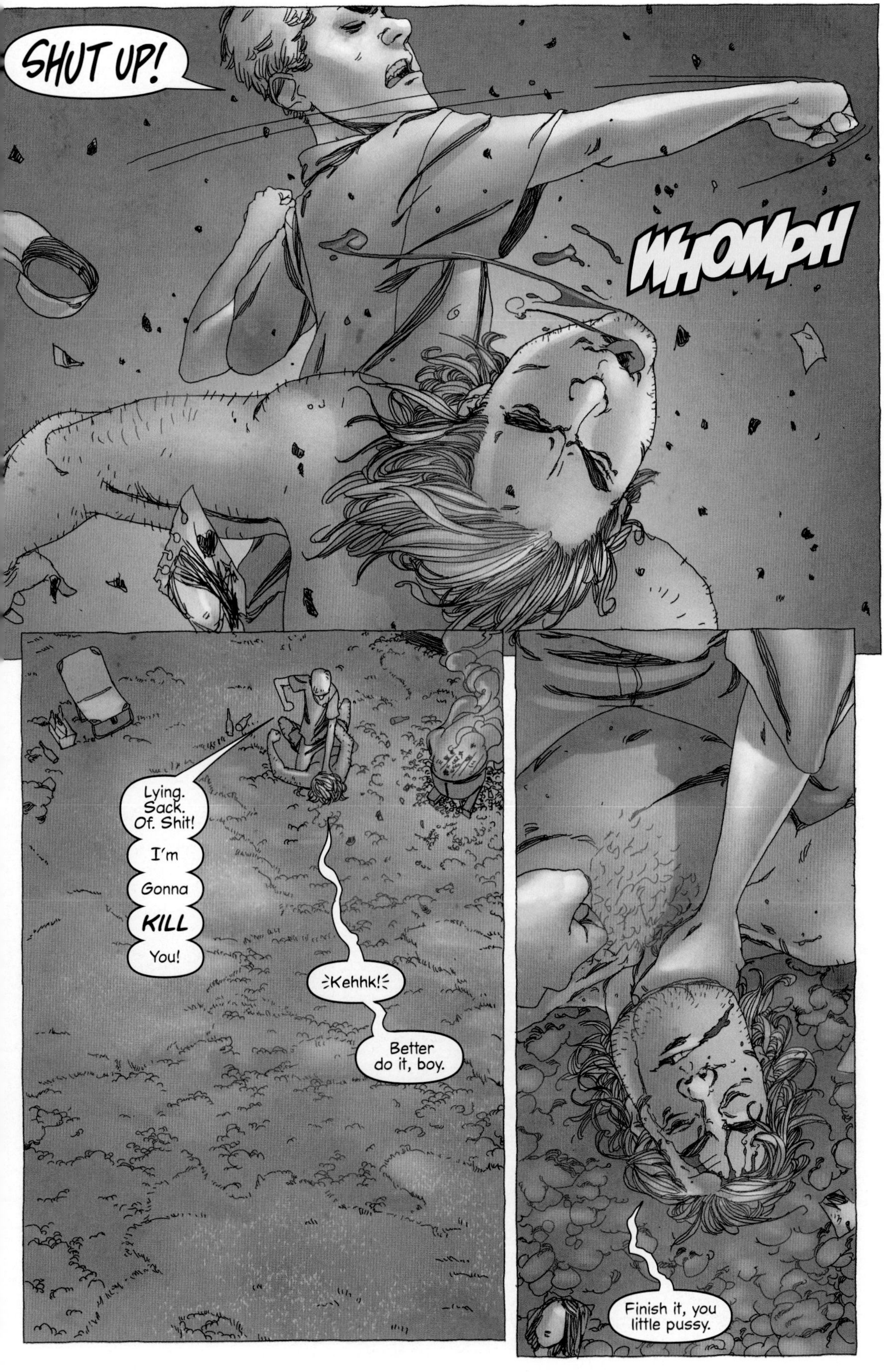
SHUT UP!
WHOMPH
Lying. Sack. Of. Shit!
I'm
Gonna
KILL
You!
Kehhk!
Better do it, boy.
Finish it, you little pussy.

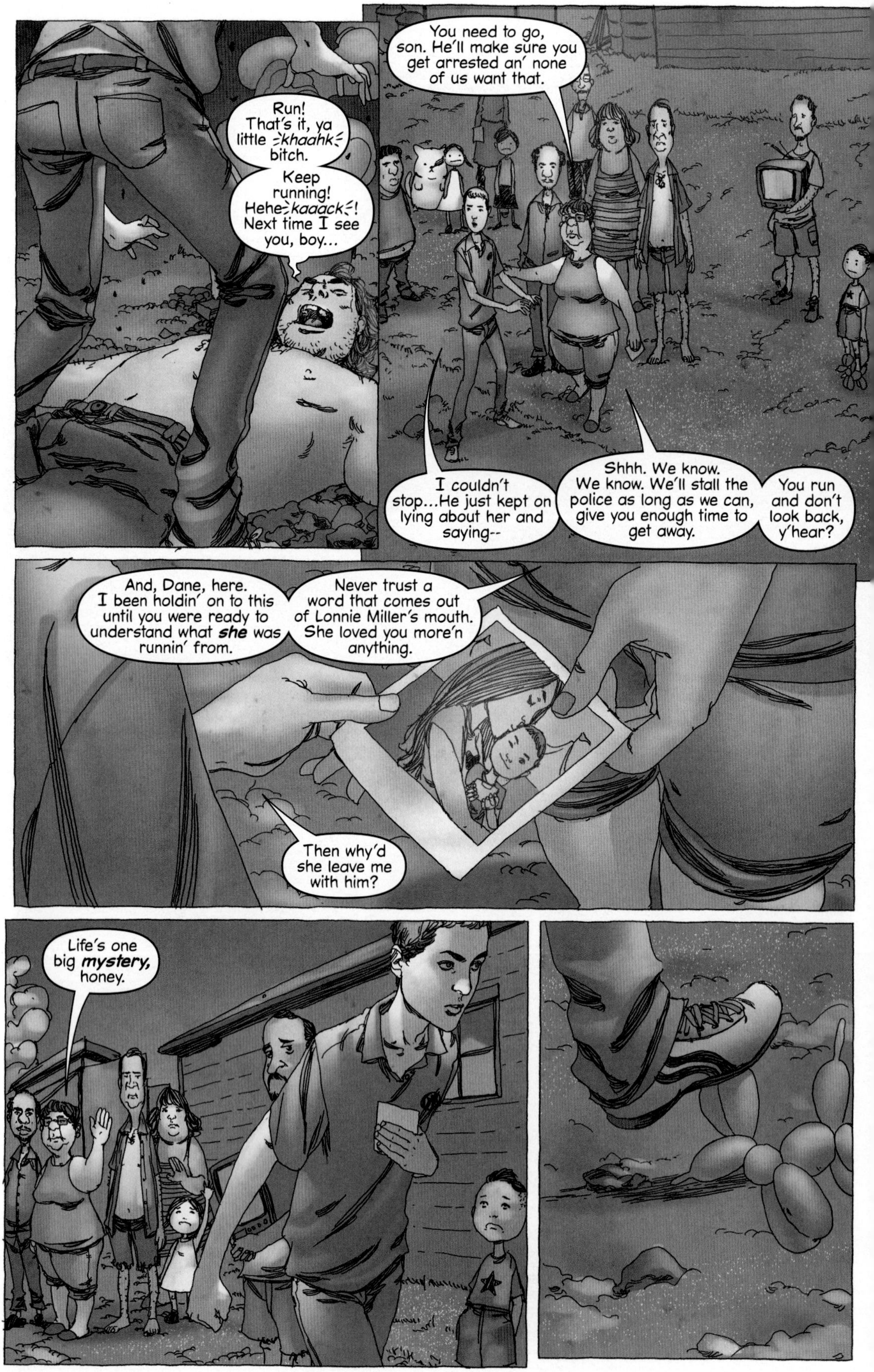

Run! That's it, ya little khaahk bitch.
Keep running! Hehe kaaack! Next time I see you, boy...
You need to go, son. He'll make sure you get arrested an' none of us want that.
I couldn't stop...He just kept on lying about her and saying--
Shhh. We know. We know. We'll stall the police as long as we can, give you enough time to get away.
You run and don't look back, y'hear?
And, Dane, here. I been holdin' on to this until you were ready to understand what she was runnin' from.
Never trust a word that comes out of Lonnie Miller's mouth. She loved you more'n anything.
Then why'd she leave me with him?
Life's one big mystery, honey.

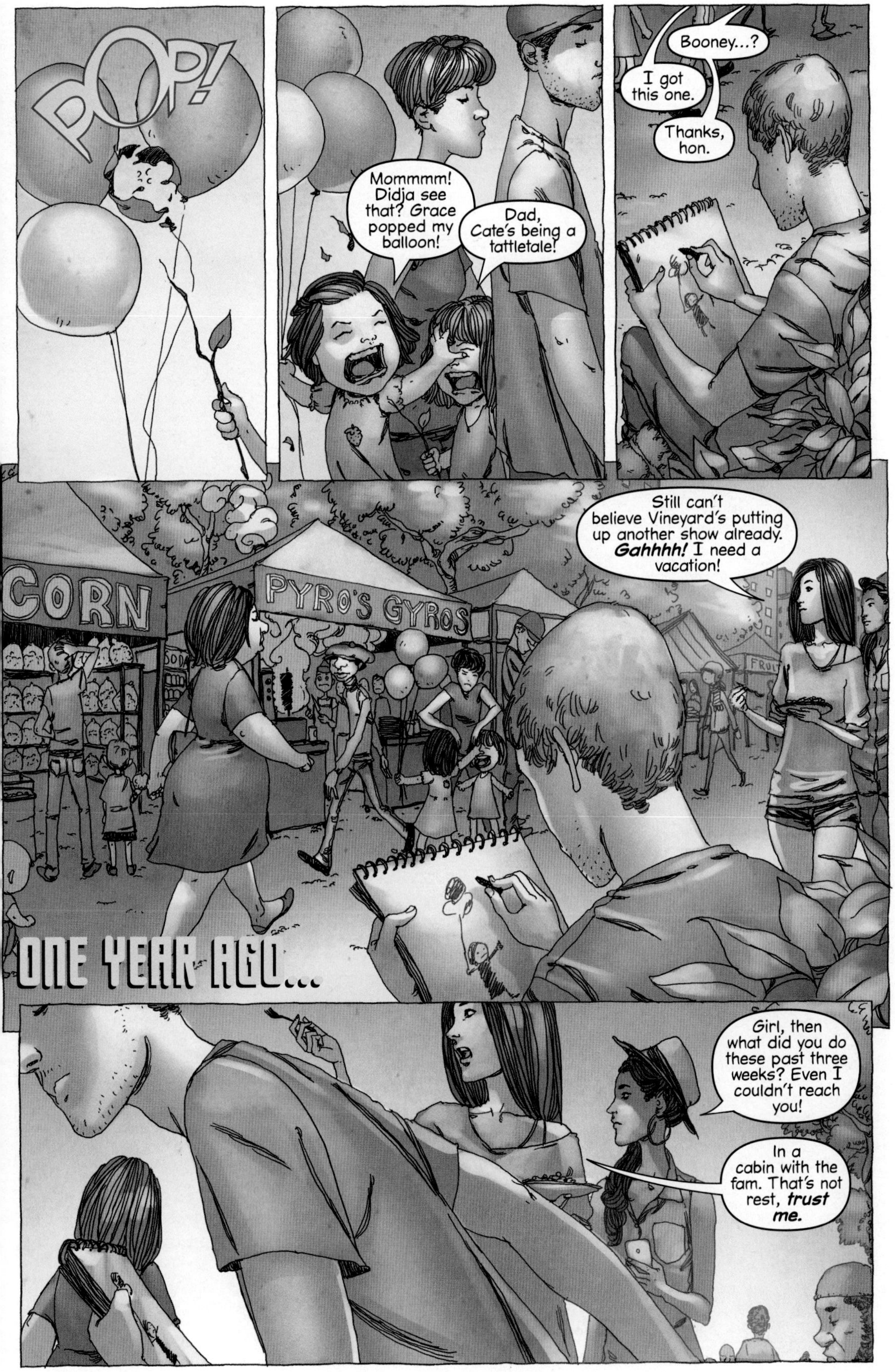
POP!
Mommmm! Didja see that? Grace popped my balloon!
Dad, Cate's being a tattletale!
Booney...?
I got this one.
Thanks, hon.
CORN
PYRO'S GYROS
Still can't believe Vineyard's putting up another show already. **Gahhhh!** I need a vacation!
ONE YEAR AGO...
Girl, then what did you do these past three weeks? Even I couldn't reach you!
In a cabin with the fam. That's not rest, ***trust me.***

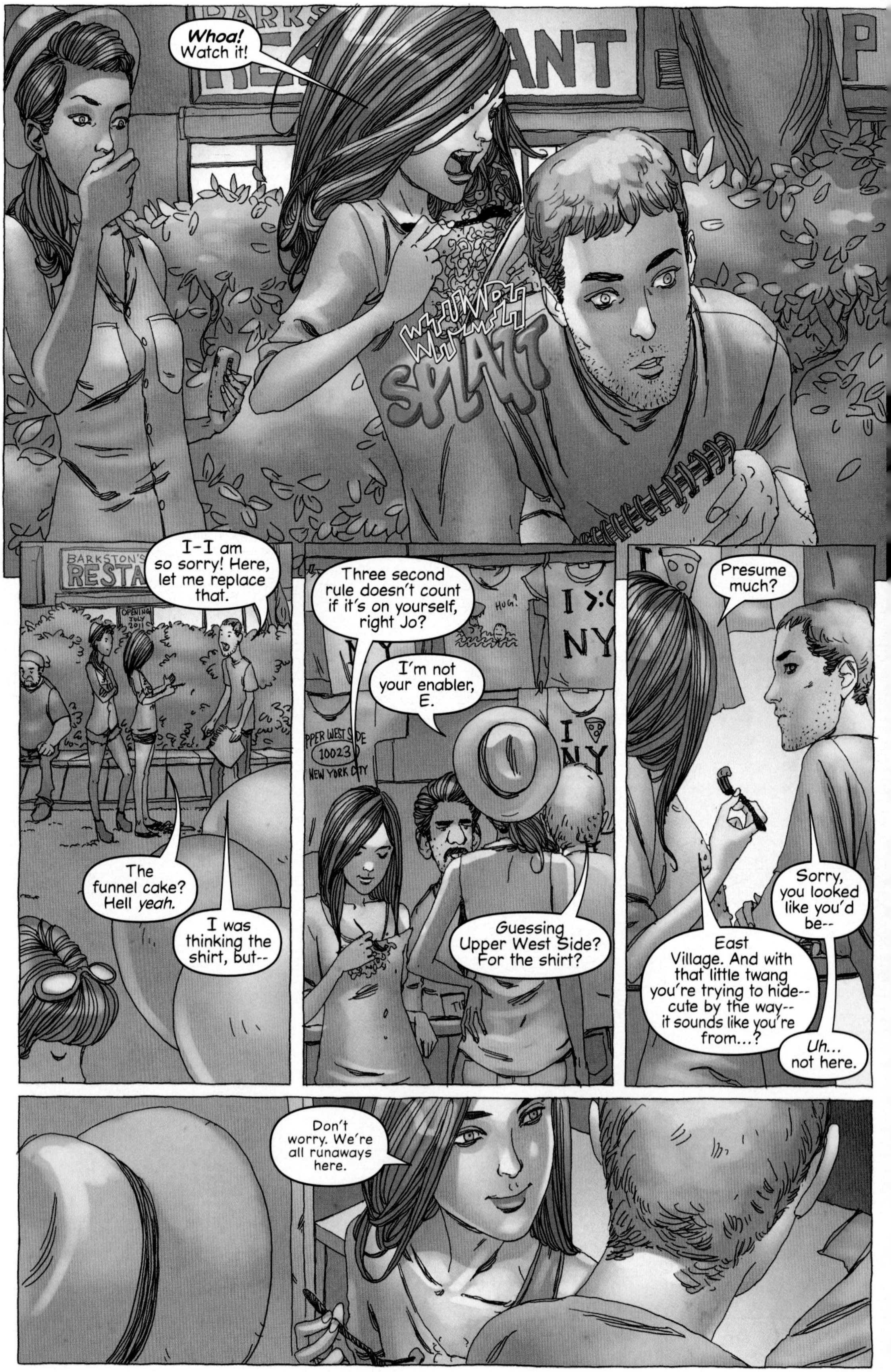

Whoa! Watch it!
WHUMPH
SPLAT
I-I am so sorry! Here, let me replace that.
BARKSTON'S RESTA
OPENING JULY 2011
The funnel cake? Hell *yeah.*
I was thinking the shirt, but--
Three second rule doesn't count if it's on yourself, right Jo?
I'm not your enabler, E.
HUG?
NY
PPER WEST SIDE 10023 NEW YORK CITY
Guessing Upper West Side? For the shirt?
Presume much?
Sorry, you looked like you'd be--
East Village. And with that little twang you're trying to hide--cute by the way--it sounds like you're from...?
Uh... not here.
Don't worry. We're all runaways here.

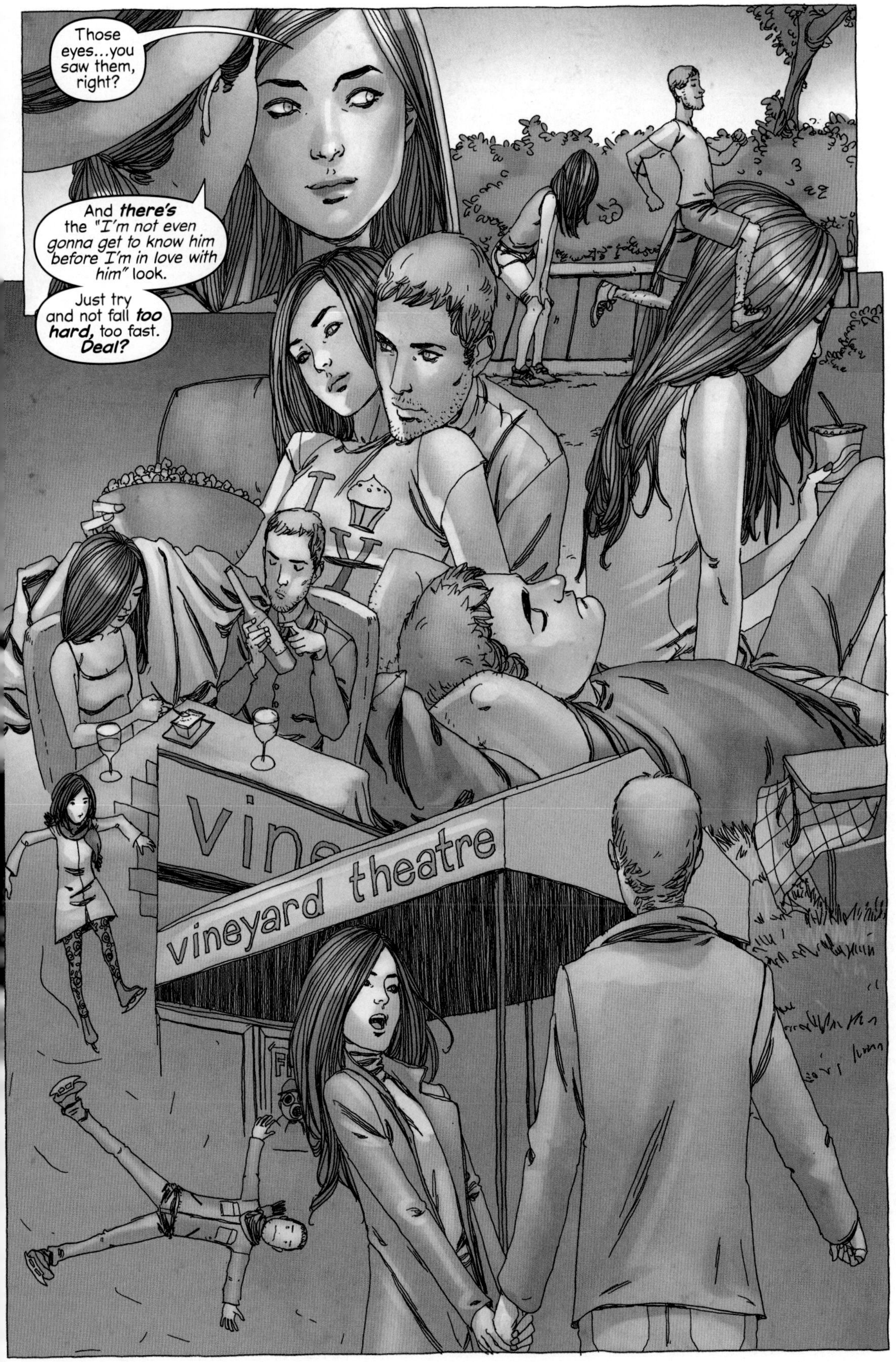

Those eyes...you saw them, right?
And ***there's*** the *"I'm not even gonna get to know him before I'm in love with him"* look.
Just try and not fall ***too hard,*** too fast. ***Deal?***
vineyard theatre

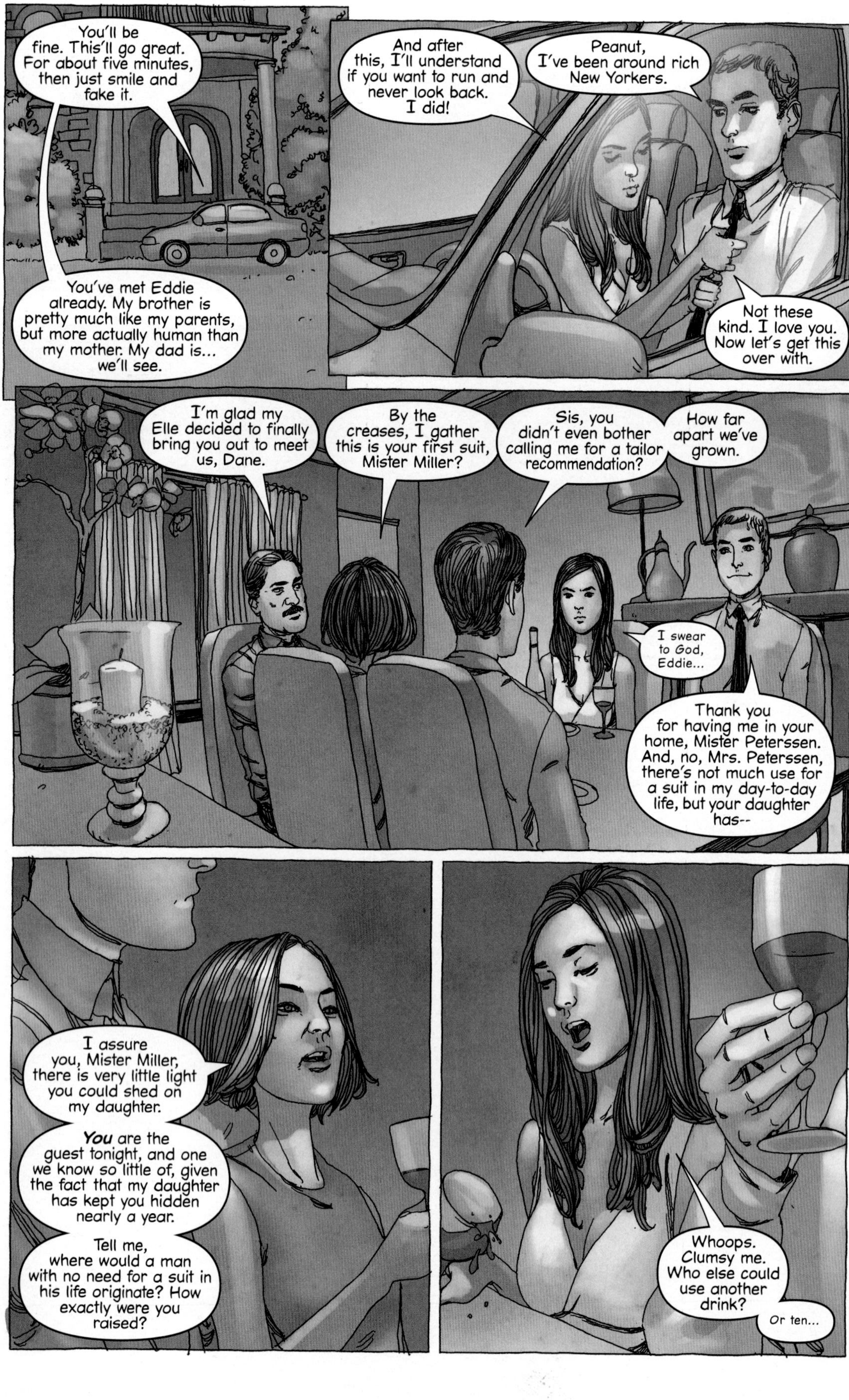
You'll be fine. This'll go great. For about five minutes, then just smile and fake it.
You've met Eddie already. My brother is pretty much like my parents, but more actually human than my mother. My dad is... we'll see.
And after this, I'll understand if you want to run and never look back. I did!
Peanut, I've been around rich New Yorkers.
Not these kind. I love you. Now let's get this over with.
I'm glad my Elle decided to finally bring you out to meet us, Dane.
By the creases, I gather this is your first suit, Mister Miller?
Sis, you didn't even bother calling me for a tailor recommendation?
How far apart we've grown.
I swear to God, Eddie...
Thank you for having me in your home, Mister Peterssen. And, no, Mrs. Peterssen, there's not much use for a suit in my day-to-day life, but your daughter has--
I assure you, Mister Miller, there is very little light you could shed on my daughter.
You are the guest tonight, and one we know so little of, given the fact that my daughter has kept you hidden nearly a year.
Tell me, where would a man with no need for a suit in his life originate? How exactly were you raised?
Whoops. Clumsy me. Who else could use another drink?
Or ten...

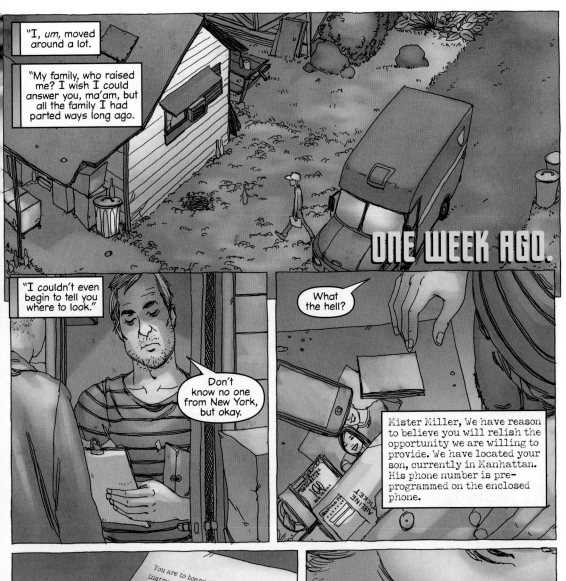

"I, *um*, moved around a lot.

"My family, who raised me? I wish I could answer you, ma'am, but all the family I had parted ways long ago.

ONE WEEK AGO.

"I couldn't even begin to tell you where to look."

Don't know no one from New York, but okay.

What the hell?

Mister Miller, We have reason to believe you will relish the opportunity we are willing to provide. We have located your son, currently in Manhattan. His phone number is pre-programmed on the enclosed phone.

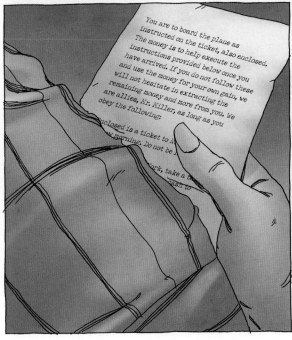

You are to board the plane as instructed on the ticket, also enclosed. The money is to help execute the instructions provided below once you have arrived. If you do not follow these and use the money for your own gain, we will not hesitate in extracting the remaining money and more from you. We are allies, Mr. Miller, as long as you obey the following:

[nclosed is a ticket to [
[morning. Do not be [

[ ]ork, take a [
[ ]ash to [

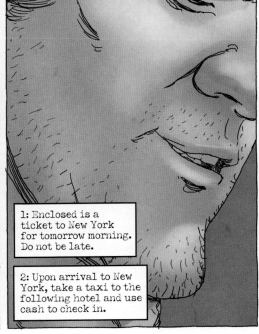

1: Enclosed is a ticket to New York for tomorrow morning. Do not be late.

2: Upon arrival to New York, take a taxi to the following hotel and use cash to check in.

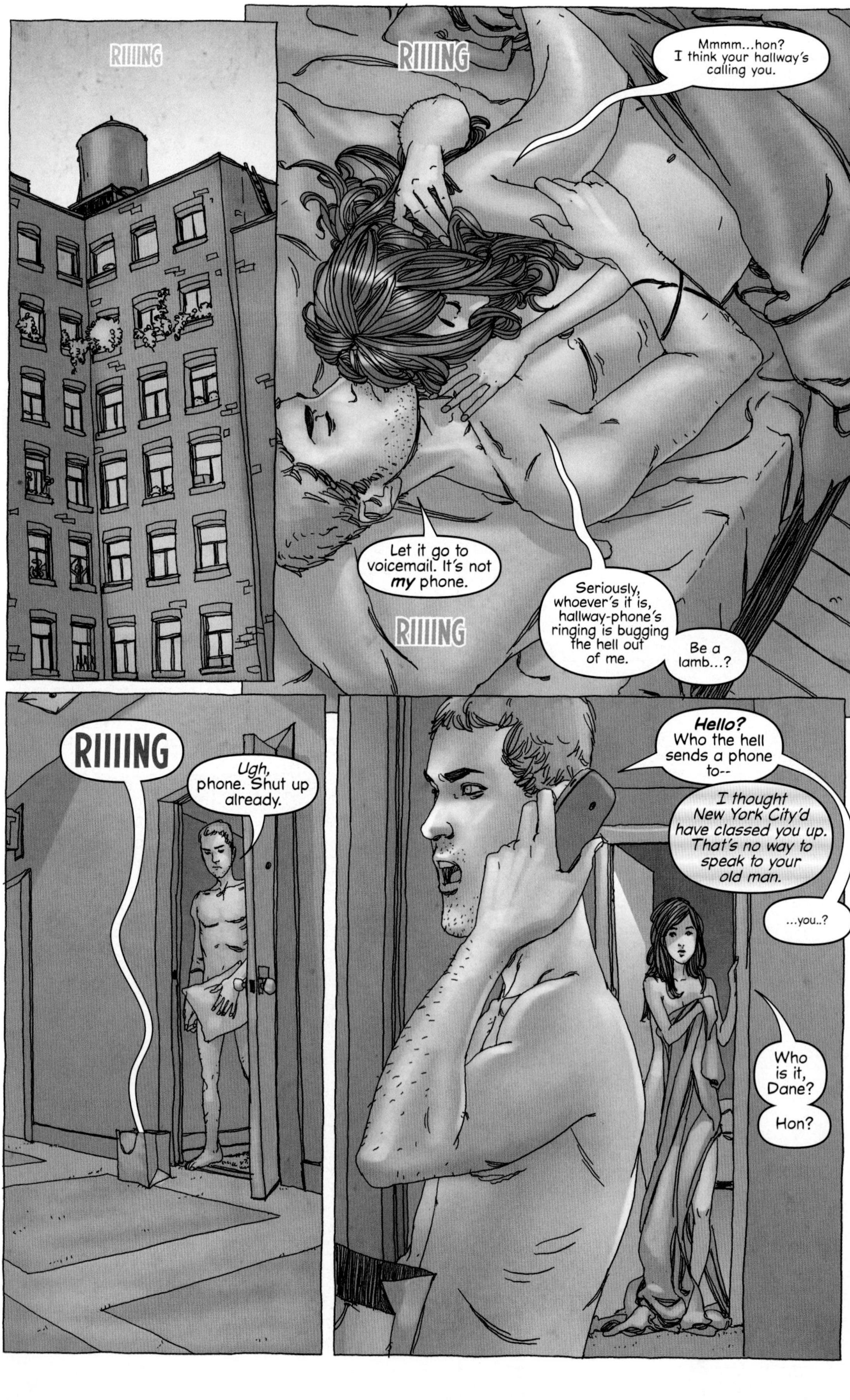
RIIIING
RIIIING
Mmmm...hon? I think your hallway's calling you.
Let it go to voicemail. It's not *my* phone.
RIIIING
Seriously, whoever's it is, hallway-phone's ringing is bugging the hell out of me.
Be a lamb...?
RIIIING
Ugh, phone. Shut up already.
Hello? Who the hell sends a phone to--
I thought New York City'd have classed you up. That's no way to speak to your old man.
...you..?
Who is it, Dane?
Hon?

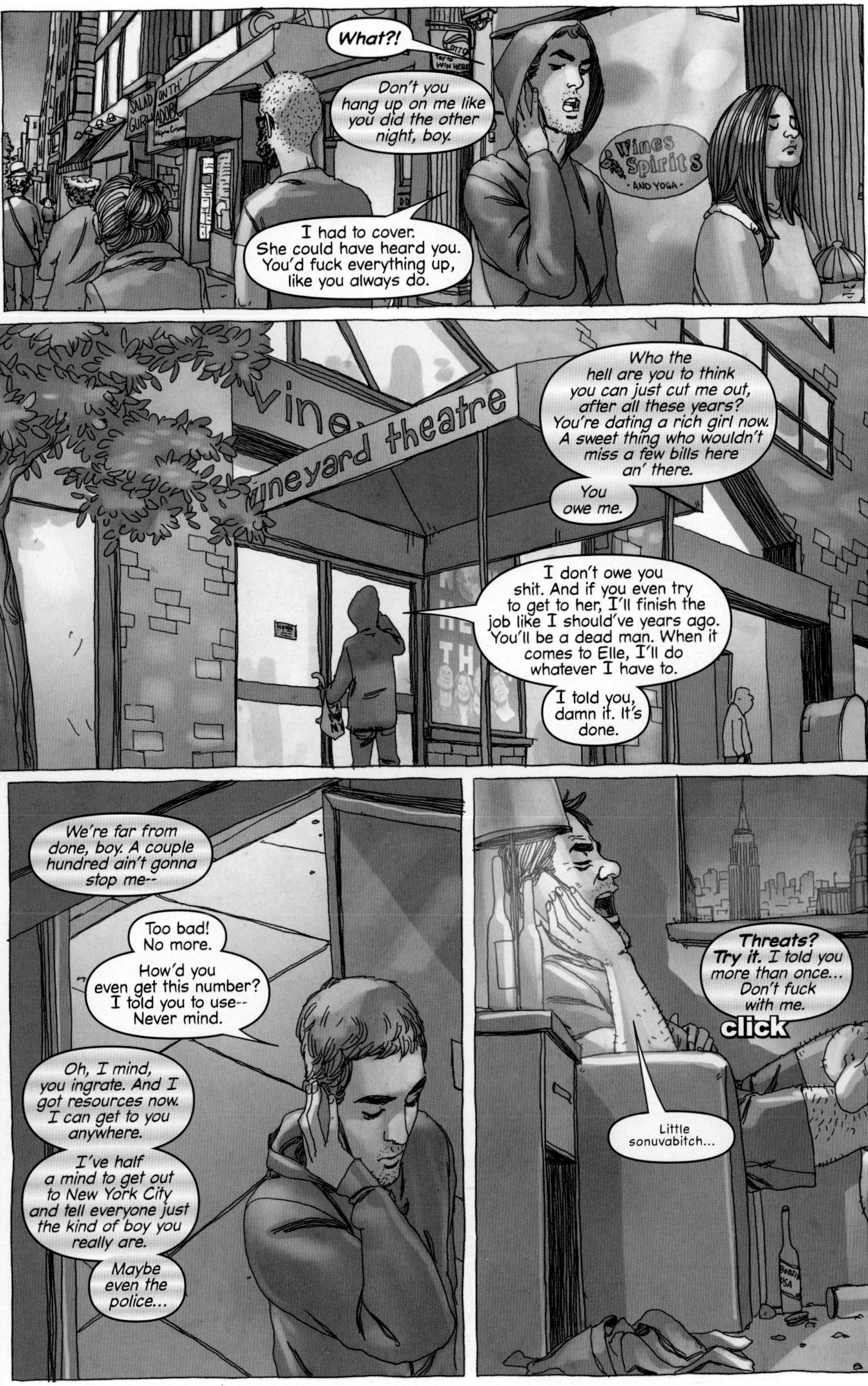
What?!
Don't you hang up on me like you did the other night, boy.
I had to cover. She could have heard you. You'd fuck everything up, like you always do.
Wines Spirits AND YOGA
vineyard theatre
Who the hell are you to think you can just cut me out, after all these years? You're dating a rich girl now. A sweet thing who wouldn't miss a few bills here an' there.
You owe me.
I don't owe you shit. And if you even try to get to her, I'll finish the job like I should've years ago. You'll be a dead man. When it comes to Elle, I'll do whatever I have to.
I told you, damn it. It's done.
We're far from done, boy. A couple hundred ain't gonna stop me--
Too bad! No more.
How'd you even get this number? I told you to use-- Never mind.
Oh, I mind, you ingrate. And I got resources now. I can get to you anywhere.
I've half a mind to get out to New York City and tell everyone just the kind of boy you really are.
Maybe even the police...
Threats? Try it. I told you more than once... Don't fuck with me.
click
Little sonuvabitch...

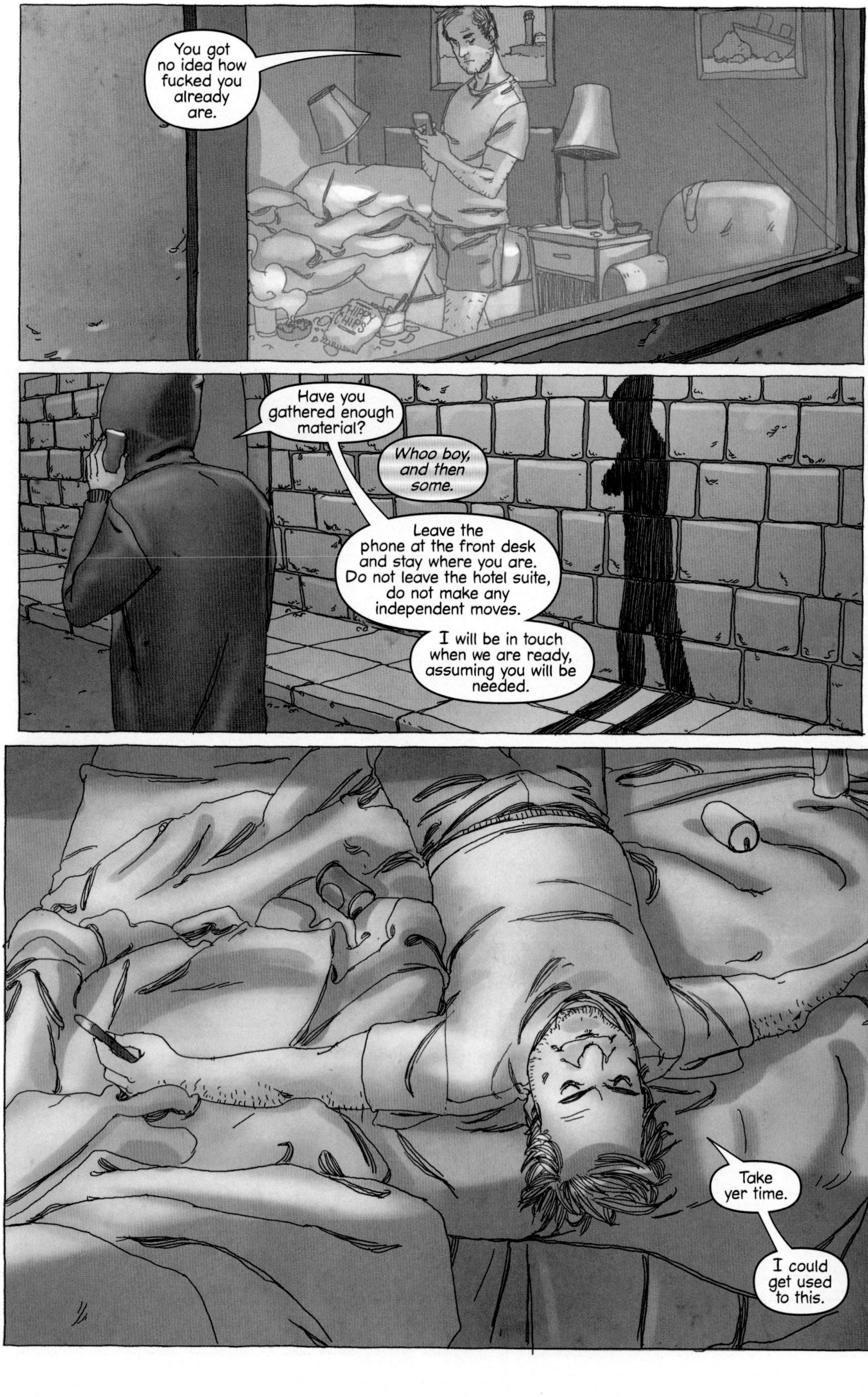
You got no idea how fucked you already are.
Have you gathered enough material?
Whoo boy, and then some.
Leave the phone at the front desk and stay where you are. Do not leave the hotel suite, do not make any independent moves.
I will be in touch when we are ready, assuming you will be needed.
HIPPY CHIPS
Take yer time.
I could get used to this.

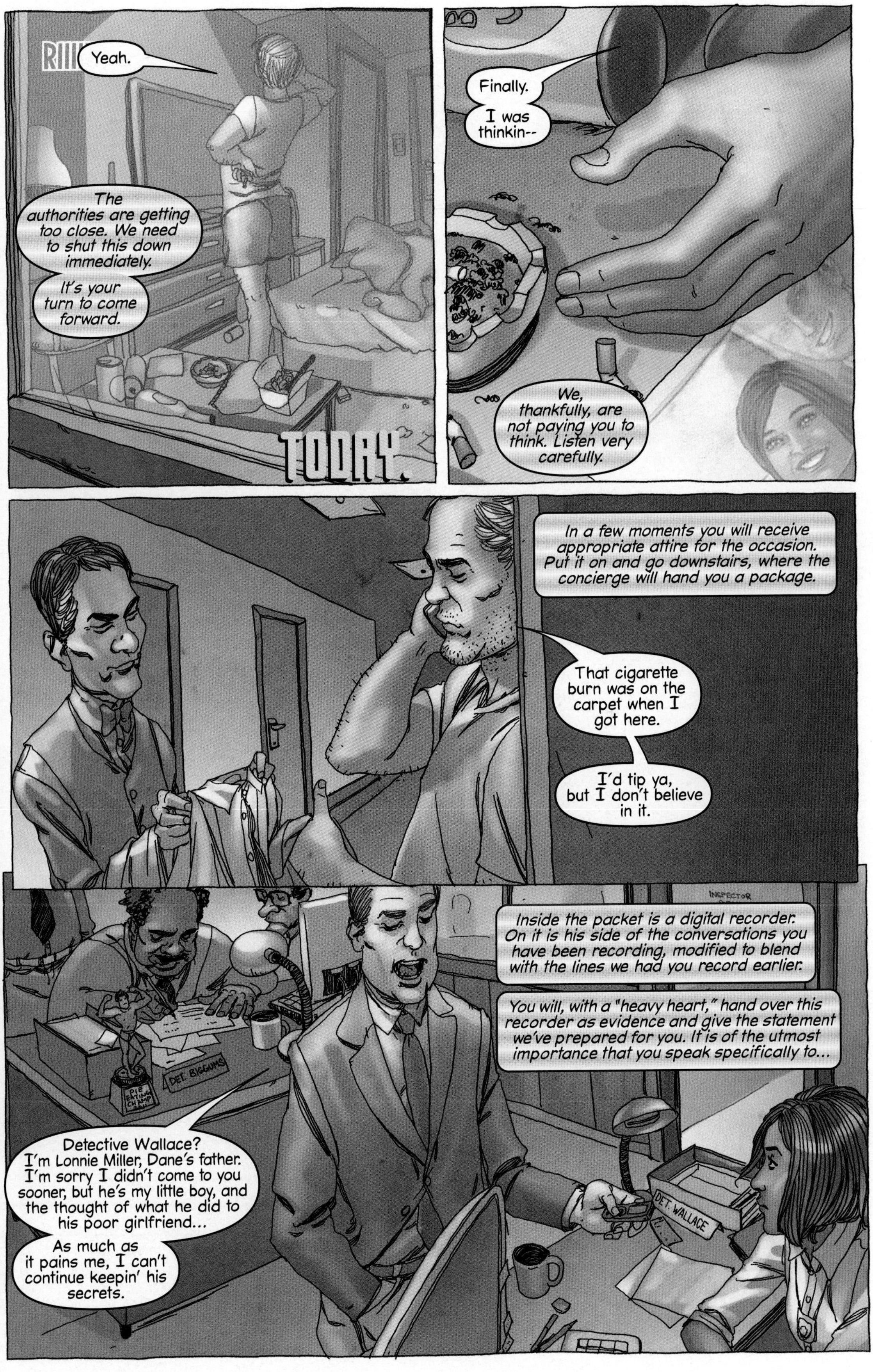
RIIII
Yeah.
The authorities are getting too close. We need to shut this down immediately.
It's your turn to come forward.
TODAY.
Finally.
I was thinkin--
We, thankfully, are not paying you to think. Listen very carefully.
In a few moments you will receive appropriate attire for the occasion. Put it on and go downstairs, where the concierge will hand you a package.
That cigarette burn was on the carpet when I got here.
I'd tip ya, but I don't believe in it.
INSPECTOR
Inside the packet is a digital recorder. On it is his side of the conversations you have been recording, modified to blend with the lines we had you record earlier.
You will, with a "heavy heart," hand over this recorder as evidence and give the statement we've prepared for you. It is of the utmost importance that you speak specifically to...
PIE EATING CHAMP
DET. BIGGUMS
Detective Wallace? I'm Lonnie Miller, Dane's father. I'm sorry I didn't come to you sooner, but he's my little boy, and the thought of what he did to his poor girlfriend...
As much as it pains me, I can't continue keepin' his secrets.
DET. WALLACE

Brrrrzzt

It's finished?

Aww, you should'a **seen** me! I was all professional an' shit.

Suits're uncomfortable as hell, but now I get why the assholes wearin' 'em feel all powerful.

Keep the suit, if you wish.

When you return to the hotel, you will find your payment, in cash, already in the safe in your room.

People use those? Cool.

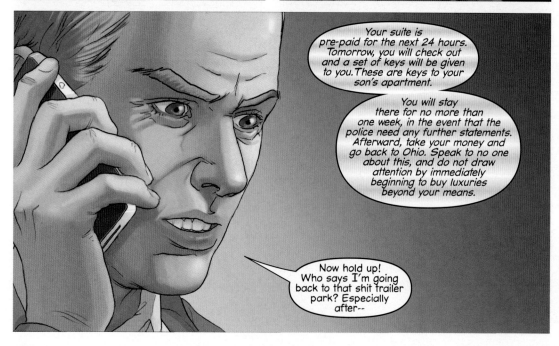

Your suite is pre-paid for the next 24 hours. Tomorrow, you will check out and a set of keys will be given to you. These are keys to your son's apartment.

You will stay there for no more than one week, in the event that the police need any further statements. Afterward, take your money and go back to Ohio. Speak to no one about this, and do not draw attention by immediately beginning to buy luxuries beyond your means.

Now hold up! Who says I'm going back to that shit trailer park? Especially after--

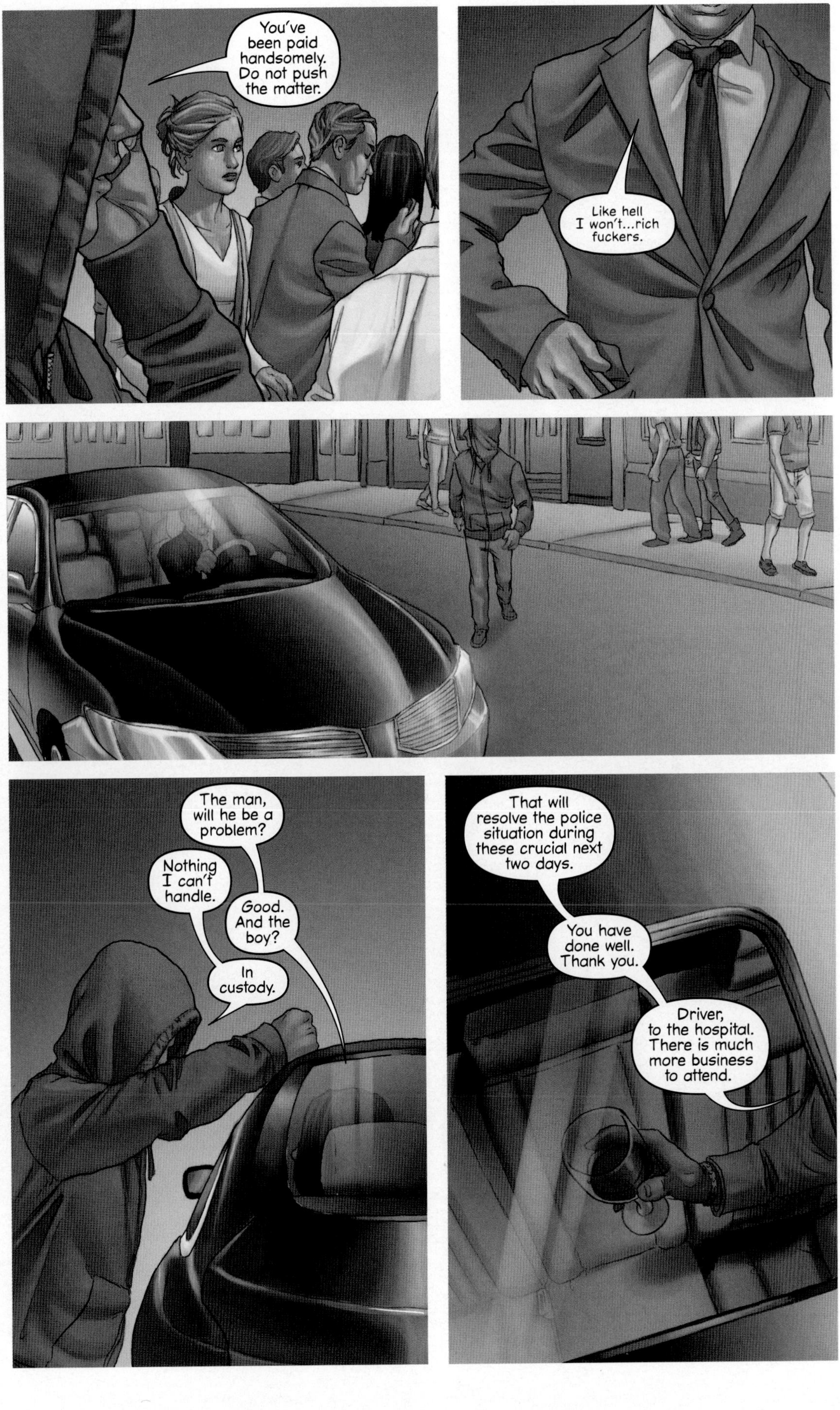
You've been paid handsomely. Do not push the matter.
Like hell I won't...rich fuckers.
The man, will he be a problem?
Nothing I can't handle.
Good. And the boy?
In custody.
That will resolve the police situation during these crucial next two days.
You have done well. Thank you.
Driver, to the hospital. There is much more business to attend.

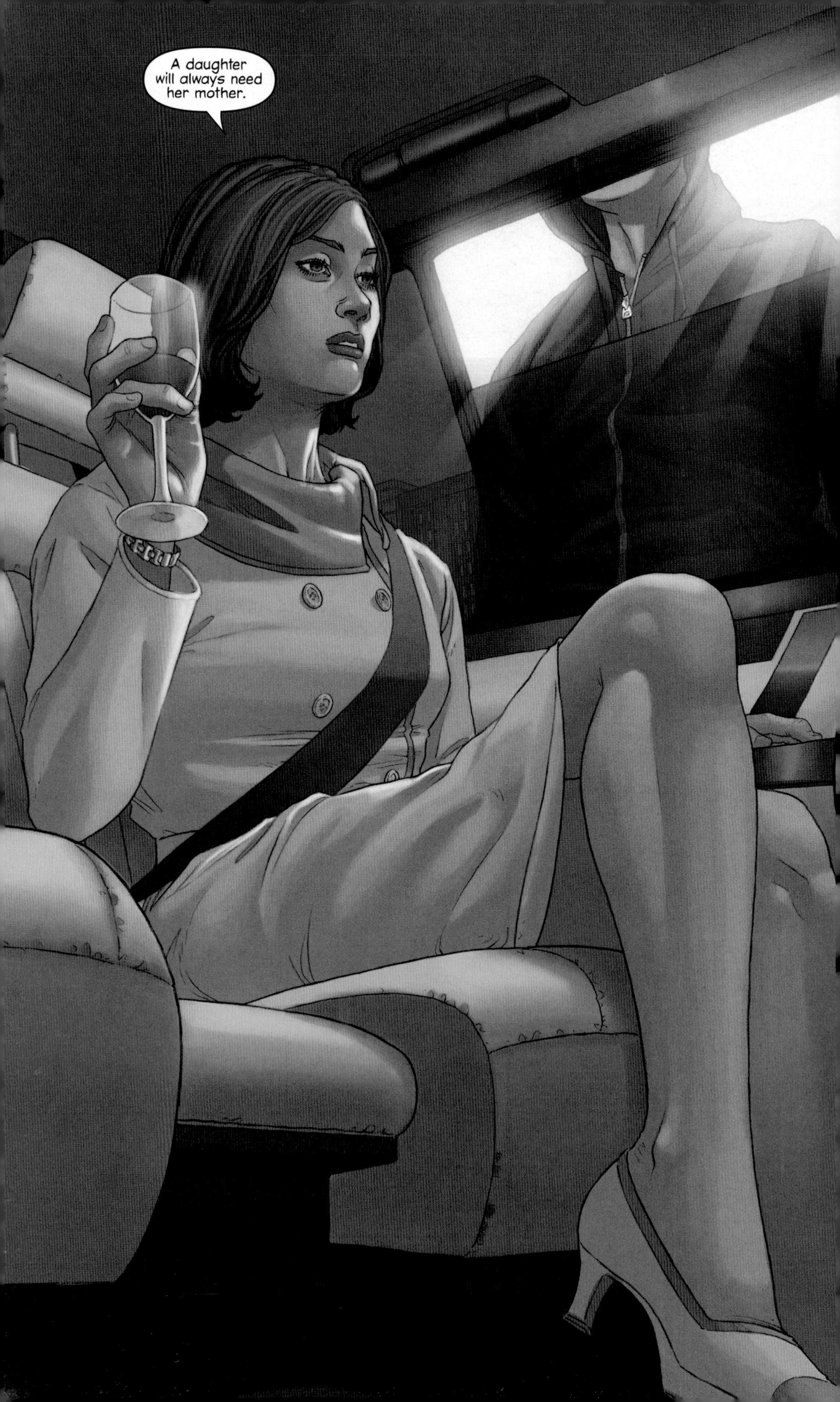
A daughter will always need her mother.

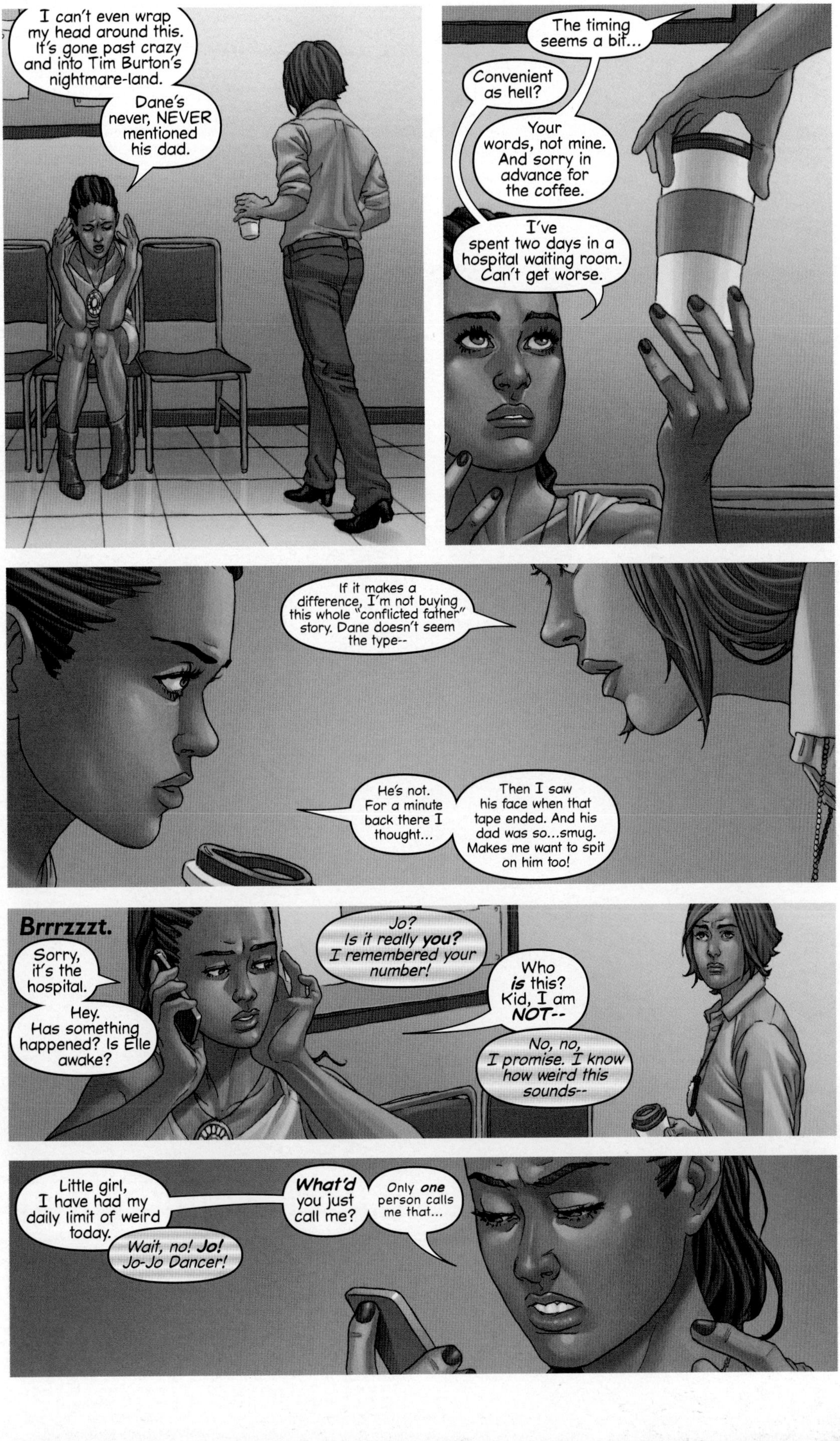
I can't even wrap my head around this. It's gone past crazy and into Tim Burton's nightmare-land.
Dane's never, NEVER mentioned his dad.
The timing seems a bit...
Convenient as hell?
Your words, not mine. And sorry in advance for the coffee.
I've spent two days in a hospital waiting room. Can't get worse.
If it makes a difference, I'm not buying this whole "conflicted father" story. Dane doesn't seem the type--
He's not. For a minute back there I thought...
Then I saw his face when that tape ended. And his dad was so...smug. Makes me want to spit on him too!
Brrrzzzt.
Sorry, it's the hospital.
Hey. Has something happened? Is Elle awake?
Jo? Is it really you? I remembered your number!
Who is this? Kid, I am NOT--
No, no, I promise. I know how weird this sounds--
Little girl, I have had my daily limit of weird today.
Wait, no! Jo! Jo-Jo Dancer!
What'd you just call me?
Only one person calls me that...

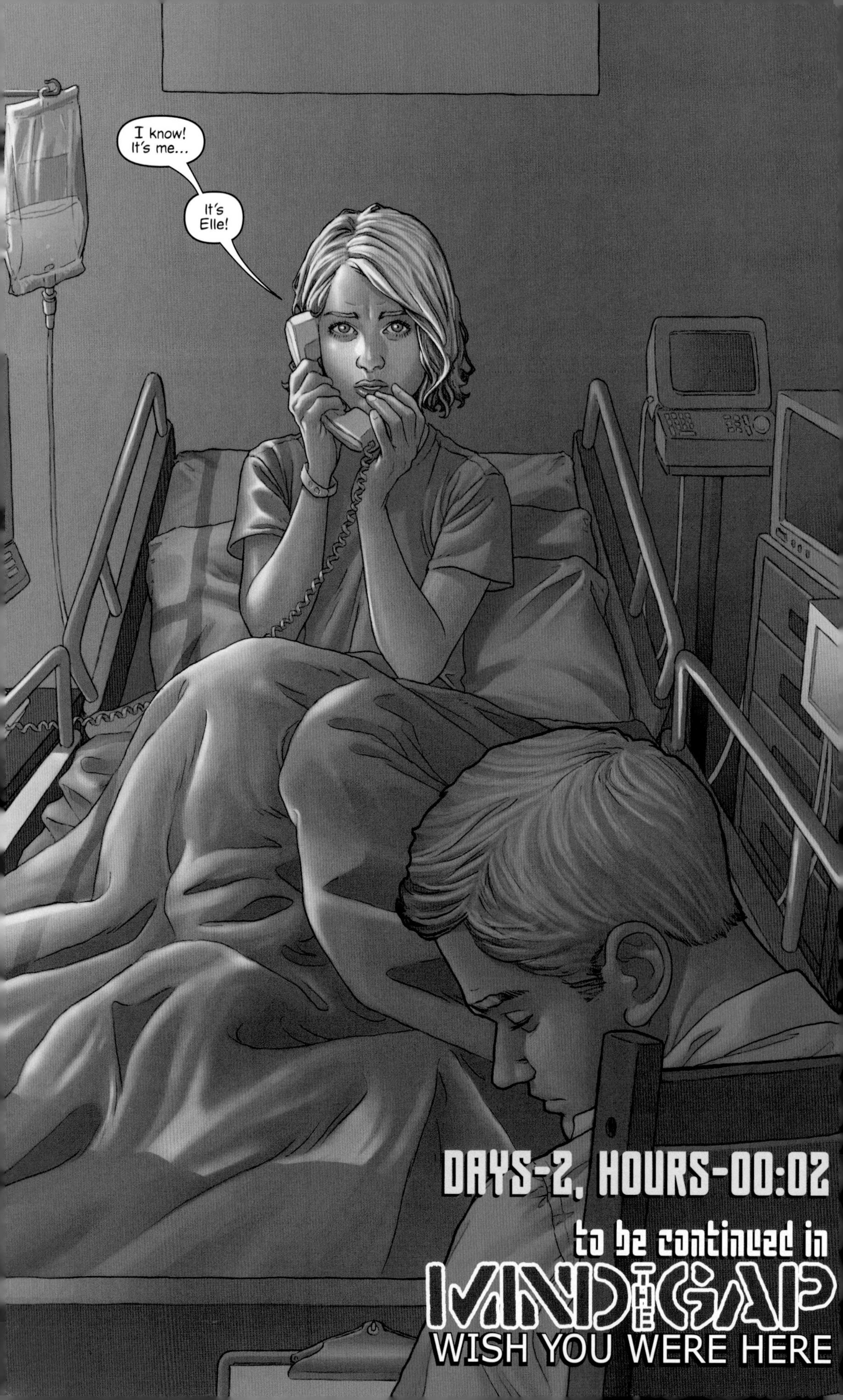
I know! It's me...
It's Elle!
DAYS-2, HOURS-00:02
to be continued in
MIND THE GAP
WISH YOU WERE HERE

MIND

VARIANT
GALLERY

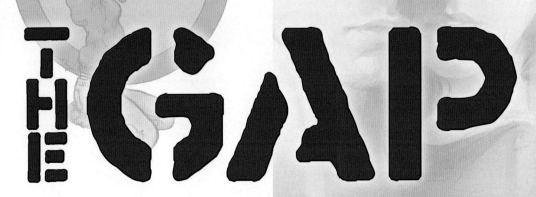

THE GAP

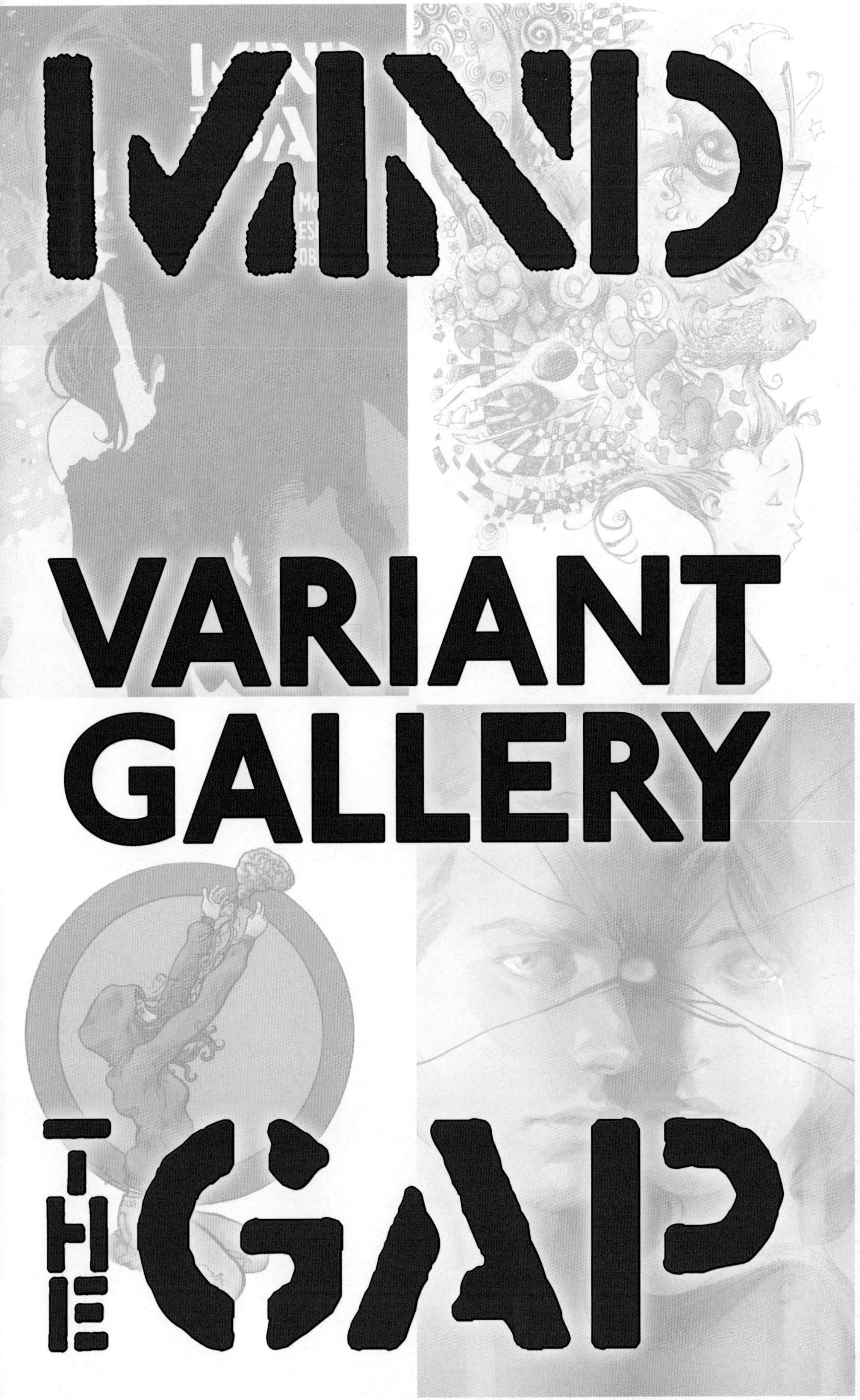

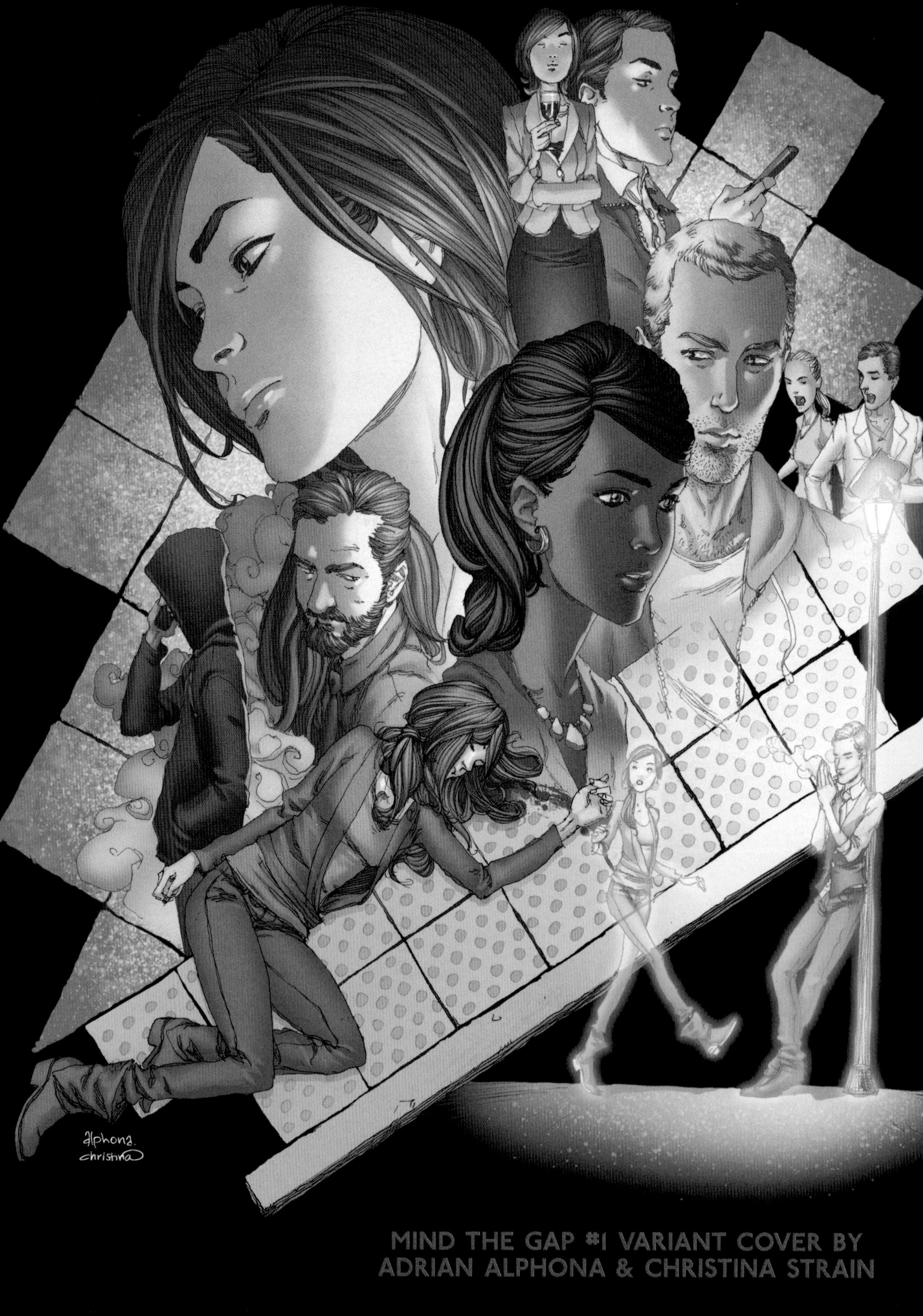
alphona.
christina

MIND THE GAP #1 VARIANT COVER BY
ADRIAN ALPHONA & CHRISTINA STRAIN

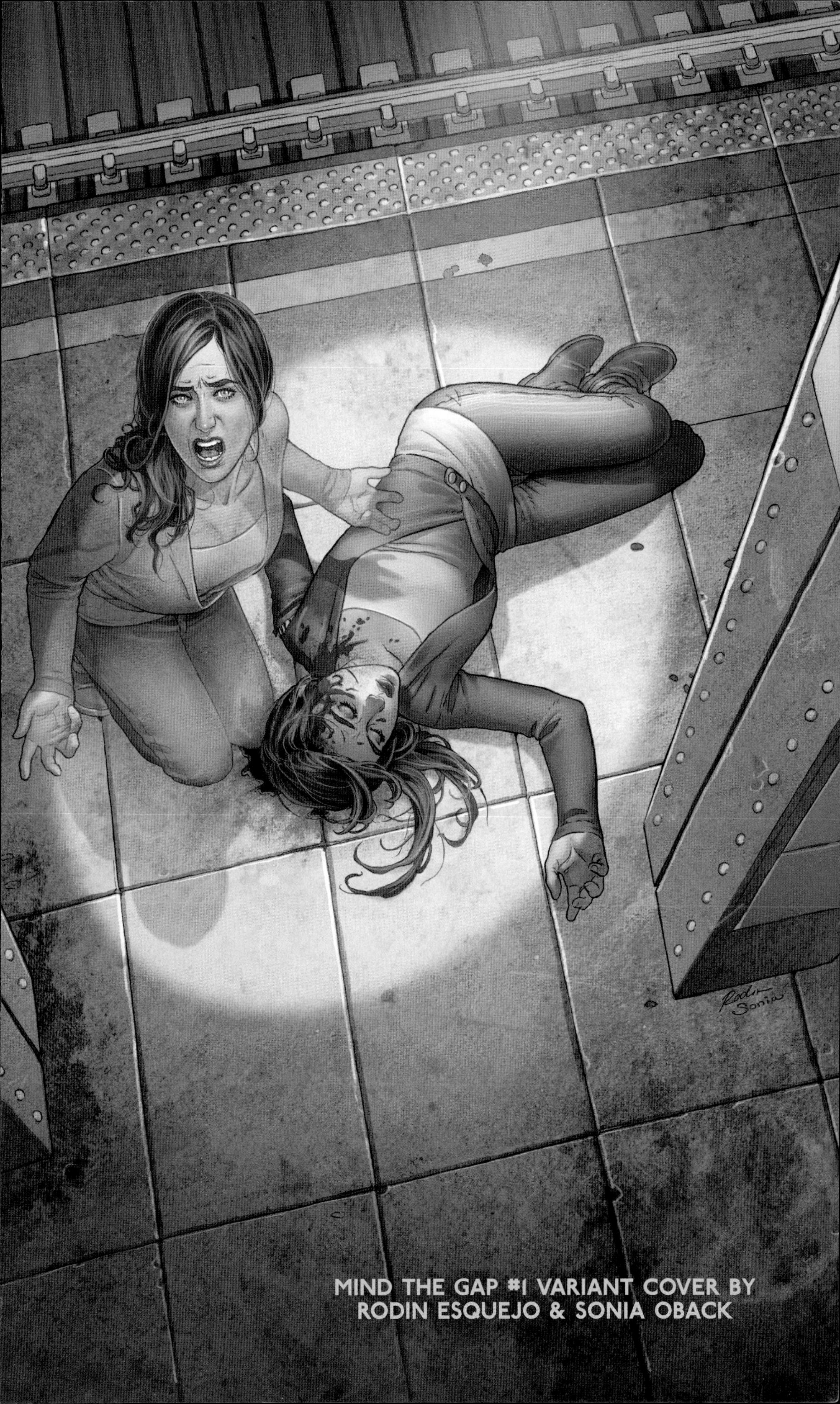
Rodin
Sonia

MIND THE GAP #1 VARIANT COVER BY
RODIN ESQUEJO & SONIA OBACK

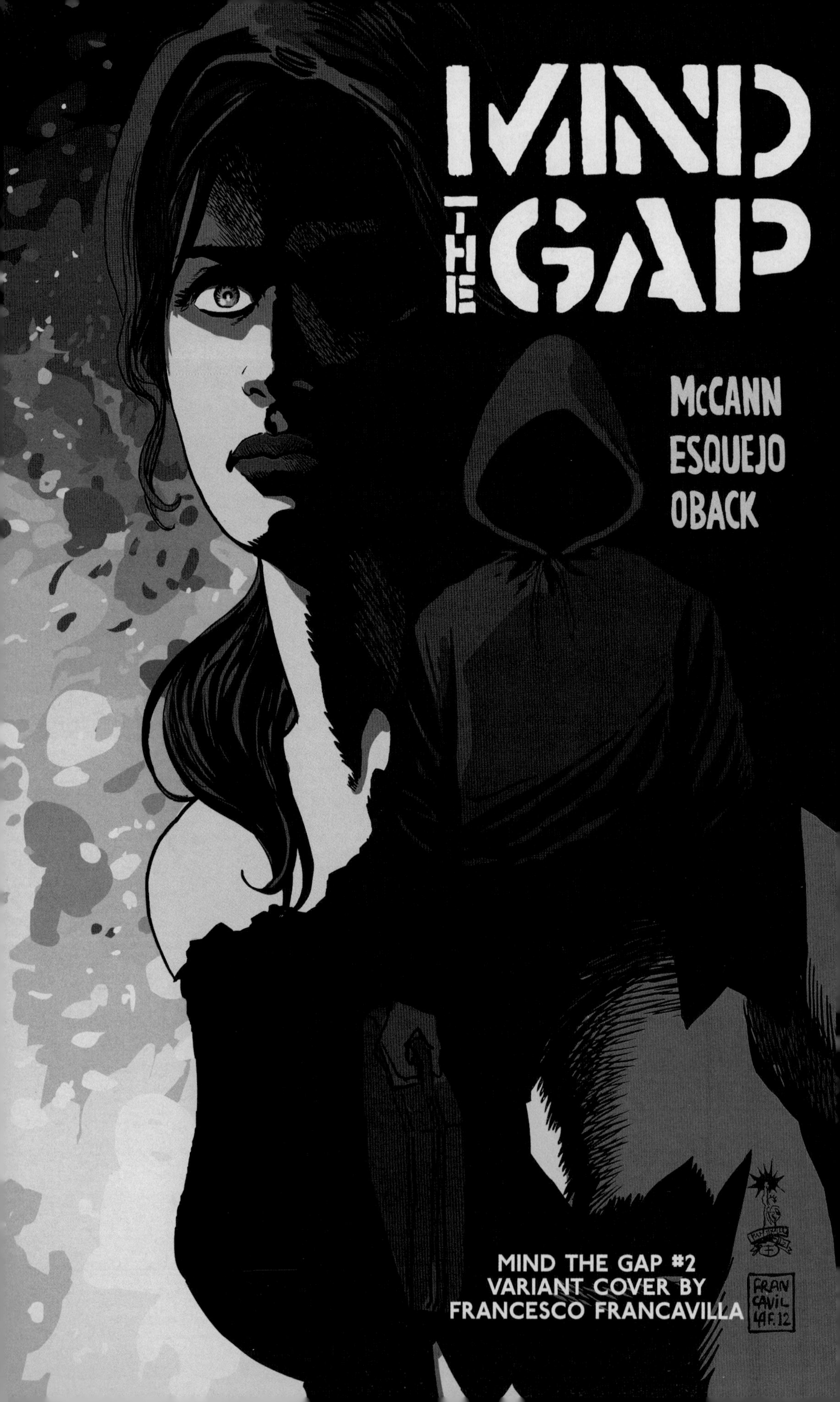
MIND THE GAP
McCANN
ESQUEJO
OBACK

MIND THE GAP #2
VARIANT COVER BY
FRANCESCO FRANCAVILLA

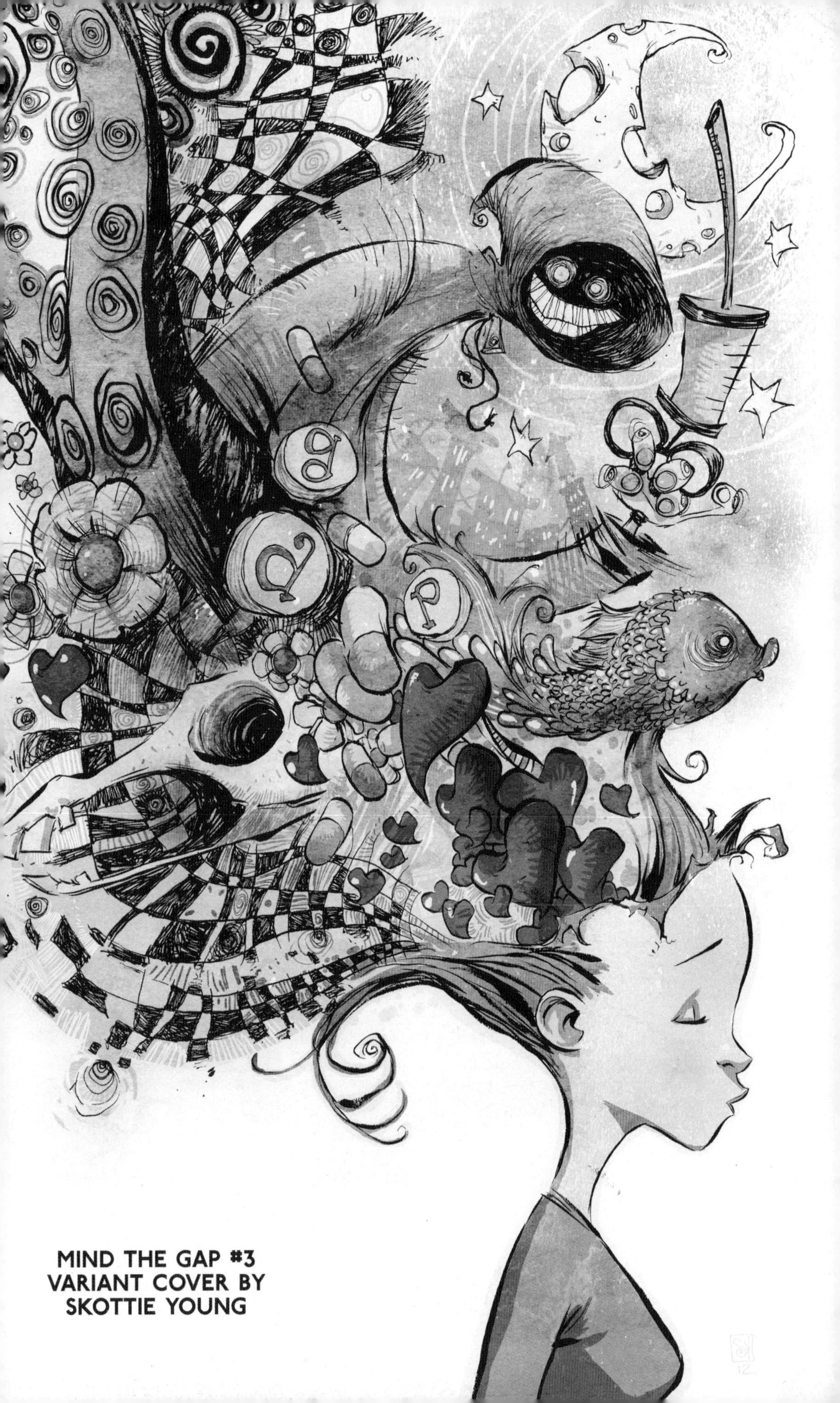

MIND THE GAP #3
VARIANT COVER BY
SKOTTIE YOUNG

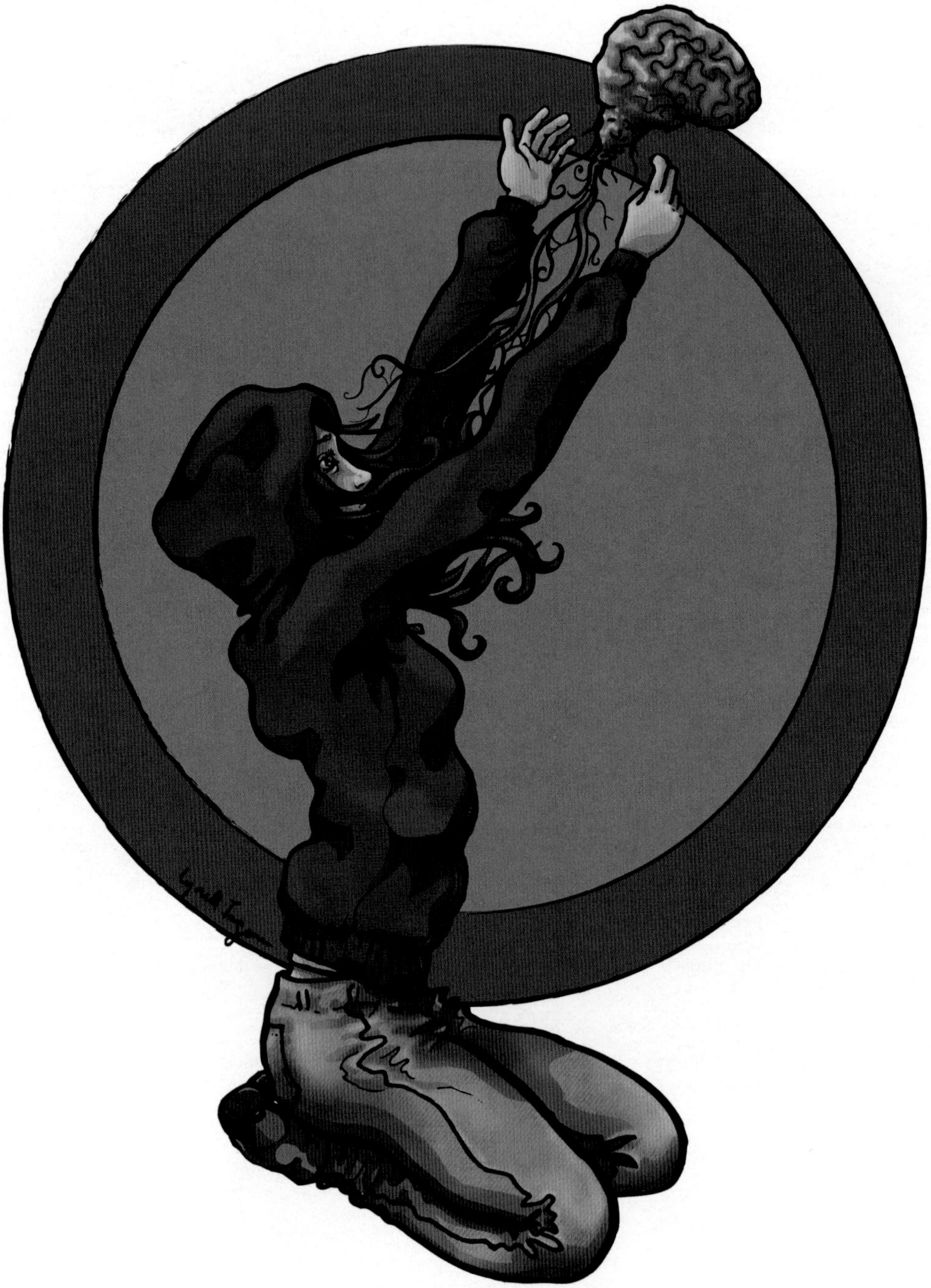

MIND THE GAP #4 VARIANT COVER BY LYNELL INGRAM

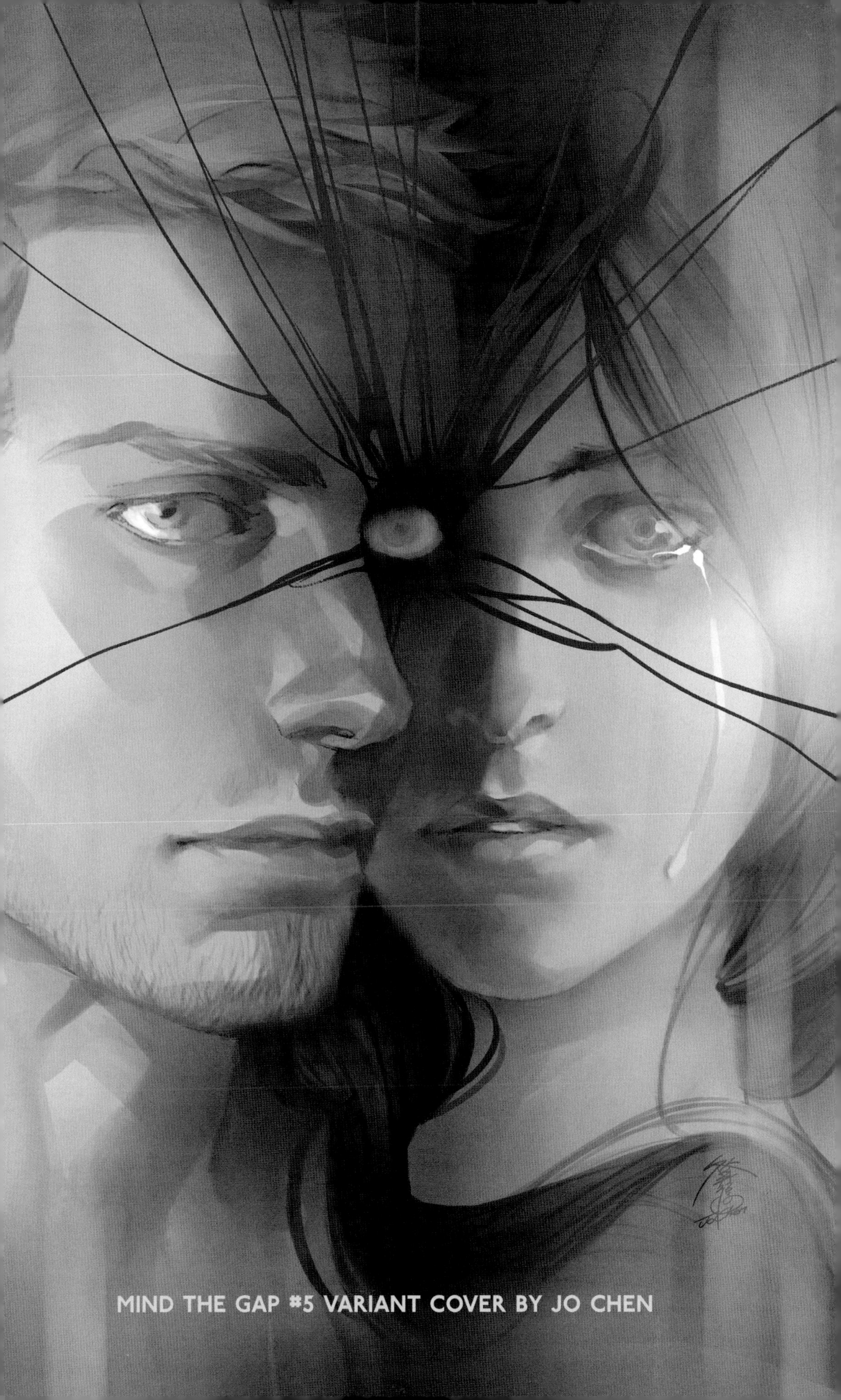

MIND THE GAP #5 VARIANT COVER BY JO CHEN

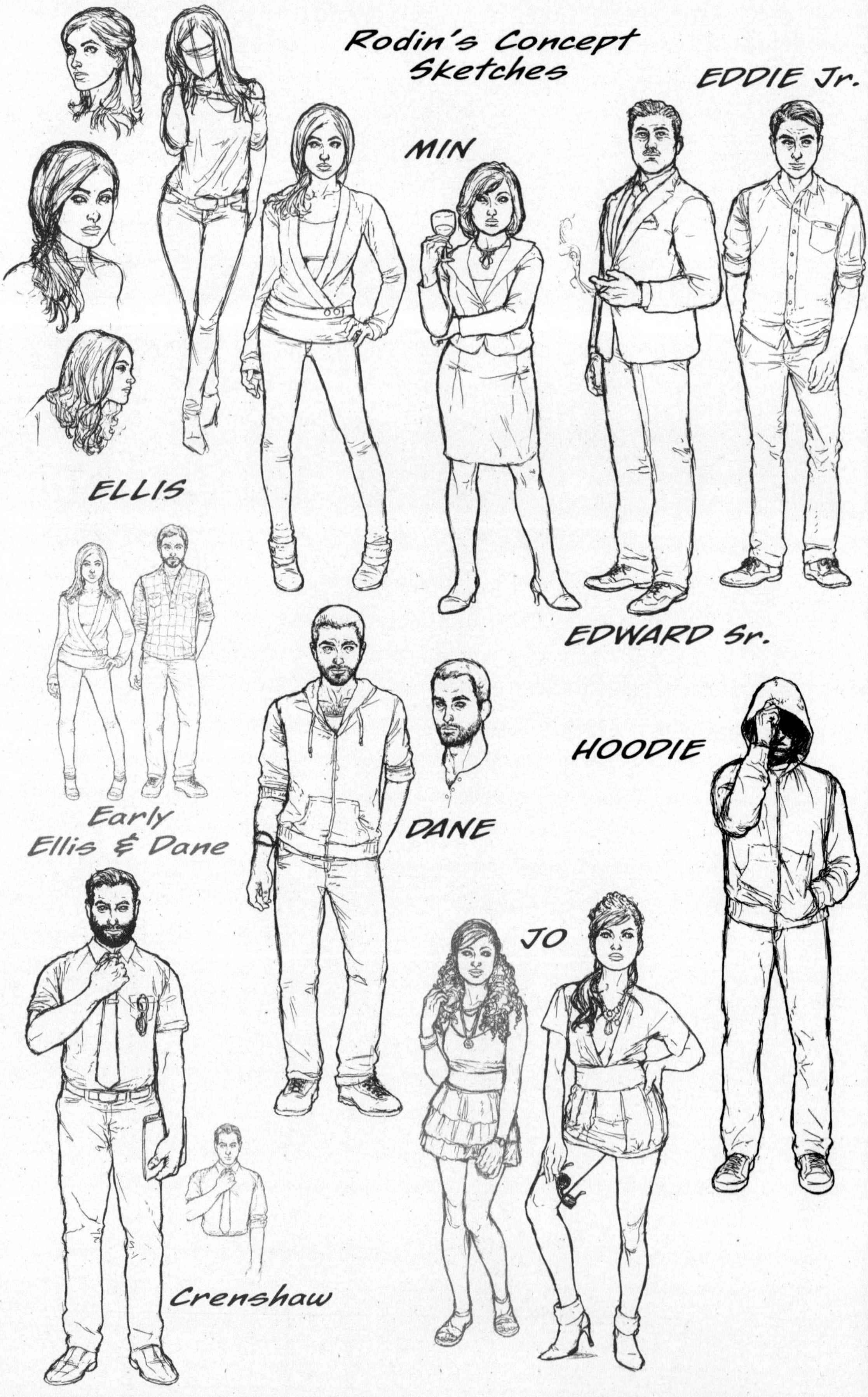
Rodin's Concept Sketches
EDDIE Jr.
MIN
ELLIS
EDWARD Sr.
HOODIE
Early Ellis & Dane
DANE
JO
Crenshaw

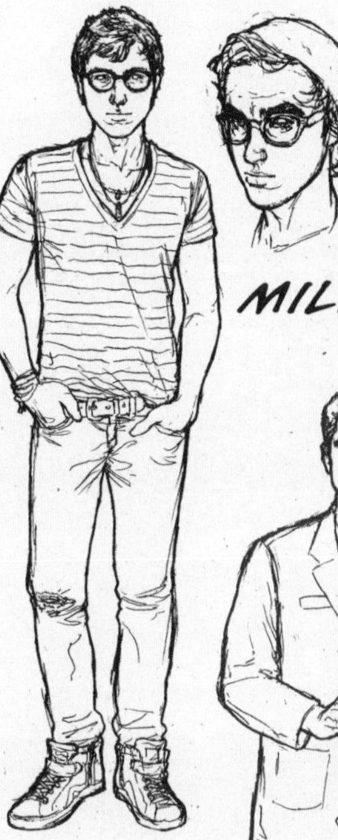

MILES

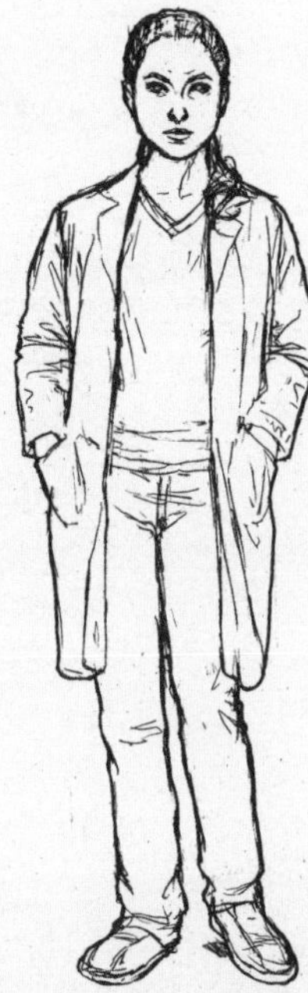

Dr. GELLER

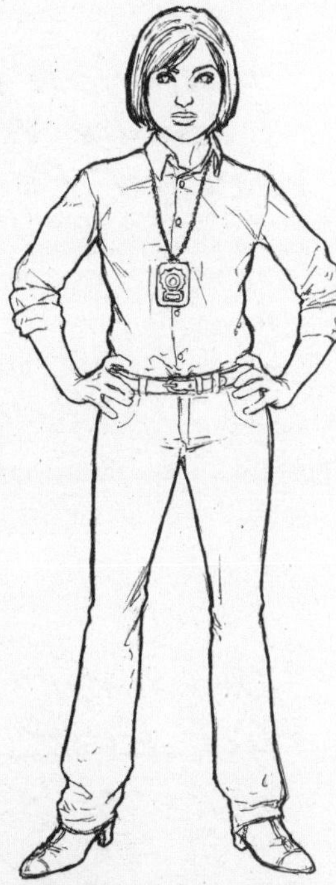

ANTOINETTE WALLACE

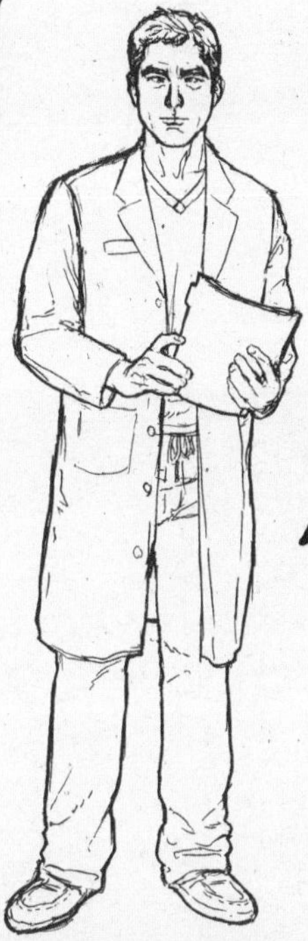

Dr. HAMMOND

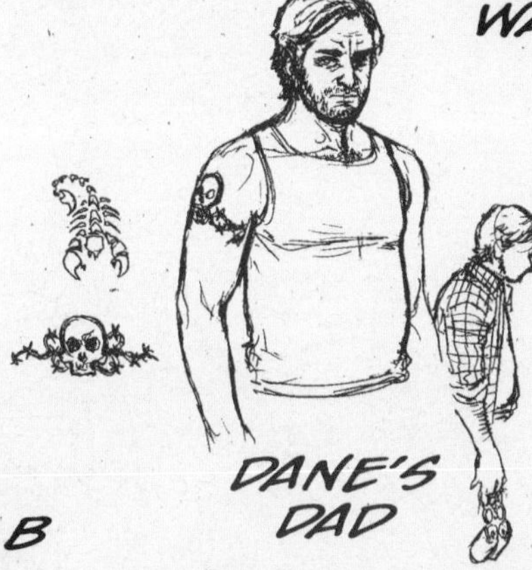

DANE'S DAD

ISSUE #1 COVER B

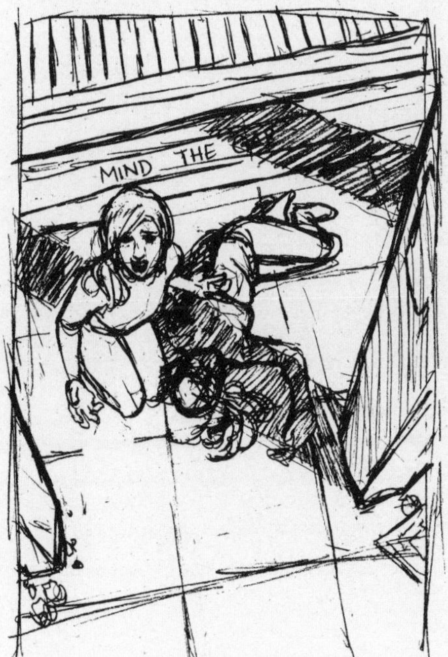
MIND THE

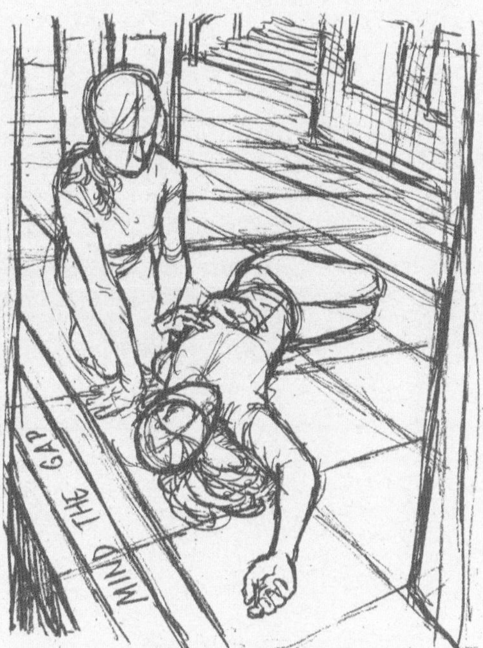
MIND THE GAP

Adrian's
Issue #1
Variant Pencils

Final Version
Without Deer

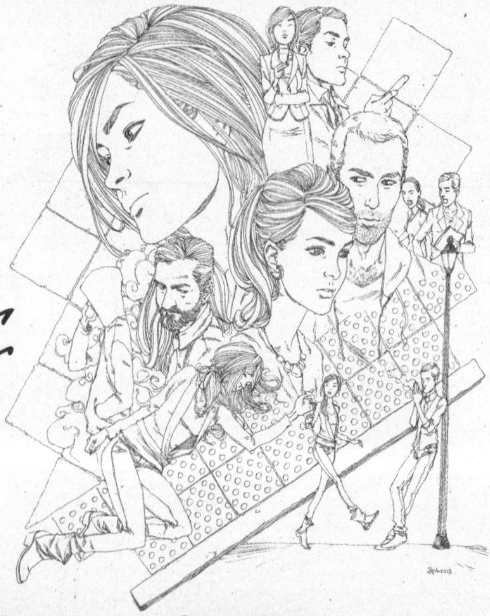
alphona

Original
With Deer

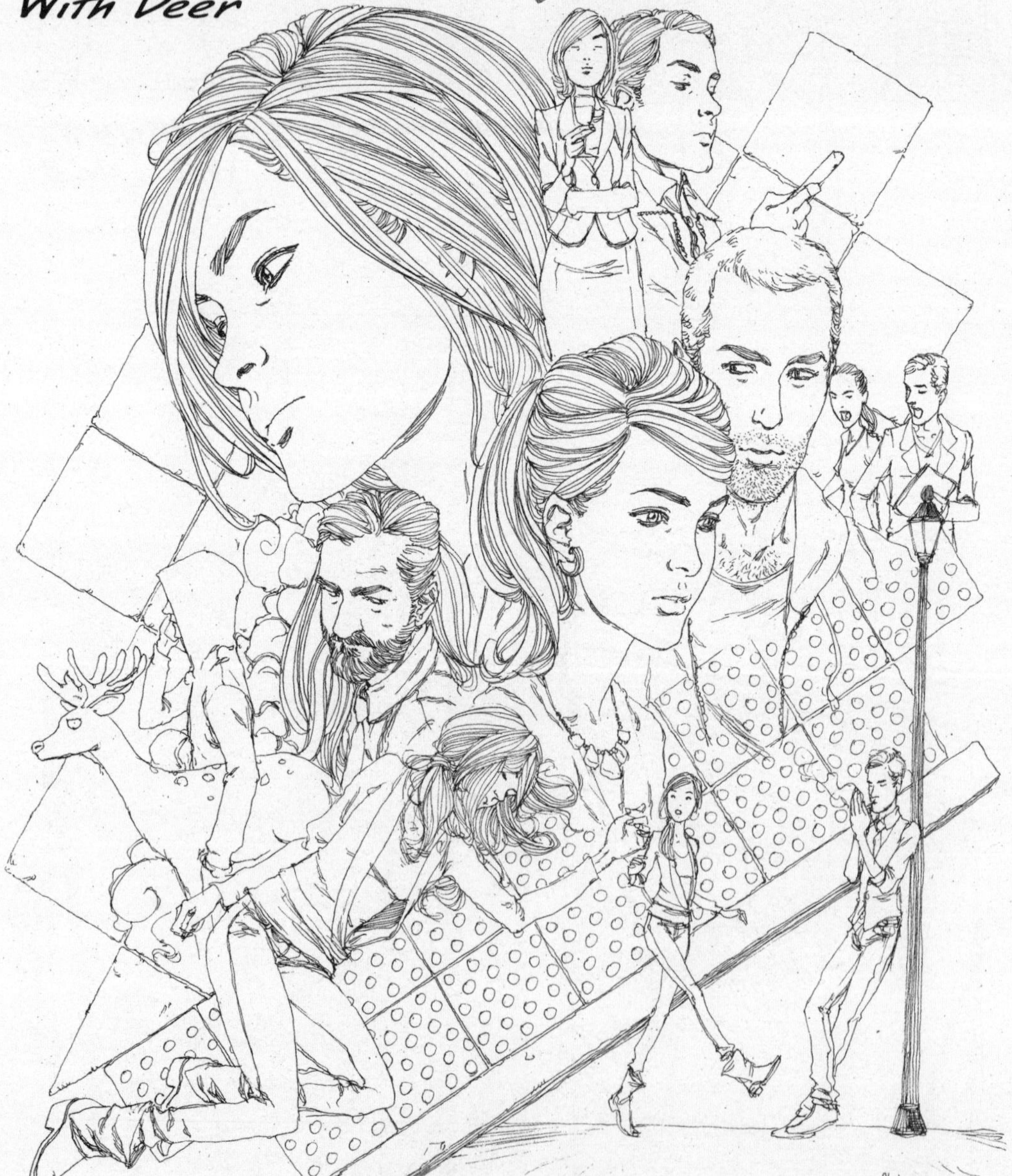
alphona.

Adrian's Concept Art

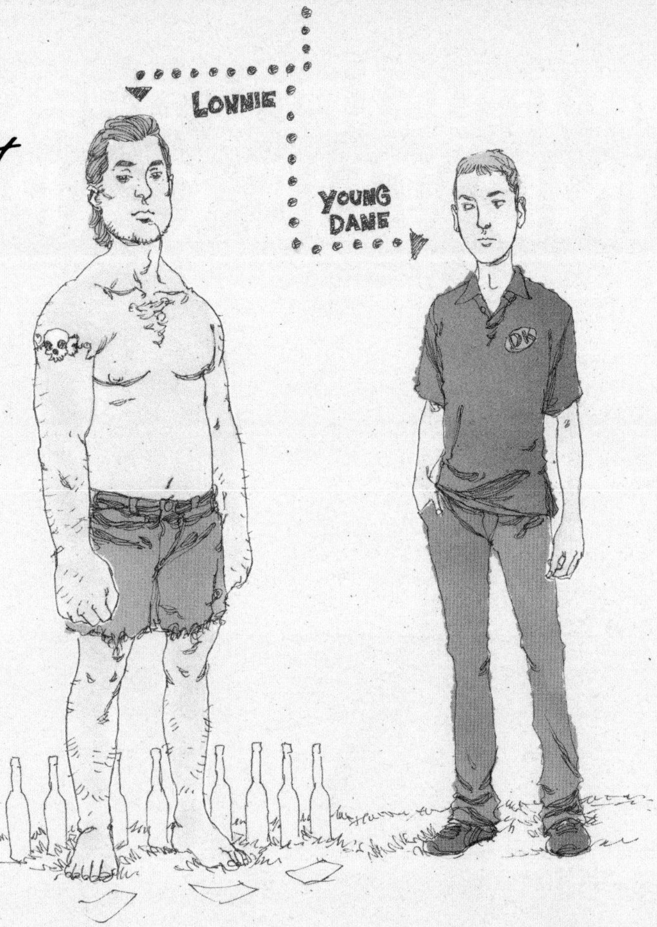
LONNIE
YOUNG DANE
DK

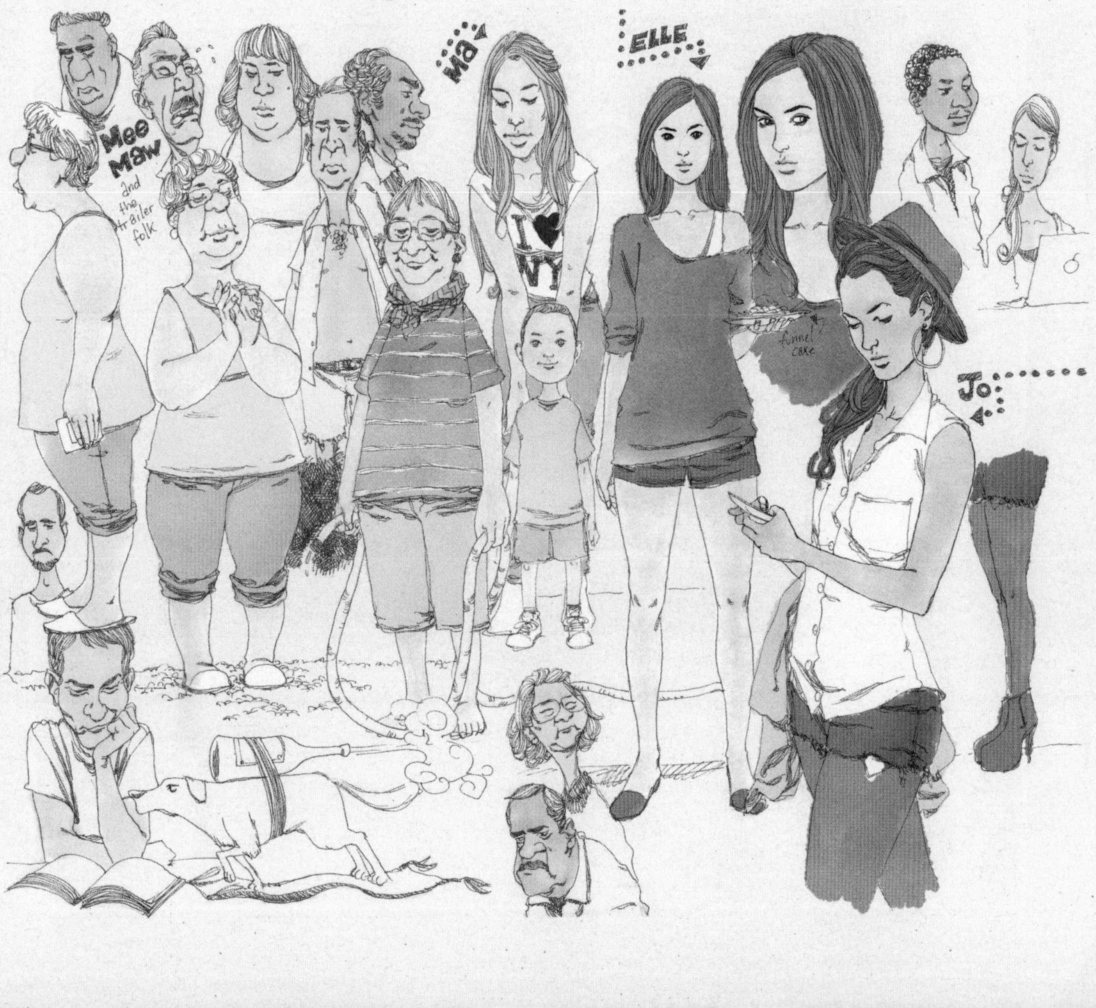
Mee Maw
and the trailer folk
MA
ELLE
I ♥ NY
funnel cake
JO

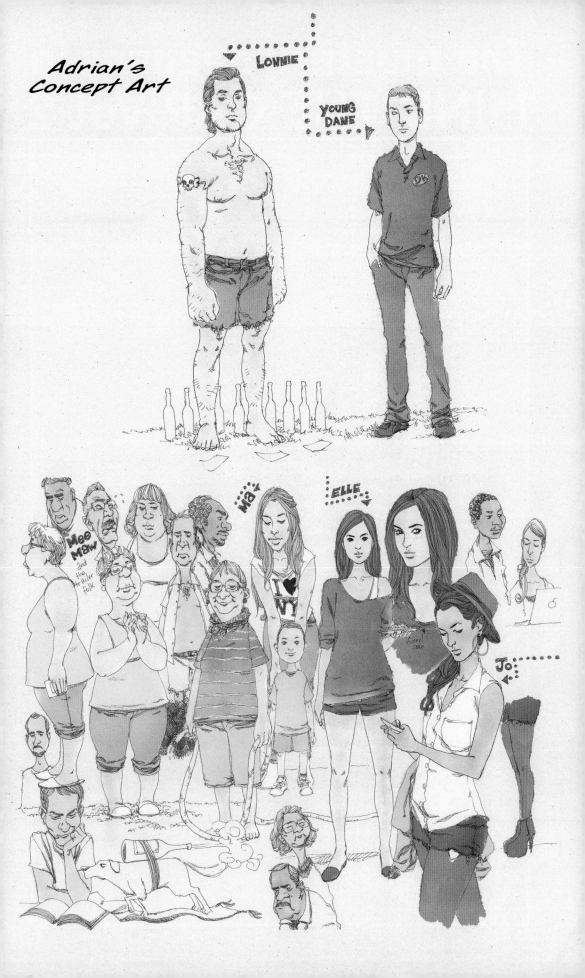

The mystery deepens in

MIND THE GAP Vol 2

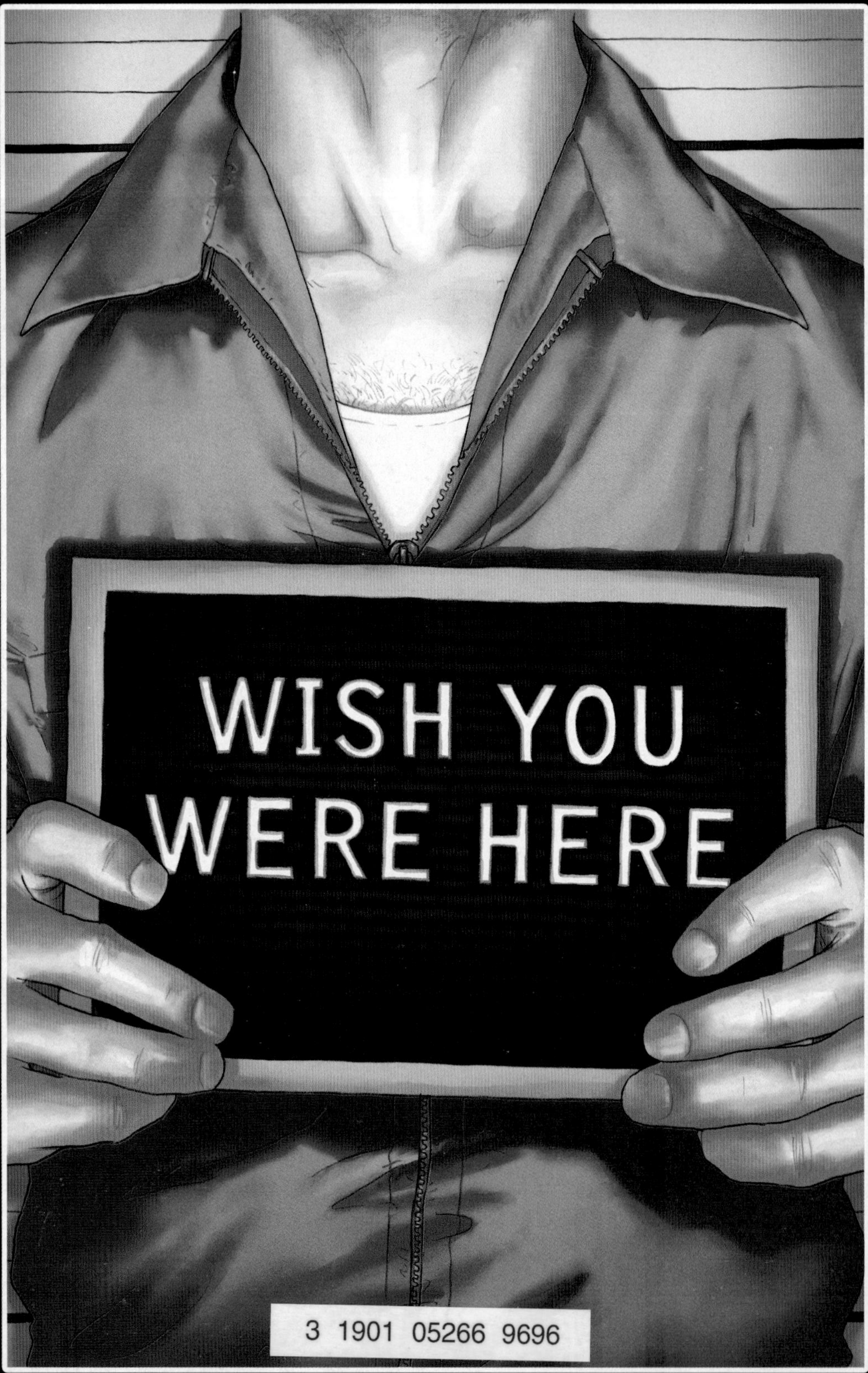
WISH YOU
WERE HERE